EQUAL AT THE CREATION:
SEXISM, SOCIETY, AND CHRISTIAN THOUGHT

Edited by Joseph Martos and Pierre Hégy

Patriarchal ideals have long played a major, even decisive role in the Christian church and in its understanding of its scriptures, community, ministry, and mission. This reality, and women's often creative response to it, form the subject of this collection.

Written by experts in church history, the articles take a close look at women's status in ancient, medieval, modern, and contemporary Christianity. Contributors explore such themes as women's role in early Christian communities, their role models in the Roman Empire, Elizabeth I's exploitation of women's cultural disadvantages, the relative autonomy of women in Catholic and Protestant churches, and their evolving roles in marriage and the ministry today.

This fascinating history of women's response to sexism in Christianity is an ideal text for courses in women's studies and church history. Lively, clear, and jargon-free, it will also appeal to anyone with a special interest in this wide-ranging subject.

JOSEPH MARTOS is a professor in the College of Arts and Sciences, and director of the Russell Institute of Religion and Ministry, Spalding University.

PIERRE HÉGY is an associate professor in the Department of Sociology, Adelphi University.

Equal at the Creation: Sexism, Society, and Christian Thought

Edited by
JOSEPH MARTOS and PIERRE HÉGY

UNIVERSITY OF TORONTO PRESS
Toronto Buffalo London

© University of Toronto Press Incorporated 1998
Toronto Buffalo London

ISBN 0-8020-0868-2 (cloth)
ISBN 0-8020-7852-4 (paper)

Canadian Cataloguing in Publication Data

Main entry under title:

Equal at the creation : sexism, society, and Christian thought

ISBN 0-8020-0868-2 (bound)   ISBN 0-8020-7852-4 (pbk)

1. Sexism – Religious aspects – Christianity.   2. Women in Christianity.
3. Woman (Christian theology).   I. Martos, Joseph, 1943–
II. Hégy, Pierre, 1937–

BV639.W7E68 1998   261.8'344   C98-930559-7

University of Toronto Press acknowledges the financial assistance to its publishing program of the Canada Council for the Arts and the Ontario Arts Council.

Contents

PREFACE vii

1 Gender Roles in Family and Culture: The Basis of Sexism in Religion JOSEPH MARTOS and PIERRE HÉGY 3

2 Gender in the Origins of Christianity: Jewish Hopes and Imperial Exigencies MARY ROSE D'ANGELO 25

3 The Aesthetics of Paradise: Images of Women in Christian Antiquity KENNETH B. STEINHAUSER 49

4 Excluded by the Logic of Control: Women in Medieval Society and Scholastic Theology MARIE ANNE MAYESKI 70

5 Ave Virginia, Regina Terrae: The Power of Culture and the Culture of Power in Renaissance England WILLIAM H. SWATOS, JR 96

6 Separation of the Sexes: The Development of Gender Roles in Modern Catholicism ELLEN M. LEONARD 114

7 Towards a Single Anthropology: Developments in Modern Protestantism WENDY FLETCHER-MARSH 129

8 Catholics and Protestants, Conservatives and Liberals: Christian Marriage Today GAILE M. POHLHAUS 143

9 Weaving New Cloth: Overcoming Sexism in Ordination
  Policies MOLLY T. MARSHALL   163

10 Understanding the Dynamics of Gender Roles: Towards the
   Abolition of Sexism in Christianity PIERRE HÉGY and
   JOSEPH MARTOS   181

   Afterword   203

   CONTRIBUTORS   207

Preface

Much has been written in recent years about sex and gender roles in history and in social institutions, especially in institutionalized religion. Excellent studies are available in books and articles on the treatment of and bias against women in just about every period, in every society, in every culture, in every religion, indeed, in just about every denomination. What did not seem to be available, as we surveyed the literature – Pierre Hégy, from a sociological perspective, and Joseph Martos, from a theological perspective – was a book on gender issues that encompassed the history of Christianity.

Being men ourselves but not fools, we dared not tread into this arena of women's concerns alone and unassisted. In true male chauvinist fashion, we at once enlisted the aid of women to do much of the work. In true egalitarian fashion, however, we tried to put gender aside and approach our task professionally and without bias. Seeking to be as representative as possible, Pierre and I invited women and men, Catholics and Protestants, Americans and Canadians, into the conversation that has resulted in the production of this book. The only things we have in common are that we are all college teachers, we all specialize to some degree in certain areas of the human sciences, and we are all sensitive to women's issues.

The book that we have jointly produced makes no claim to be a definitive text. We wanted to write not for academicians and scholars (who already have enough to read) but for people like our students – individuals in the process of educating themselves about the great issues that shape our society and its institutions. Some do this by going to college and taking courses; others do it by picking up books such as this one, reading and thinking about them, and perhaps discussing them with their friends. We do not believe that all education takes place in the classroom. To be sure, we each learned a great deal by doing the research – outside the classroom – that led to the writing of our individual contributions.

Apart from the introduction and conclusion, the eight historical chapters divide the Christian centuries into more or less standard groupings – chapter 2, the first century; chapter 3, the classical or patristic period; chapter 4, the Middle Ages; chapter 5, the Renaissance; chapters 6 and 7, the modern age; and chapters 8 and 9, contemporary times. Each investigates some of the ways in which women were treated differently from men, especially in marriage and ministry. They do not provide a detailed inspection; rather, each offers a window into a particular period of Christian history that sheds light on the ways in which women are regarded and treated today. They are also written from the perspective of North American mainline Protestant and Catholic Christianity, and they do not attempt to treat topics that would be of interest, for instance, to Orthodox or Hispanic Christians. Nevertheless, we hope that readers who find the chapters illuminating will be encouraged to learn more about gender roles in society and church institutions.

On behalf of our collaborators in this effort, we would like to thank those who made this book possible, especially our students, from whom we have learned so much; our colleagues, who shared ideas with us; our families, which sometimes had to bear with our reclusiveness; our institutions, which gave us the time to learn and write (especially those that provided us with financial assistance to attend the 1995 convention of the Society for the Scientific Study of Religion to meet one another and discuss our work in progress); and the University of Toronto Press (especially Ron Schoeffel), for its encouragement and support of this project.

EQUAL AT THE CREATION

1

Gender Roles in Family and Culture: The Basis of Sexism in Religion

JOSEPH MARTOS and PIERRE HÉGY

Every human culture has treated men and women differently. This was true, as far as we can tell, in prehistoric societies, and we have records showing that it has always been true in the civilizations that have preceded ours. It is also the case in every society and in every culture in the world today, whether that culture be tribal, nomadic, sedentary, agricultural, industrial, or postindustrial. Differential treatment of men and women according to their sex appears to be endemic to the human condition.

The differentiation of gender roles does not always favour one sex over another, however. The dominant pattern in human history (and prehistory) gives greater power and privilege to males rather than females, and it is commonly referred to as 'patriarchy,' from Greek roots meaning 'father' and 'rule.' The opposite pattern, 'matriarchy' or mother rule, is overt in some cultures and covert in others, but it is definitely in the minority both in the past and in the present. A balance of power between the sexes, such as might be found in an 'egalitarian' society, is even more rare. It exists in a limited number of tribal cultures; in small, experimental communities; and in some contemporary marriages. It is also alive in the human imagination, especially among people who are oppressed, persecuted, and powerless. The vision of such a society appears to have existed in the imagination of Jesus of Nazareth, and there is good evidence that the earliest Christian communities were, if not totally egalitarian, considerably less patriarchal than the societies that surrounded them.[1]

The existence of gender roles in a religion founded by someone who apparently favoured greater gender equality is something of an anomaly, especially when during most of that religion's history the bias in favour of men has been so great that it merits the name 'sexism.' In the chapters below, we see how women have been regarded and treated in Christian history, especially in marriage and ministry. Some chapters emphasize gender roles in the Christian community; others, patriarchy and sexism or the unequal treatment of women. The business of this opening chapter is to introduce some basic concepts and to lay a groundwork for what follows. The closing chapter inquires about possibilities for the future.

Gender Roles

The purpose of gender roles in nature and society is, in a word, efficiency. Closely connected are survival and satisfaction, for gender roles assist in the survival of biological and social groups, and they also contribute to the satisfaction of individuals within groups. Gender roles are an efficient social mechanism for ensuring group survival: when all know their place, the group functions well. Gender roles are also an efficient means of providing individual satisfaction: when everyone knows his or her place, individuals have a sense of belonging and purpose.[2]

In an evolutionary scheme of things, gender roles are an outgrowth of the process of diversification and specialization in nature. The simplest one-celled creatures are not much different from one another, and their one cell must do everything that a living organism is capable of doing in order to survive – namely, ingesting, excreting, and reproducing. In multi-celled plants and animals, cells begin to diversify and specialize in function: in plants, leaves look and function differently from roots, and so on; in animals, eyes and ears, hair and feather follicles, nervous systems and digestive systems are composed of specialized cells performing diverse functions. If an individual is a community of cells, the development of cell roles makes possible the evolution of larger and more complex individuals.

At the societal level, individuals themselves are analogous to cells. As a solitary individual, the survivor of a shipwreck on a deserted island must do everything for himself or herself, much as an individual paramecium must do everything for itself. Unlike the single-celled creature, however, the solitary human and in fact all solitary animals cannot reproduce alone. Early in evolutionary development, even before the full differentiation of animals from plants, sexual specialization emerged as a means of ensuring diversity and adaptability in reproduction – a simple and efficient method of guaranteeing the survival and evolution of species. Sexual specialization in mammals and primates brought with it the development of sex roles, or tasks that individuals of one sex performed either exclusively (such as nursing the young) or predominantly (such as hunting). Sex roles in the animal world ensure that the work of the group (flock, pack, pride, herd, and so on) gets done and that the individuals in the group know their status and function within it. In many species of animals, social differentiation occurs on the basis not only of sex but also of size and strength; hence the pecking order of chickens and the dominance hierarchy of horses and deer. In mammals with more complex brains, such as primates, social differentiation takes place on the basis of other factors as well, such as age and family relationships.[3]

Human social diversification and specialization are even more complex. Hence it is proper to speak about gender roles rather than sex roles. Sex roles deal primarily with place and function with regard to reproduction and survival; gender roles include these but also entail a great variety of social, symbolic, and satisfaction functions as well.[4] Gender roles define not only how girls relate to boys and how men relate to women but also how girls relate to other girls and to women, how males of any age relate to various places and activities, and so on and so forth. In other words, gender roles move beyond simple sex roles and involve the complexity of human society and culture.[5]

As noted above, the vast majority of human cultures were and still are patriarchal in structure. Whenever one sex dominates another in a culture, however, the reason is commonly not efficiency but the symbolic exercise of power. Gender roles are of course found in egalitarian societies: a finite number of tasks need to be accomplished by a group (such as foraging, fishing, trapping, constructing dwellings, rearing children, and making clothes and tools), and in simple societies these are often parcelled out to one sex or another, though not always to the same sex in each society. Patriarchy and matriarchy, however, are cultural expressions of power – usually over the food supply.[6]

In prehistoric societies, since males were free of the physical restrictions that pregnancy and nursing place on females, they were able to develop hunting skills that put them in control of tasty and nutritious protein in the form of meat. Hunters could command favours in return for the food that they supplied, and they could also demand obedience and subservience. Patterns of power and control, once established, could be readily perpetuated, even in agricultural societies where women's work equalled that of men. Thus patriarchy or male dominance, once initiated in prehistoric hunting-gathering societies, tended to predominate in ancient agricultural civilizations.[7]

Even today the patriarchal ordering of society continues wherever men are the primary providers for the family, and even where women work equally hard as men women are not equally rewarded. Patriarchy entails the inherent injustice of perpetually unequal treatment of the sexes, not to mention the myriad injustices and insults that derive from the abuse of power. Yet patriarchal forces are today diminishing under the pressure of women's increased educational, economic, and political power. Moreover, patriarchal structures are themselves under attack by women and men alike, who are philosophically committed to the existence of human rights, who are morally bound to the promotion of fairness, and who are religiously inspired by the gospel of Jesus.

Patriarchy in Western Culture

Though many cultures around the world have been ruled by patriarchal social structures, Christianity has been influenced mainly by patriarchy in Middle Eastern and European cultures. A brief review of those cultures serves both as an overview of this book and as an introduction to its chapters.

Ancient Israel

Relations between the sexes in the ancient Mediterranean world were what can be called 'utilitarian' or 'instrumental.' Family structures and marriage customs show that women were largely regarded as commodities to be used by men for their benefit and for that of families headed by men.[8]

Biblical narratives from Abraham forward describe an Israel that was unquestionably and unquestioningly patriarchal. The main characters in Jewish legend and history are male; men are the actors, and women are (along with animals, land, and other possessions) acted on. The most important women in biblical literature (such as Sarah, the wife of Abraham, and Miriam, the sister of Moses) play minor roles at best. Abraham, Isaac, and Jacob – father, son, and grandson – are referred to by biblical scholars as patriarchs, and all three were polygamous. Each in his turn headed an extended nomadic family, and just as each had many oxen and camels, he also had a number of wives. The children to whom the wives gave birth were considered the children of the patriarch, and for the most part female offspring are not even mentioned in the surviving narratives.

In the book of Genesis, Abraham passes off Sarah as his sister (and therefore sexually available to local potentates with whom Abraham is currying favour), as does Isaac, his wife Rebecca (Gen. 12:10–20; 20:1–7; 26:1–11), though in none of the cases does the deception result in the wife's being sexually used by a man who is not her husband. Similarly, Lot offers his two daughters to the men of Sodom to use as they will in exchange for safety, and the girls avoid this fate only because the men will not be deterred from their intention to violate the rules of hospitality (Gen. 19:4–11). The power of the male head of household to dispose of the females under his authority, however, is never questioned. Of course, power of a father over children extends to sons as well, as is clear from the story of Abraham and Isaac (Gen. 22:1–14). Patriarchal authority in some societies is absolute.

Though stories of the great men in Hebrew literature at times intimate the existence of romance, the love in question is akin more to the love of a teenage boy for a flashy car than to the mutual attraction of mature adults. Jacob falls in love with Rachel, who is shapely and beautiful, rather than with her older sister Leah; but their father, Laban, makes Jacob take Leah as a condition for getting Rachel, so Jacob is able to start married life with two wives instead of one (Gen. 29:15–30). Earlier in the narrative, Isaac was not so lucky: he never laid eyes on the girl whom his father had obtained for him until she arrived to be his wife (Gen. 24:62–7). The stories do not even mention the girls' feelings about their fate or about the men to whom they are given.

The patriarchs and later the kings of Israel had concubines as well as wives, concubines being females to whom the head of a household had sexual access but to whom no family responsibility was owed. Thus concubines and their children could be dismissed if their presence was unwanted for any reason. According to the biblical history, the servant Hagar and her son (by Abraham) Ishmael were sent into the desert after Abraham had a son by his wife, Sarah (Gen. 21:8–14), and later Abraham sent away the sons of other concubines who might be rivals to Isaac (Gen. 25:6). Esau, Isaac, and Jacob had children by a number of wives and concubines, as did David and Solomon later (cf. II Sam. 3:2–5; I Kings 11:3). Solomon's seven hundred wives and three hundred concubines were listed shortly after his gold and ivory, his chariots and horses (I Kings 10:14–29). The king did not have a personal relationship with these women; they were his property.

The Ten Commandments in their historical context were originally addressed to Israelite males and regarded primarily their relationship with other Israelite males. The commandments 'Thou shalt not kill' and 'Thou shalt not steal,' for example, forbade killing and stealing from other Israelites (cf. Ex. 20:1–17); this left Israelites free to kill and plunder their neighbours, which they did when they could get away with it. The original sexist nature of the Decalogue is clear in Ex. 20:5, which speaks about fathers, sons, grandsons, and great-grandsons, but not about women. Verse 17 was obviously addressed to men, for it enjoined the listeners to refrain from coveting a neighbour's house, wife, servant, ox or donkey – things that could be owned only by men. Thus the commandment against adultery was a prohibition against ruining another man's possession; adultery in the Jewish world was not so much a sexual sin as a violation of a property right.[9] Since men could acquire and dispose of property, men could divorce their wives, but women had no parallel right (Deut. 24:1–4). Indeed, the question did not even arise, for how could a possession get rid of its owner?

Graeco-Roman Culture

Marriage in ancient Greece and Rome was with few exceptions an arrangement between parents (that is, fathers) or their surrogates, not between the spouses themselves. Marriage relations were instrumental, centred on the preservation of the family name and the continuation of the state. Husbands and wives were not expected to have a close relationship: rather, theirs was a practical division of labour, with the man interacting on behalf of the family in the public sphere and the woman remaining in the domestic sphere. Men sought companionship not with their wives but with other men, as did women with other women. Men were also allowed to satisfy their sexual desires with women other than their wives, while the converse of course was forbidden to women.[10] Indeed, men were not expected to be sexually attracted to their own wives, and women were not supposed to be sexually attracted to men at all. To have children, they performed their 'marital duty.'[11]

Though women wielded some power in the home, men governed the structure and functioning of public society. The confinement of women to the home and the non-confinement of men made possible a public life entirely dominated by men. Men could become successful through education in rhetoric and law, and they could advance through military and political skill; such opportunities were not available to women. In Greek city-states and in the Roman republic, men could divorce their wives with relative ease. When dismissed from her husband's house, the woman returned to her father, while all assets and children remained with the father of the family, the *paterfamilias*. The wife, being a commodity or family asset, owned nothing.[12]

The *paterfamilias* enjoyed an absolute right over all of his assets, including his children. He could order an infant born with some defect (especially if it were female) to be taken out to an uninhabited area and left to die. He could punish his own children with impunity, and even beat them to death. He could also order the death of a child who had not yet reached adulthood, but understandably this male prerogative was seldom invoked. The family and public implications of such a decision might be harder to live with than the obstreperous offspring.[13]

The radical imbalance in favour of men began to be righted somewhat in the later years of the Roman republic and the early years of the empire, at least for women in the higher social and economic orders. When men went off to war, their wives were left in charge of domestic affairs – both those that were normally in their province and now those that entailed relationships outside the home as well. Women thus gained economic power, and, if their husbands did not return from their military exploits, they kept it – at least until they married again. Enjoying their new-found freedom, and given the scarcity of eligible men, widows often chose not to remarry until their sons came of age and inherited their father's property. Some women, however, chose to parlay their position and wealth into concessions from would-be suitors.[14]

By the time of the Roman empire, women as well as men could freely enter into marriage without their parents' consent, and women as well as men could divorce their spouses. According to Roman law, if marriage was by consent of the spouses, when the consent ended so did the marriage. Still, few children could afford to marry without their parents' consent. Among the common people, and especially in rural areas, girls were still given away or handed over at the onset of puberty to the boys (or the older men) to whom they were betrothed. They thus passed from the possession of their father to the possession of their husband, never being legal or social persons in their own right.[15]

When the Roman empire in the fourth century adopted Christianity as its state religion, not much was different for women than it had been under the worship of the old pagan gods. Though women had experienced some equality with men in the earliest days of the Jesus movement, by the end of the first century this innovation was beginning to be lost, and by the time the once-outlawed religion became socially acceptable, equality had absolutely vanished.[16]

In Christianity as in Judaism before it, the inequality in the social status of women was linked with inequality in religious functioning. Whereas the religions of Greece and Rome accepted women as priestesses and prophetesses, classical Christianity from the second century onward (in contrast with early Christianity in its first decades) began excluding women from religious leadership. In other words, ancient pagan religions did not necessarily link social status and religious roles: even though women in general had inferior social status, women with special roles in religion had a social status superior to that of the average man. Christianity, however, did not permit this to happen: the inferior status of women barred them from any religious role that placed them over men.[17]

The inferiority of women was ideologized by classical Christian (i.e., male) authors. Religious intellectuals developed an ideology that justified the low social position of women and explained why women could not aspire to leadership in the church. One key element in this ideology was the idea that woman was created after man. Another element was the belief that a woman committed the first sin. These two concepts were repeated over and over by male Christian writers from the second century on.

They can be found even in one of the books of the Bible, the First Epistle to Timothy, written not by Paul but by a later writer using his name, around the end of the first century. At one point, the author declares, 'I do not allow women to teach or have any authority over men; they must keep quiet. For Adam was created first, and then Eve' (I Tim. 2:12-13). Even though the fact that one creature is made before another does not imply that the earlier is better than the later (in the first account of creation, for example, the other animals are created before human beings), this author uses the creation of Adam before Eve to prove that men are superior to women and therefore that women cannot be given authority over men. The illogic of the argument is a sure sign of ideological thinking.

The second element in the ideology of male superiority follows closely on the first. 'It was not Adam who was led astray but the woman: she was deceived into transgression' (I Tim. 2:14). Again here, there is no logical connection between being the first to sin and being inferior, though there is perhaps a psychological or a symbolic connection. That is, the idea of woman's subordination to man can be symbolically expressed in a story that assigns blame to the first one to do something wrong. Such psychological and symbolic connections are likewise symptomatic of ideological thinking.

The Christian ideology of patriarchy, or the set of ideas used to explain and justify patriarchy, was not limited to these two concepts, but they were crucial to its becoming accepted. Once male leaders in the church were able to find first Old Testament texts and then New Testament texts that could be used to exclude women from leadership, the fate of women was sealed. The social hierarchy of the Graeco-Roman world became the ecclesiastical hierarchy of the Christian church, and the Bible was used to prove that the subordination of women was ordered by God.[18]

Medieval Christendom

Just as women in ancient Rome had been able to assume roles normally assigned to men during periods of war, women at the beginning of the Middle Ages were able to achieve leadership roles in society and the Church during the turbulent period popularly known as the Dark Ages. These women were the exception rather than the rule, but there was enough looseness in the social structure to allow at least some females to penetrate the barriers that had excluded them from leadership in the Christianized Roman empire.

The leadership roles in the church that women were able to assume were few enough: as Christian girls were married off to pagan boys, they could be evangelizers, taking the faith to an increasing number of Germanic tribes; as founders and abbesses of monasteries, they could be monastic leaders of celibate women's communities and occasionally of paired communities of women and men; as mystics and saints, they could be spiritual guides to women and men alike. These roles were relatively minor when compared to the overall governance of the church, and they were also new, for they had not existed in the now-defunct empire. In the fluid situation that accompanied barbarian invasion and settlement, women were able to take initiatives and do things that were intelligent and creative, regardless of the fact that females had not done them before. The decline of scholarship during the Dark Ages also helped women, for men were less aware of the ideological arguments that centuries before had been used to keep Christian women in positions of subservience to men.[19]

Whatever freedom women had achieved in the Roman empire with regard to marriage, moreover, was lost in the Middle Ages. Germanic culture dictated that a woman be transferred from the household of her father to the household of her husband; in this respect, Germanic custom was similar to the custom of the ancient Israelites. Thus girls were never allowed to choose their own husbands, but since boys were usually not given a choice by their parents either, there was not much disparity of privilege. Unlike the Jews, however, the new Christians of northern Europe had virtually no tradition of divorce (though exceptions could be made when politically arranged marriages became politically inexpedient). The permanence of Germanic marriage, when buttressed in the twelfth century by an ideological usage of selected biblical texts, became the indissolubility of Christian marriage.[20] Thus women in medieval Christianity were locked into patriarchal marriage arrangements that were by definition almost always disadvantageous to them.

If the eleventh century saw the end of the Dark Ages (by the year 1000, virtually all the tribes of Europe had been converted to Christianity), the twelfth century saw the dawning of a new era of scholarship. Monastery writing rooms developed into schools as monks began finding the leisure actually to read and attempt to comprehend the manuscripts that had been preserved through centuries of copying by hand. Cathedral schools grew as medieval cities grew, and they evolved into a new type of academic institution – the university – which brought together scholars from all the known arts and sciences. Western Europe came in contact with the East when crusaders returned home with loot that included writings by early Christian theologions, Greek philosophers, and Islamic intellectuals. In the universities, a method was devised to compare and contrast similar and opposing viewpoints of human and divine authors. Since it was developed in schools, it was called the scholastic method, and the intellectual style that it fostered was known as scholasticism.

The thirteenth century saw the high point of scholasticism as it was practised by such capable and brilliant scholars as Albert the Great, Thomas Aquinas, and Bonaventure. These men (there were no women scholastics because formal education was exclusively male) produced a new synthesis of ancient and contemporary, pagan and Christian thinking. Since the writings from which they drew, however, were inherently patriarchal, the medieval synthesis they produced was unavoidably patriarchal as well. The ancient ideology of women's inferiority was rediscovered and given currency. In addition, since the scholastics had access to ancient philosophical writings, the theological arguments of the past were now reinforced by philosophical arguments as well. Women could now be proven to be inferior because of 'natural' differences between the sexes: men were by nature fit to think and rule, whereas women were by nature more emotional and in need of being ruled. The ideology of male superiority was thus supported not only by ideas found in scripture but also by those supposedly inferred from nature.[21]

Needless to say, whatever freedom women had experienced during the social flux of the Dark Ages was stifled by the social stability of the high Middle Ages. Thanks to the scholastics, moreover, Christian society was provided with both theological and philosophical explanations of why women were – and therefore should be – subject to men. This situation did not change in the fourteenth and fifteenth centuries, either, as the later Middle Ages blended into the early Renaissance.

Modern Europe

If modern Europe emerged from its medieval matrix during the Renaissance, modern Christianity broke from medieval Christianity during the Protestant Reformation. The Reformation was a religious expression of the cultural revolution that was occurring during the Renaissance.

The Protestant Reformation – as well as the so-called Catholic Counter-Reformation which began about a half-century afterward – brought about a host of structural and theological changes in Christianity. Martin Luther in 1517 challenged the authority of the hierarchy to offer promises of salvation, to collect church taxes, and to restrict the reading of the Bible. Luther's doctrine of salvation by faith rather than by works removed incentives to the monastic life, his extolling of marriage over celibacy encouraged monks and nuns to marry, and his interpretation of the priesthood of all the faithful made ministry available to all who felt called to serve the church.

Not much later, Ulrich Zwingli and John Calvin took the momentum of Luther's reform and used it to develop even more revolutionary practices and doctrines. All sacraments were eliminated except baptism and the Lord's supper (i.e., eucharist), for these were the only two that were clearly attested to in the New Testament. The complex international structure of the Roman church was replaced with a simpler model of the local church found in the epistles and in the Acts of the Apostles. The philosophical explanation of Christian doctrine, common in both patristic and scholastic theology, was discredited and gave way to a purely theological mode of explanation that relied heavily on a more literal interpretation of scripture.

In none of this revolutionary activity, however, was anything done to change the low social status of women. The patriarchy of the Middle Ages passed through that of the Renaissance to become the patriarchy of modern culture – essentially unchallenged and unchanged. The academic justifications for the subjugation of women changed from being partly philosophical to being purely theological and from being based on church doctrine to being based on scriptural teaching, but the subjugation of women remained. The intellectual appreciation of womanhood changed from the honouring of the Blessed Virgin and virgin saints to the exaltation of the married women of the Bible, but this did not shift the status of women. If anything, the low social status of women was reinforced by the high theological esteem they were given: women were taught that a life of obedience and submission to men was praised and rewarded by God. At most, some of the social roles available to females changed (they could no longer be celibates, monastics, or mystics; rather, they should all be married, housewives, and mothers), but their low social status relative to men was unaltered.[22]

The Catholic Counter-Reformation attempted to meet the challenge of the Protestant Reformation by cleaning house, but it did little to rearrange the furniture. The Catholic church reformed its methods of appointing bishops, training priests, and celebrating the sacraments, but it did not alter any of the ecclesiastical structures that had evolved during the first fifteen centuries of Christianity. Women's monastic orders remained, and new religious orders were approved to perform charitable works outside convent walls, but these orders of women always had to be under the supervision of men. Catholic married women, like their Protestant counterparts, were expected to be subservient to their husbands.

Just as the medieval organization of Catholicism remained intact during the modern centuries, so also did the scholastic justification of that organization and the position of women at the bottom. Though Catholicism never raised the Pauline utterances about the role of women to the level of church doctrine, it justified the subjugation of women in the practical sphere of church law by appealing to those same texts. In a church sharply divided between clergy and laity, women were never admitted to the ranks of the clergy, yet females in religious orders (like those in Catholic families) did not have status in their own right. Nuns were considered 'married to God' or 'married to the Church,' so even though they were celibate and single they were metaphorically regarded as married and therefore subject to the wills of men – that is, to the male clergy to whom they were accountable.[23]

The increasing secularization of modern culture posed a greater challenge to medieval patriarchy than did traditional Protestantism. In the eighteenth and nineteenth centuries, some women began to break the mould into which men would cast them by being poets and playwrights, novelists and painters, even though they often enough had to hide their authorship under male pseudonyms. Pioneer women in the frontier territories of North America escaped many of the social restrictions of civilization by being equal partners with men, who, for their own reasons, prized the freedom of the wilderness over the security of civilization. In the nineteenth century and increasingly in the twentieth, women of genius and courage moved into fields previously dominated by men, creating professional roles for themselves primarily in education and health care but also, to a lesser extent, in science and business. Slowly the assumptions and structures of religiously reinforced patriarchy were being bypassed and challenged.[24]

In Christianity itself, the greatest room for the expansion of women's roles was found at the fringes of modern denominationalism, in radical groups such as Quakers and Shakers; in utopian communities such as Oneida in New York, Harmony in Indiana, and the Amana colonies in Iowa; and in holiness movements such as pietism and perfectionism, revivalism and pentecostalism. The belief in congregational autonomy, present in some Protestant traditions, permitted independently-minded congregations to call women as well as men to the ministry. Likewise, the belief in the freedom of the Holy Spirit, prevalent in some evangelical traditions, allowed certain Protestants to affirm that charisms of leadership and ministry could be bestowed on anyone God chose, including women.

Opposition to the slave trade in Europe had been spearheaded by Protestant evangelicals who found slavery detestable on human grounds and contrary to the fundamental teachings of the New Testament, even though isolated texts could be dug up to support the practice. When the British slave trade was abolished in 1808, evangelicals turned their attention to the United States, where slavery itself was still legal. Many in the abolitionist movement, especially as it spread to mainstream Protestant denominations in the northern states, were women who did the drudge work of organization and solicitation, even though the most prominent speakers against slavery were men. None the less, the experience of working for the liberation of others raised the consciousness of women, and they began to notice the parallels between the servitude of blacks and their own subjugation. After the American slaves were emancipated by presidential decree and enfranchised by constitutional amendment, women began working for their own civil liberties.[25]

Women succeeded in securing the right to vote in Canada in 1918, and in the United States in 1920, partly by shaming democratic governments with the fact that half their citizens were excluded from democracy, and partly by persuading the public that women who served heroically as nurses in the world war and who supported the war effort at home deserved the franchise. The Second World War likewise broke down stereotypes and ideologies of female inferiority, this time because women served not only as nurses but also in the armed forces (though not yet in battle positions) and because women proved themselves in European resistance movements and in North American factories. After the war, women were expected to step aside and resume their deference to men, but this return to the sexism of the past lasted only through the 'happy days' of the 1950s.

The Beginning of the End of Patriarchy

Women since the nineteenth century had been striving for equality of status, largely in the public arena of civil rights, but it was not until the twentieth century that the social upheaval of two world wars and their aftermath began to make this possible. During the wars, women out of necessity took on roles of a higher status than those normally assigned to them by society, proving that they could competently fill them. Just as women in ancient Rome gained economic power when their husbands and sons were away at war, and just as those in medieval Europe gained social power during the turmoil of the barbarian invasions, so also their successors in the twentieth century gained both economic and social power by doing in wartime what they were not permitted to do in peacetime.[26] They did this by moving into the labour force, securing the right to vote, and demanding the rights of citizens.

One of these rights is education, and during the 1950s and 1960s women increasingly took advantage of relatively inexpensive college and university programs to pursue undergraduate and graduate degrees. Economic changes in the 1970s made it increasingly necessary for households to have two incomes in order to increase (and in many cases to maintain) the standard of living achievable in earlier decades on a single income. The 1970s also saw great changes in the divorce laws of many nations, and, with the introduction of no-fault divorce (i.e., by mutual consent rather than by court litigation), divorce rates climbed to new heights. Divorced women found themselves thrown into the workforce, and, having to support themselves and dependent children, they could no longer afford to work for the same low wages with which they had been content as married women working for supplemental income. Women with higher education and professional job skills began to demand equal pay for equal work.[27]

All these factors fuelled the feminist movement of the 1960s and 1970s, as did the general social ferment of that era. Disillusionment with the Cold War that replaced the promised peace following the Second World War, disenchantment with the arms race and the U.S. war in Vietnam, reaction against conformism and rigid social expectations, and dissatisfaction with blatant racial inequality led young people especially to question the roles assigned to young and old, blacks and whites, women and men. Women's liberation burst onto the scene along with black liberation, gay liberation, and other protest movements, all rebelling against the rules and structures imposed by an essentially patriarchal culture. At the same time, changes in the law implementing legal equality regardless of race, gender, and other factors made it possible for females to move into social roles previously reserved for males. Women became heads of households, blue-collar workers, career professionals, middle managers, business executives, and government officials in increasing numbers. Many of the roles into which they moved increased their social status because of the power these positions offered and because of the salaries they commanded.[28]

Virtually all the major cultures in the world are still patriarchal in structure, but in Western culture and others affected by Western culture women are playing many roles previously available only to men and achieving status open in the past only to men. At the same time, however, it must be admitted that the status that they are acquiring is status as defined by patriarchy. For example, higher-paid work has more prestige than lower-paid work, paid work in general has more prestige than unpaid work, intellectual skill has more prestige than manual labour, and work with adults has more prestige than work with children. Activity that produces immediately tangible benefits is more highly rewarded and has a higher status than that which produces benefits that are socially important but less immediate or less tangible, such as the education of the young or the preservation of the environment. Moreover, people are respected more for what they do (and especially the wealth they generate) than for who they are, and accomplishments are more esteemed than relationships. Patriarchal values predominate, even though women move into positions formerly filled only by men.

If the patriarchal structure of Western society is less rigid than it was a century ago, it is far from being replaced by a social structure that is truly egalitarian. Men grossly outnumber women in management and executive positions in business and government, men and women tend to enter different professions, with the higher-paid professions dominated by men, and men continue to earn higher salaries for comparable work even in the same profession. This continued inequality is not the only heritage of patriarchy, however, for the privileges extended to males were historically and still are given predominantly to males who are white. The culture of patriarchy therefore manifests itself not only in sexism but also in racism and in every other social structure in which the division of labour is based not on the aptitude of individuals to do certain types of work but on prejudice in favour of one group and against others. Patriarchal bias exists whenever the availability of opportunity is based not on aptitude but on factors that have little or nothing to do with the task to be performed – gender, skin colour, religion, nationality, marital status, sexual preference, and so on – for all these preferences in Western culture have been determined by dominant males.

All this being acknowledged, however, it is still true that Western culture appears to be less severely patriarchal than it was a half-century ago, a century before that, a century before that, and so on. Though patriarchy is far from disappearing, there seems to be a tendency towards a more egalitarian ordering of social opportunity, based not on stereotypes but on abilities. This is not to say that the trend could not be reversed; it is only to say that a trend appears to have begun.[29]

Sexism in Contemporary Christianity

As was noted at the beginning of this chapter, the existence of gender roles is not necessarily a matter of injustice. In foraging cultures and tribal societies in which sex defines many social roles, the group cannot survive without the contributions of women and men alike. Moreover, very often social roles are defined by factors other than sex (such as family of origin and hereditary occupation), and individuals are not able to escape the duty to fill those roles. Injustice arises not from the mere division of labour but from the ability of those with greater power (men, royalty, the wealthy, and so on) to coerce those with less power to do their will without fairly compensating them. Systemic injustice exists when the more powerful can exploit the less powerful in a systematic way that is built into the structures of society and is accepted by oppressors and oppressed alike. The medieval feudal system of landed gentry and landless serfs, the exploitation of miners and factory workers in the industrial revolution, and the use of child labour and migrant workers today are all examples of systemic injustice.

What makes sexism unjust is not the difference in social roles assigned to women and men but the difference in status between those roles and the concomitant difference in power between women and men. (For instance, men may choose to adopt lower-status roles usually assigned to women, such as child rearing, but women cannot enter higher-status positions reserved to men. Thus women are unable to break through the 'glass ceiling' that prevents them from climbing too high on the corporate ladder.) As a result of the difference in status and power, men can oppress and exploit women, receiving from them much more than they are given in return. In this sense, the evil of sexism exists even when it is not recognized as injustice but is accepted as the way things are. In this sense, too, Christianity has been sexist, if not from the time of Jesus, then from the time that leadership in the church became predominantly male.[30]

Sexism in Christianity today shows up primarily in the areas of ministry and marriage. Marriage in Western culture has always been patriarchal and therefore sexist, and patriarchal marriage in Christian culture has from the first century been supported with an ideological interpretation of scripture and nature. Ministry in Christian organizations has, from the second century on, excluded women from leadership positions except vis-à-vis children and other women.[31] Ministry in the sense of service has never been denied to women, as long as their service did not raise their status.

The visibility of sexism in organized religion is heightened today by the relative decline of sexism in secular society. Though Western culture remains patriarchal, most Western countries are ideologically committed to legal equality and opposed to sexual discrimination. Though some Protestant churches share this egalitarian ideology, Catholic, Orthodox, and other Protestant churches (and they comprise the majority in the Christian world) do not. The bulk of organized Christianity is therefore at odds with the stated (if not always lived-out) ideology of contemporary Western culture in the area of sexual justice. Sexism or sexual discrimination is the assignment of gender roles based on reasons that are not related to the different physical capabilities of men and women.[32]

Gender roles are unjust when they are not based on gender-related reasons (for example, only women can bear children, and men generally have more upper-body strength than women) but are symbolic expressions of power. In today's society, there are no tasks that cannot be performed by women as well as men because the tasks of contemporary society are increasingly related to intelligence rather than to musculature. In a factory, for example, a woman can operate a fork lift, and on a dairy farm a woman can install a milking machine. Conversely, a man can do just about any job that has been stereotyped as women's work, such as nursing and teaching small children. What makes for difference in performance and preference is a variety of factors (such as intelligence, physical size, agility, personality, and training), of which sex may be a factor in some cases (for example, modelling women's clothing), but not many.

When gender is used as a symbolic expression of power, its application is discriminatory and unjust. That is, when gender (like race, ethnicity, skin colour, religion, political affiliation, or sexual preference) is the basis on which a decision is made regarding an individual in a certain role, then, unless gender is related to the ability to fulfill the role, using it as a basis of judgment is unjustifiable. The deliberate use of gender as a determinant of judgment or selection is nothing less than a naked exercise of power – that is, the power to make decisions based on personal preferences rather than objective reasons. Even the undeliberate or unconscious use of gender in judgment or selection is an unjust exercise of power, only more subtle and concealed. Discrimination against women exists when men are able to do things that women are prevented from doing not by their own limitations but by men.[33]

Applying these criteria to issues in marriage and ministry, it becomes clear that sexism based on patriarchal patterns of power still survives in Christianity. Conservative evangelical churches promote the concept of headship in marriage, according to which the husband is the head of the Christian household and the wife is obliged to be submissive to him.[34] Even in churches and denominations that do not espouse the doctrine of headship, however, the cultural pattern of marriage that generally persists among members is some form of patriarchalism, according to which men have rights and privileges (such as not having to do housework in addition to working outside the home) that women do not have. To the extent that these Christian bodies do not actively fight the sexual bias in Western culture, they are in collusion with that culture and tacitly approve of sexism. Finally, some churches, such as the Roman Catholic, subject women to sexual rules regarding birth control and abortion which women have had no hand in drafting and are in no position to revise. These churches institutionalize sexism with regard to marriage because men alone have the power to formulate the doctrines that define marriage and the morals that regulate it.[35]

Likewise with regard to ministry, sexism is overt in some churches and covert in others. Higher-status ministerial roles have been traditionally reserved for men, so even in those denominations that have adopted policies that allow women equal access to all church positions, the statistical fact is that men still hold the majority of senior positions and the social reality is that women are not often called by congregations to those positions. In addition, some churches bar women from ordination on theological grounds, and so they prevent women both from serving in the ordained ministry and from making church-related decisions that are the prerogative of the ordained clergy.

From the historical and sociological perspective espoused in this volume, it matters little whether the theological arguments supporting the exclusion of women from ordination – or for that matter, proving the headship of husbands over wives – are valid. Arguments are only as sound as their premises, and it is quite logical that conclusions drawn from sexist premises would be equally sexist. Our concern is with the historical records and sociological facts that expose the existence of sexism rather than with its legitimation or delegitimation. We leave the endorsement or criticism of sexism to others.

NOTES

1 The definitive study of this evidence is Elisabeth Schüssler Fiorenza, *In Memory of Her: A Feminist Theological Reconstruction of Christian Origins* (New York: Crossroad, 1983). See also Ben Worthington III, *Women in the Earliest Churches* (New York: Cambridge University Press, 1988).
2 On the social construction of gender roles in primitive (foraging) societies,

see Claire M. Renzetti and Daniel J. Curran, *Women, Men and Society: The Sociology of Gender* (Needham Heights, Mass., Allyn and Bacon, 1989), chap. 4, especially 49–54.

3 See Linda Marie Fedigan, *Primate Paradigms: Sex Roles and Social Bonds* (Montreal: Eden Press, 1982). For a more popular treatment, see Desmond Morris, *The Naked Ape: A Zoologist's Study of the Human Animal* (New York: McGraw Hill, 1967).

4 'Gender roles are the tasks and activities that a culture assigns to the sexes.' Conrad Philip Kottak, *Cultural Anthropology*, 6th ed. (New York: McGraw Hill, 1994), 241.

5 See Ernestine Friedl, *Human Nature: An Anthropologist's View* (New York: Holt, Rinehart and Winston, 1975).

6 Ernestine Friedl, 'Society and Sex Roles,' *Human Nature* (April 1978), reprinted in *Anthropology 94/95* (Guilford, Conn.: Dushkin Publishing, 1994), 124–9.

7 On sexist patterns in tribal societies, see Peggy Reeves Sanday, *Female Power and Male Dominance: On the Origins of Sexual Inequality* (New York: Cambridge University Press, 1981).

8 On the place of women in ancient Israel, see Kevin Harris, *Sex, Ideology and Religion: The Representation of Women in the Bible* (Totowa, NJ: Barnes and Noble Books, 1984), 30–76. On marriage in the Old Testament, see David R. Mace, *Hebrew Marriage: A Sociological Survey* (New York: Philosophical Library, 1953), 121–59.

9 See Evelyn Stagg and Frank Stagg, *Women in the World of Jesus* (Philadelphia: Westminster Press, 1978), 21–2; also 'Adultery' in John L. McKenzie, *Dictionary of the Bible* (Milwaukee: Bruce Publishing Co., 1965), 14.

10 The controlling issue here is paternity – that is, a man's knowledge of his own offspring so that he could pass his family's property to his heirs. If a woman had access to many men, her husband would not know which of her children was his. In the words of Apollodorus of Athens: 'We have courtesans for pleasure, concubines to look after the day-to-day needs of the body, wives that we may breed legitimate children and have a trusty warden of what we have in the house.' Quoted in W.K. Lacy, *The Family in Classical Greece* (London: Thames and Hudson, 1968), 113.

11 See Sarah B. Pomeroy, *Goddesses, Whores, Wives, and Slaves: Women in Classical Antiquity* (New York: Schocken Books, 1975), 62–5. For primary documents, see Mary R. Lefkowitz and Maureen B. Flint, *Women's Life in Greece and Rome* (Baltimore: Johns Hopkins University Press, 1982).

12 See, for example, Everett Fergusen, *Backgrounds of Early Christianity*, 2nd ed. (Grand Rapids, Mich.: William B. Eerdmans, 1993), 65–72; also Edward

Schillebeeckx, *Marriage: Secular Reality and Saving Mystery* (London: Sheed and Ward, 1965), vol. II, 4–17.
13 See Jane F. Gardner, *Women in Roman Law and Society* (Sydney: Croom Helm, 1986), 6–7.
14 See J.P.V.D. Balsdon, *Roman Women: Their History and Habits* (London: Bodley Head, 1962), chap. 2.
15 Gardner, *Women*, 11–12.
16 See Jean LaPorte, *The Role of Women in Early Christianity* (New York: Edwin Mellen Press, 1982), 109–32; also relevant articles in David M. Scholer, ed., *Women in Early Christianity* (New York: Garland Publishing, 1993).
17 See Ross Shepard Kraemer, *Her Share of the Blessings* (New York: Oxford University Press, 1992).
18 A helpful survey of the history of women in Christianity can be found in the chapter on Christianity by Rosemary Radford Reuther in Arvind Sharma, ed., *Women in World Religions* (Albany, NY: SUNY Press, 1987), 207–33.
19 See Suzanne Fonay Wemple, 'Women from the Fifth to the Tenth Century,' in Christiane Klapisch-Zuber, ed., *Silences of the Middle Ages*, which is volume II of *A History of Women in the West* (Cambridge, Mass.: Harvard University Press, 1992), 169–201.
20 For a detailed treatment of this development, see Schillebeeckx, *Marriage*, 33–94. For a summary, see Joseph Martos, *Doors to the Sacred: A Historical Introduction to Sacraments in the Catholic Church* (Liguori, Mo.: Triumph Books 1991), 360–7.
21 See Eleanor Como McLaughlin, 'Equality of Souls, Inequality of Sexes: Woman in Medieval Theology,' in Rosemary Radford Reuther, *Religion and Sexism: Images of Women in the Jewish and Christian Traditions* (New York: Simon and Schuster, 1974), 213–66.
22 For general background, see Steven Ozment, *When Fathers Ruled: Family Life in the Reformation* (Cambridge, Mass.: Harvard University Press, 1983).
23 For example, see Elisabeth Schüssler Fiorenza and Mary Collins, eds., *Women – Invisible in Theology and Church* (Edinburgh: T&T Clark, 1985), especially the articles in Part II.
24 See Georgia Harkness, *Women in Church and Society: A Historical and Theological Inquiry* (Nashville, Tenn.: Abingdon Press, 1972), chap. 4; also Barbara Sinclair Deckard, *The Women's Movement: Political, Socioeconomic, and Philosophical Issues* (New York: Harper and Row, 1975), chap. 10.
25 See Ellen Carol Dubois, *Feminism and Suffrage: The Emergence of an Independent Women's Movement in America, 1848–1869* (Ithaca, NY: Cornell University Press, 1978).
26 See, for example, Karen Anderson, *Wartime Women: Sex Roles, Family Rela-*

tions, and the Status of Women during World War II (Westport, Conn.: Greenwood Press, 1981).

27 On this period, see William L. O'Neill, *Feminism in America: A History*, 2nd ed. (New Brunswick, NJ: Transaction Publishers, 1989), 308–25.

28 These and other developments are amply described in Flora Davis, *Moving the Mountain: The Women's Movement in America since 1960* (New York: Simon and Schuster, 1991). See also Deckard, *The Women's Movement*, chap. 12.

29 For an overview, see Rita J. Simon and Gloria Danziger, *Women's Movements in America: Their Successes, Disappointments, and Aspirations* (New York: Praeger Publishers, 1991).

30 See, for example, J. Kevin Coyle, 'The Fathers on Women and Women's Ordination,' and Rosemary Radford Reuther, 'Misogynism and Virginal Feminism in the Fathers of the Church' in David M. Scholer, ed., *Women in Early Christianity* (New York: Garland Publishing, 1993), 117–67 and 262–95, respectively.

31 Such is the so-called order of widows. See Bonnie Bowman Thurston, *The Widows: A Women's Ministry in the Early Church* (Minneapolis: Fortress Press, 1989).

32 For a collection of protests against sexism, see Alice L. Hageman, ed., *Sexist Religion and Women in the Church: No More Silence!* (New York: Association Press, 1974).

33 See Jean Lipman-Blumen, *Gender Roles and Power* (Englewood Cliffs, NJ: Prentice-Hall, 1984).

34 See, for example, John MacArthur, Jr, *The Fulfilled Family* (Chicago: Moody Press, 1985), chap. 2.

35 See Mary Daly, *The Church and the Second Sex* (New York: Harper and Row, 1968), especially chap. 2. For a broader perspective, see Karen McCarthy Brown, 'Fundamentalism and the Control of Women,' in John Stratton Hawley, ed., *Fundamentalism and Gender* (New York: Oxford University Press, 1994), 175–201.

2

Gender in the Origins of Christianity: Jewish Hopes and Imperial Exigencies

MARY ROSE D'ANGELO

Retrieving the story of Christian beginnings has always been a deeply political act. For most of the history of scholarship, the politics of this retrieval has been hidden. But in the last thirty years, widespread changes in theories of historical scholarship, the growth of feminism, and the emergence of political theologies have made it easier to see the ways in which sexual and imperial politics formed both the origins of Christianity and the explanations of those beginnings by later Christians and by historical investigators.

  This chapter argues that Jewish hopes of a new and transformed world made the movement begun by Jesus and his companions and the communities of the early Christian mission forums for participation and leadership for women. This thesis is a deliberate attempt to correct earlier (and some fairly recent) approaches to the question that have claimed that the teaching of Jesus and the more 'liberated' roles of women in Roman society released women from the restrictive and demeaning status to which 'patriarchal Judaism' assigned them.

  According to these interpretations, 'Jewish society' represents the problem: the patriarchal social setting whose rigid gender arrangements were (however temporarily) disarrayed by the 'solution': the message of Jesus, or the 'brokerless kingdom,' or the 'radical wisdom' of the Jesus movement.[1] Both feminist and non-feminist interpreters have framed the question in this way, generating an implicitly and sometimes explicitly anti-Jewish apologetic in Christian treatments of the issue. This apologetic, which has been repeatedly remarked by the Jewish feminist theologian Judith Plaskow, has become the object of real, though not always effective, concern among many feminist scholars.[2] It has recently been exacerbated by naïve use of social scientific and especially anthropological terms and categories of analysis among both feminist and non-feminist interpreters.

To elicit an understanding of the experiences of women in the beginnings of Christianity without reverting to anti-Jewish triumphalism, feminist interpretation must do two things. First, it must delineate the difference between the ways in which the communities that began Christianity accepted and revised gender practices and the ways in which the patriarchal interests of later Christian churches have represented them. Second, it must concentrate on the Roman paradigm of patriarchy and the ways in which it impinged on both Judaism and the early church. By 'patriarchy' I mean a social system in which a limited number of privileged males have power over women, children, and less privileged males. In Roman society, these privileged males are designated 'fathers' (*patres* and *patresfamilias*); among the less-privileged males are slaves, freedpersons, clients, and even unemancipated sons. This power is formally termed *patria potestas* (paternal power) and is extended beyond the household by patronage. At the apex of this system are the *patres* and *patres conscripti* of the senate and (after 31 BCE) the emperor. After 2 BCE, the title *pater patriae* formalized the emperor's status as the paterfamilias of the Roman people and the empire.[3] Augustus's consolidation of his imperial power was accompanied by legal measures to strengthen the patriarchal family.[4]

In fact, the roles that women assumed in the beginnings of Christianity had precedents in contemporary Jewish and Roman social settings but received new meaning (and in some settings wider accessibility) from the eschatological horizon within which they were performed. In Christianity, women's roles became a source of conflict in part because the communities' origins in the Jewish hope for radical change by God's reign were increasingly accommodated to the 'family values' of Roman imperial propaganda.

Gender in the Gospels and Reconstructions of the Context of Jesus

Recent reconstructions of Jesus' career have largely attempted to see him in the context of an itinerant movement, usually designated the Jesus movement. Gerd Theissen's description of the movement in sociological terms represented it as prophetic (charismatic, driven and attended by manifestations of spiritual power) and as anti-patriarchal – that is, the movement encouraged, perhaps even required, its members to reject their duty to the father of the family, the family's sustenance and substance, and its continuation, and to go on the road to preach the good news of God's reign.[5] Elisabeth Schüssler Fiorenza, by pointing out that the movement appears to have included women, radically changed the meaning of this description of the movement as antipatriarchal.[6] The presence of women on the road in the movement implies a challenge not just to the generational order of patriarchy but also to the gendered ideology, which (in Jewish, Greek, and Roman societies) assigned men to the city or political realm and women to the household or domestic realm. She described the Jesus movement as a 'discipleship of equals.'[7]

I have suggested two shifts in this perspective that further revise the understanding of gender in the origins of Christianity. The first is to rethink the term 'Jesus movement'; this phrase not only implies the exclusive leadership of Jesus but also assumes that his person was the content of the message. The older (and well-tested) scholarly observation that Jesus preached not himself but the reign of God suggests that those who were attracted to the movement attached themselves not primarily to the person of Jesus but rather first and foremost to the promises of God's reign. Thus 'reign-of-God movement' better represents this reality than does 'Jesus movement.'

Second, this observation, coupled with Theissen's description of the movement as charismatic, implies that the members saw themselves not primarily as followers, disciples, of Jesus (as the next generation saw them), but as prophets of, participants in, God's reign. Thus the movement was less a 'discipleship of equals' than a community of shared prophecy. While it cannot be shown that the movement at all times extended equality to women, the gospels give substantial evidence that women were participants and leaders in the movement, impelled by sharing in the prophetic spirit that animated it. Thus the female and male members of the movement were less the followers and disciples of Jesus than his companions in following and going out to meet the reign of God.[8]

Using the gospels as evidence for the context of Jesus and his companions in the reign-of-God movement presents many problems. Mark, probably the earliest of the four gospels of the New Testament, was written near or (more likely) after the fall of the temple (70 CE) – that is, approximately forty years after the death of Jesus. More important, the gospel writers sought to re-present Jesus – to make him newly present in the communities for whom they wrote. This is true not only of the four gospels in their final forms, but also of their sources, whether oral or written (like Q, the collection of sayings widely believed to be the common source of Matthew and Luke), as well as of those surviving gospels that never attained canonical status (such as the *Gospel of Thomas* and the *Gospel of Mary*).

Thus the Jesus of the gospels acts in and speaks to and for communities of the late first and early second centuries. Sayings of Jesus have been revised to suit their needs, and questions or objections that are put to him often articulate the issues the communities understand themselves to be facing. The other figures in the gospels, whether unnamed antagonists and recipients of miracles or named disciples who figure in individual stories, tend to represent positions within or related to the evangelists' communities. When names are remembered and used, this is probably because the names are famous enough to have been known and important to those communities. Both the canonical gospels and other materials that reflect the traditions about Jesus include the names of women as well as men among those who belonged to the circle around him.

The Reign-of-God Movement: Who Were Its Members?

In the conventional view, Jesus was surrounded by a council of twelve male disciples (followers) appointed by Jesus as his apostles (missionaries, emissaries) and understood to be his deputies and heirs. Women, if included at all, are taken to be supporters of the men who attend to their physical needs through donations of money or labour. But this picture, which derives from the gospel of Luke and Acts, obscures the evidence of the other (and earlier) sources, in which the role of the twelve is less clear and the participation of women more varied. Paul (whose writings are the earliest in the New Testament) appears to see the twelve primarily as witnesses to the resurrection (1 Cor. 15:5). If Q (one of the sources of Matthew and Luke) refers to the twelve at all, it may understand them as an eschatological council, the twelve judges of the twelve tribes (Matt. 19:28, Luke 22:30).[9]

The traditional assumptions about the twelve rely almost entirely on the picture in Mark (another source of Matthew and Luke), which depicts a special group of twelve male disciples who function as close companions of Jesus and whose names are listed in 3:16–19: Simon (nicknamed Peter), James and John (the sons of Zebedee, nicknamed the 'sons of thunder'), Andrew, Philip, Bartholomew, Matthew, Thomas, James (son of Alphaeus), Thaddeus, Simon the Canaanean, and Judas

Iscariot. In Mark 6:7–13 the twelve are sent out 'two by two' as Jesus' ambassadors who extend the mission of preaching, exorcism, and healing, and they are models for the early Christian mission.

They are by no means the only companions of Jesus/disciples in the gospel. After the selection of the twelve, the author speaks of 'those that were around him with (including) the twelve' (4:10) as the recipients of secret teaching; 'disciples' in Mark seems to refer to this larger group (4:34; see also 7:2, 15, 17; 8:27, 33–4, 9:29, 31), which also goes on the road with him to Jerusalem and his death (10:10, 13, 24, 46, 11:1). In Mark, this group includes women disciples; in 15:40–1, this gospel refers to women 'who followed him in Galilee and ministered to him' as watching the crucifixion from afar. The words 'followed' and 'ministered' indicate that these women are disciples; the note that they had followed in Galilee implies that they were on the road with him.[10] Three women are named: Mary Magdalene, Mary the mother of James and Joses, and Salome.

Both Matthew and Luke take over Mark's picture of twelve especially close male disciples and a group of other disciples that includes women. In differing ways, each of these authors defines the picture further and in so doing tends to limit the roles of the women disciples further. Both copied the list of twelve male disciples more or less intact, identifying the missionaries as apostles (Matt. 10:2, Luke 6:13). Matthew arranged the list in pairs, apparently linking the partners who went out 'two by two.' The tendency of this author to identify the twelve as the 'twelve disciples' pushes the women (and other male disciples) into the background. But women are not excluded from discipleship. Luke identifies the twelve as 'the apostles' and specifically excludes women from apostleship (Acts 1:21–2), but he does recognize women disciples, both before and after Jesus' death and resurrection (Luke 10:38–42, Acts 9:36). Moreover, this author confines the ministry of the women on the road with Jesus to patronage, with them supporting the mission out of their means.

Unlike Matthew and Luke, the gospel of John appears to have been independent of Mark, at least in its early stages of development, and it speaks with a very different voice. John refers to the twelve in only two settings.[11] The function of the twelve is never explained in John. They are never explicitly identified as apostles; 'apostles' does not designate a special group in John.[12] No list of the twelve is ever given, and it is possible that the author of John never knew such a list. But John does include twelve famous disciples: the unnamed disciple distinguished by the title 'beloved' (probably introduced in 1:36–9, see also 13:21), Andrew (introduced 1:36–40), Peter (1:41–2), Philip (1:34), Nathanael (1:45–51), Judas Iscariot (6:66–71), Martha, Mary, and Lazarus (11:1–44), Thomas (11:16), Judas not the Iscariot (14:22), and Mary Magdalene (19:25, 20:1–18). As with the disciples of Mark's list, only a few of these figures play major roles in the fourth gospel.[13] Without a list, it is impossible to say for certain whether the women disciples were seen by the author as among the twelve. But perhaps Luke's insistence on the requirement of maleness for membership in the twelve (Acts 1:21–2) offers backhanded evidence that some early Christian communities did count women among the members of the twelve as well as among the apostles.[14]

The three women whom Mark places at the cross (Mary Magdalene, Mary the mother of James and Joses, and Salome) deserve special attention. The author claims that the first two also saw where Jesus was buried (15:47) and that all three found the tomb empty on the third day (16:1–8). The decision to name specific women is apologetic; the author wishes to specify witnesses who can link the death of Jesus, his burial, and the tomb. The witnesses are women and 'far off'; the political nature of the alleged crime and its penalty would have endangered anyone showing overt sympathy for Jesus. Though all four gospels include the names of specific women witnesses at least at the tomb, and it is probable that Matthew and Luke use Mark's narrative as one of their sources, the only name all four have in common is that of Mary Magdalene. The differing names are likely to have been chosen because the women were on some level famous – that is, known by the potential readers to have been active in the movement.

This fame is sometimes hard for later readers to discern. The three women in Mark 15:40 and 16:1 are a good example. Mary the mother of James and Joses (Mark 15:40, 47, 16:1) appears to be taken over in Matthew's accounts of the cross (27:56), burial (27:61), and empty tomb (28:1); she may be understood by Mark to be a relative of Jesus (6:3; cf. Matt. 13:55).[15] Salome (Mark 15:40 and 16:1) is dropped from Matthew and Luke and makes no appearance in John.[16] But she does appear in the *Gospel of Thomas*, where she challenges Jesus and, on the basis of his reply, declares herself his disciple.[17] Mary Magdalene is by far the most famous of these women for later readers. Following Mark, Matthew places her at the cross, burial, and tomb (27:56, 61, 28:1); this gospel adds a brief narrative in which she and 'the other Mary' are the first to see the risen Jesus (28:9–10). Luke also mentions her at the empty tomb

(24:10).[18] In John she plays a more prominent role; a witness to the cross (John 18:25), she is also the sole discoverer of the empty tomb and the first of the disciples to meet the risen Jesus (John 20:1–2, 11–18). The protagonist of the *Gospel of Mary*, who is a visionary and appears to be also an apostle, is probably Mary Magdalene, as is the Mary who is an interlocutor of Jesus in *Gospel of Thomas*.[19] The *Gospel of Philip* calls her the companion of Jesus and claims that he loved her more than all the other disciples and kissed her frequently, apparently because her response to his teaching showed her to be more enlightened than the others.[20] The *Dialogue of the Savior* also seems to regard her as the most enlightened of the disciples.[21]

Both Mary and Salome reappear in the later, composite work called *Pistis Sophia*, where they show themselves to be dialogue partners of deep understanding.[22] Thus there are limited but fairly widespread traditions about these two women which identify both of them as disciples, and Mary Magdalene as an apostle; Mary Magdalene bore the title 'apostle of the apostles' until at least the tenth century.[23] But there is also a darker side to Christian traditions about Mary Magdalene and Salome. Luke 8:1–3 already identified Mary Magdalene as one from whom seven devils had gone out; the proximity of this note to Luke's story of the sinful woman (7:36–50) is likely to have contributed to the portrait of Mary as prostitute and penitent that eventually obliterated her status as witness and apostle. Salome's name became attached to the unnamed daughter of Herodias, who is made the occasion of John the Baptist's death in Mark 6:17–29.[24] The *Protevangelium of James* introduces a Salome in the role of doubter of Mary's virginity; she is punished and converted (19:18–20:12).[25]

Martha and Mary, who appear both in Luke 10:38–42 and in John 11:1–12:8, offer an especially striking example of the complexities involved in trying to discover what it was like for women to participate in the reign-of-God movement. Most believers and in fact preachers recall these women only as they are depicted in Luke's very short, exemplary story. This story appears to pit the two women against each other and shows Jesus affirming the silent Mary who 'sits as his feet' – i.e., learns from him as a disciple – against a complaining, bustling Martha, who is busy with what is seen as the women's work of serving. The story is thus often read as permitting women to step out of the gender roles assigned to them, but at the cost of denigrating women who engage in the work of sustaining life. The stories in John 11:1–12:8 present a quite different picture; they show the two women acting in concert on behalf of their brother (11:17–44) and in gratitude for his restoration to them (12:1–8). In John's version Martha in particular is an example of faith (11:20–7).[26]

What then lies behind the two different versions? Should one be accepted over the other? The two stories have only the most minimal common traits. In both, Martha is said to serve/minister (*diakonein*; Luke 10:39–40, John 12:1), while Mary is designated as 'sister.' In both, Martha welcomes Jesus (Luke 10:38, John 11:20); this may imply that she is the owner of the house. This scant information suggests that behind these stories lies the memory of two famous women who formed a pair of missionaries, like the pairs in Matt. 10:1–4. They were known and remembered as Martha the *diakonos* (minister; cf. Rom. 16:1, Phoebe the *diakonos*/minister of the church of Cenchreae) and Mary the sister (*adelphe*), just as Paul signed letters as Paul the *apostolos* with a companion (for example, Sosthenes, I Cor. 1:1) designated 'the brother' (*adelphos*).[27]

The stories told of Martha and Mary in the gospel of John appear in other versions with unnamed women as their protagonists.[28] Thus it seems likely that Martha and Mary were remembered primarily because of their roles in the (post-resurrection) early Christian mission; these roles are commemorated by the titles 'minister' (*diakonos*) and sister (*adelphe*). The narratives in which they appear in Luke and John are less insights into the history and character of these particular women than vehicles for these authors' theological concerns and their assumptions or prescriptions about gender.[29]

Thus women appear to have been participants and even protagonists in the reign-of-God movement. This does not necessarily mean that the women within the movement achieved full equality or that all gender prescriptions and barriers were lifted and equality was explicitly espoused by the movement as a whole. The point here is not that the participation of women in the reign-of-God movement was unexampled in Jewish or Roman contexts, or that Jesus 'liberated' women from Jewish or Graeco-Roman patriarchy, or that 'Jesus was a feminist.' Rather, the point is that the picture of Jesus surrounded by twelve male disciples, with women only as supporters or as listeners, results from the Christian sexual politics of later readers rather than from univocal evidence in the texts. The reign-of-God movement was far more the project and the product of women than later generations of Christians have been willing to acknowledge. How then should this movement of women as well as men be understood?

Gender in the Origins of Christianity 33

Reading Gender in the Reign-of-God Movement: The Problem

A variety of recent reconstructions of the context of Jesus attempt to appeal to women or to present Jesus in the light of feminist concerns. Some argue that Jesus rejected the system of purity and impurity that they attribute to most sects of Judaism of the time, depicting Jesus as rejecting the prescriptions of Leviticus in such narratives as the woman with the flow of blood and the daughter of Jairus (Mark 5:21–43).[30] The idea that Jesus aroused hostility by open commensality or inclusion of the socially marginal has been given a feminist twist. The synoptic sayings on divorce are sometimes taken as Jesus' rejection of patriarchal marriage or of inequality within marriage.[31] Some rereadings of Jeremias's theories that Jesus used 'abba' as an address to God and conveyed by it an understanding of God that was uniquely intimate have claimed Jesus's use of 'father' as a non-patriarchal divine title.[32]

Each of these approaches involves a number of problems. The historical evidence for these conclusions is often slender. In some cases, Jesus is presented as liberator to women, but no attention is given to women as active participants in the movement.[33] Nearly all treatments are flawed by invidious comparison between Jesus or the Jesus movement and Judaism. Even Schüssler Fiorenza's sophisticated presentation of the Jesus movement as a renewal movement within Judaism contrasts Jesus' *'basileia* concept' as a practice of 'inclusive wholeness' to a dominant ethos that equated God's reign with 'holiness.'[34]

As well as reinforcing or encouraging Christian anti-Judaism, these approaches distort the lives and history of ancient Jewish women by producing pictures of ancient Jewish gender relations that are badly skewed. There is in fact little evidence that ritual purity had a major influence on the lives of women in Galilee in the first century or that Jesus reacted against it.[35] Nor is it the case that Jewish women were confined to female space or domestic roles, or that Jewish practices in marriage and divorce were as absolute as they are often taken to be.[36] These pictures are produced by a collaboration of the apologetic interests of nineteenth- and twentieth-century scholarship with those of the gospels. Centuries of scholarly investigation of the New Testament under the auspices of the great imperialist cultures (Germany, England, France, and the United States) have read the gospels in light of 'Jewish background' and 'Hellenistic influences,' effectively masking the Roman imperial interest with which these modern empires identified, often quite explicitly. In addition, Christian commentators have sought to show that Jesus and therefore Christianity were superior to Judaism.

The gospel writers are motivated by at least two apologetic concerns. The first and simplest is an appeal to the Roman imperial interest. Thus the gospel narratives depict Pilate as executing Jesus not in an attempt to eliminate a threat to empire but in a concession to the Jews. A second apologetic concern is the need for a theological explanation for the death of Jesus and the fall of the temple; both are explained by adopting the earlier biblical attempts to explain the suffering of the Jews as the result of their own 'hard-heartedness' (the so-called Deuteronomistic theology); thus the gospel writers claim that the Jews refused to listen to Jesus as they refused to listen to the prophets. This apology forms not only the passion narratives but also all accounts between Jesus and specific parties of Judaism in the gospel. The Jews of the gospels, in particular the Pharisees, scribes, and lawyers who debate with Jesus, are straw Jews, characters set up by the gospel writers to offer a contrast to Jesus.[37]

Is it then possible to consider the meaning of women's participation in the reign-of-God movement without reiterating and exacerbating the anti-Jewish apologetic of the gospels and later Christian interpretation of them? To do so, it is necessary to make two steps in rethinking the meaning of the movement itself. First, it is essential to move from contrasting the movement with Judaism towards understanding the movement as one among a number of manifestations of Jewish resistance to the Roman order. Second, it is also important to understand that resistance as spiritual resistance, spiritual in the literal sense of spirit-driven, charismatic, and prophetic.

Reign of God as Resistance to Rome

Seeing the reign-of-God movement as resistance to Rome requires attending to two aspects of the movement frequently acknowledged but on the whole poorly absorbed: that Jesus died in the interests of Rome and that the reign-of-God movement offered an alternative to the Roman imperial order.[38] The charge against Jesus and the method of his execution make clear that he died as an enemy of Rome. The gospels seriously misrepresent the role of the Jews in the death of Jesus, in that they place the motivation and initiative with the Jewish leaders, claiming that Pilate was forced into collaborating with them. Pilate was not subject to pressure from the high priests; rather the high priests held office and indeed officiated liturgically only at the sufferance of the procurator.³⁹ If indeed the Jewish high priests played any role in the death of Jesus, then the picture in the gospels must be reversed: the high priests may have collaborated with Pilate, whether in the interest of preserving their relationship with him or as an expedient towards saving themselves and the people as a whole from reprisals. Jesus died for the sake of Rome's imperial interest.⁴⁰

This is obscured for most twentieth-century Christians because Christian interpretation is accustomed to presenting Jesus' life as a conflict with the Pharisees over religious ideas and practice and his death as the result of envy on the part of the Jewish leaders. But it was to the Roman imperial occupation that the preaching of God's reign spelled a threat.⁴¹ Josephus, a first-century Jewish historian attempting to explain the early-first-century context of the Jewish revolt of 66, describes a 'fourth school of Jewish philosophy.' Its major tenet was a rejection of human (especially foreign Roman) rule, God being the only ruler and lord; its adherents would die rather than acknowledge another ruler or lord.⁴² In the first century, the announcement of God's reign must have implied for most hearers, especially Romans: '*God*'s reign – not the emperor's.'

Much recent research on the Jesus of history has focused on whether Jesus saw the reign of God as a future or a present reality. This old question has been hardened by the recent tendency to make an absolute separation between apocalyptic expectation and wisdom.⁴³ But the attention that it receives obscures other aspects of the reign in the gospels and the writings of Bible and early Judaism. First, the word 'reign' (like 'world' in Paul and John) refers less to a spatial or temporal reality than to a population. This observation does not exclude temporal and spatial references – a population has both temporal and spatial aspects. Some very ancient sayings in the gospels reflect the understanding of the reign as a populace: 'Blessed the poor ... *of them* is God's reign' (i.e., composed of them; Matt. 5:3); 'let the little children come to me; *of such* is God's reign' (Mark 10:14). The expressions 'of them' and 'of such' should probably be read not as possessive but as expressing the composition of the reign. Thus 'to the enter the reign of God' (Mark 10:15, 23, 24, 25; Matt. 5:20, 18:3; John 3:5) is to join the movement, to go on the road with God's reign.

Second, the reign of God refers to God's powerful activity within the world. The proclamation that 'the reign of God has come near' can be transposed into a sentence with God as subject: 'God reigns (will reign).'⁴⁴ The introductions to the parables might be retranslated, 'God reigns like' or 'God acts like.' When the women and men of the movement proclaimed God's reign by choosing to go on the road, they both claimed to be God's reign and went out to meet its definitive manifestation. Unlike the gospel of John, the synoptic gospels refer to only one passover. Thus the time frame from Jesus' appearance as the disciple of John the baptizer to the crucifixion may well have been less than a year; the preaching career of Jesus and the movement need have been no more than a few months. It is possible for virtually the entire movement to have been literally moving for that amount of time.[45]

An analogy can be seen in another itinerant movement about fifteen years after Jesus' death, led by a prophet named Theudas.[46] According to Josephus, Theudas had led a 'huge crowd with all their possessions' to the Jordan, where God was to part the waters for them. Presumably, they expected God to lead them into the possession of the land, as in the days of Moses and Joshua. This expectation implied freedom from imperial rule both to Theudas and his companions and to the Roman procurator Coponius, who sent troops to slaughter the greater part of them. There is no reason to believe that Theudas's movement was a violent revolution or included only men; indeed, desert traditions behind Theudas's new exodus and entry would have assumed that women and children alike were to enter through the Jordan as well.

These traditions appear to also have influenced the itineracy of the reign-of-God movement, which distanced its members from the patriarchal household, a relatively certain means of imperial control. Women as well as men left the recognizable, controllable bounds of the family and the settled communities in which each householder, each father, was responsible for those subject to him – wives, children, and slaves – to the local authorities and ultimately to the emperor, the father of his country. By going on the road, they moved out of the imperial rule and into the reign of one God and father. Like Theudas's new exodus, the reign-of-God movement incurred Roman wrath; when it ascended to the holy city for the Passover festival of liberation, the Romans exacted a penalty for its expectations by executing Jesus.

Reign of God as Spiritual Power

The second significant aspect of the movement is its spiritual and prophetic character. This spirit-driven character should be imagined not on the heroic model through which the prophets of the Hebrew Bible are usually read, but in the context of the communal prophecy that characterized early Christianity. This means not just conceiving Jesus as prophet but locating him as one prophet within a prophetic movement. Traces of the prophetic and spiritual activity of others remain in the gospel narratives, which give evidence that Jesus was not the only prophet in the movement – that others also acted as prophets, proclaiming God's reign and manifesting God's spirit in cures and exorcisms. The gospels remember this obliquely in the passages in which Jesus commissions and sends out the disciples. An even more significant example is the memory of the woman who anointed Jesus (Mark 14:1–11; Matt. 26:1–16; John 12:1–11).[47] Her deed is prophetic, the deed of Samuel anointing Saul and David or of Nathan (with Zadok the priest) anointing Solomon; she designates Jesus as messiah/christ (anointed). Unlike the disciples, who are commissioned for their prophetic deeds, this woman is depicted as acting without direction or even permission from Jesus: *she* commissions him, announcing the word of God that comes to her, for and to him.

The movement's charismatic character meant a sharing of spiritual power not only because miracles were done by others as well as by Jesus but also because miracles as manifestations of spiritual power appear to have been participatory. The Gospel of Mark reflects the early view that faith and participation on the part of the one seeking miracles are a prerequisite for the disbursement of spiritual power. The most striking example is the story of the women with the flow of blood in Mark 5:24–34. She herself prescribes the means of her cure, which she accomplishes with a touch that brings forth power from Jesus. His address to her merely affirms the cure that has already taken place. In 6:5 (on an incident immediately following this narrative), the author comments that Jesus could do no miracles in his home place 'because of their lack of faith.' The other miracle narratives (in particular Mark 9:14–29) make clear that this comment is by no means incidental but rather essential to the author's understanding of how miracles work. In all these cases, the argument I am making is not that any of these individual narratives are historical but rather that together they preserve memories of the character of the movement in which the doing of miracles and prophetic deeds is an attribute not only of Jesus but one shared among the women and men of the movement.

Recognizing the prophetic character of the movement both before and after Jesus' death also suggests that words of Jesus remembered in the gospels are at least in part the product of the prophetic activity of the community. This is because the male and female prophets of the community continued to speak after the resurrection, when they experienced the spirit in which they spoke as the spirit of Jesus; the 'word of the Lord' that came to them was the word of Jesus the risen Lord. The second-century prophetic movement that called itself the new prophecy provides an analogy to the earliest Christian experience of the spirit; a number of the oracles of its first prophets, Montanus, Priscilla, and Maximilla, begin with the words 'I am' and resemble the 'I am' sayings of the gospel of John. At least some sayings of Jesus in the gospels are likely to have originated as sayings of the risen Lord Jesus articulated by the prophets.[48] As narratives about Jesus became increasingly important, they were given settings in stories about Jesus' life.

Even sayings that were part of the reign-of-God movement and antedated Jesus' death and resurrection might have originated with others of its prophets than Jesus. For instance, the prophetic activity of the movement may have been the origin of at least some beatitudes before the death of Jesus.[49] The gospels preserve one context in which beatitudes were uttered that has received little attention. In at least three settings, listeners respond to the revelatory pronouncements with a beatitude. In Luke 11:27-8 and *Gospel of Thomas* 79, an unnamed woman responds to Jesus with a beatitude that acknowledges the power in his teaching. Jesus, in response, corrects her with a beatitude on the hearer. A (male) fellow guest in Luke 14:5 responds to Jesus' beatitude on potential hosts with a blessing on those who will eat bread in God's reign.[50] Jesus responds to Peter's confession in Matthew with a beatitude that acclaims the revelation that Peter has received.

Similarly, the beatitudes may have originated as prophetic responses to the movement's great revelation, 'God's reign has come near.' Traditional interpretations of this proclamation envisage it as announcing a message from God whose implications were revealed in full to Jesus, while some more recent attempts see it as unveiling a social program carefully thought out by him. But the proclamation had deep resonances in Jewish religious consciousness. Its meaning must have come largely not from the specific content provided by Jesus, but from the hopes and expectations of the women and men who heard this proclamation: justice for the poor; an end to hunger, landlessness, and homelessness; and freedom from the Romans' taxes and their idolatrous rule.[51] When Jesus (or one of the female or male prophets of the reign) proclaimed 'God's reign has come near!,' another of the prophets (or Jesus) would have responded, 'Blessed the poor! Of you is God's reign!' From another prophet, or at another time, the proclamation could have elicited the response, 'Blessed the hungry! They shall be filled!' or 'Blessed the weeping! They shall have the last laugh!'

Such prophetic responses might easily become an extension of the preaching itself, repeated by a preacher or his or her companions as they moved from village to village. As such, they would serve both as prophetic and apocalyptic pronouncements and as gnomic sayings enshrining the wisdom of God's reign. In this view, Jesus functions as a prophet among his companions, women and men who also are prophets, who also speak revelations of how and in whom God reigns. The beatitudes represent their prophecy and their wisdom as well as his.[52]

Rereading Gender in the Reign-of-God Movement

In the picture that I have drawn above, women took part and assumed leadership in the reign-of-God movement not because it offered liberation from 'patriarchal Judaism' but in response to a particular (though not necessarily unique) conjunction of Jewish experience and Jewish hopes.[53] The reign of God as a movement of resistance to Rome which would evoke God's definitive act of redemption was formed by the memories of the Exodus; the Jewish tradition of prophecy grounded the experience of the spirit as word and power for women as well as for men.[54] Where exodus traditions in themselves might have reinforced familial and gender roles by stressing the family structure, the urgency of hope combined with the prophetic character of the movement conspired to suspend them. Gender roles were not so much directly challenged as superseded by the urgency and power of God's reign. The spirit itself was an experience of power for the women of the movement.

An analogy can be found in the evangelical revival movements of the nineteenth-century United States, where women embraced ecstatic experience more readily than men and through it asserted leadership in the first generation of revivals. As revivals helped to create and were absorbed by the new bourgeois social order, they were increasingly gendered; ecstatic manifestations and female leadership were increasingly relegated to the margins of the movement.[55]

Early Christianity and Roman Patriarchy

Similar shifts occurred after Jesus' crucifixion and resurrection. The reign of God as resistance to the Roman order gave way to the message of Jesus' death and resurrection as God's deed and the catalyst of God's reign in the traditions reflected in canonical New Testament. As far as possible, Jesus' death was distanced from its political context by attributing it to the envy of the Jews.[56] God's reign became more the future reward of present suffering than God's power-filled community. In traditions such as that behind the *Gospel of Thomas*, the reign was internalized and (apparently) depoliticized.[57]

Even so, women's leadership did not cease. The missionary character of the early movement and its apocalyptic expectations continued the urgency that once had derived from the proclamation of God's reign, and, along with the spirit-oriented character of most branches of the early Christian mission, it helped to provide a forum for women's activity. But increasingly gender became a point of conflict; it became necessary to modify, reassert, or explicitly challenge the gender norms of the Roman imperial world.[58]

Romans 16 is an especially valuable window into the continued participation of women in the movement. Romans was written to a community that Paul had not founded and in fact had never visited. In Romans 16 – the greetings of the letter – Paul appears to name as many members of the community by name as he can in an attempt to garner support for his journeys to Jerusalem and Rome itself and his proposed mission to Spain. This suggests that the people greeted are persons of influence, and probably also known to Paul, and therefore missionaries themselves. A striking number are women, and the women greeted in Romans seem to function in the same range of missionary roles as men.[59] Most notable among them is Junia, who, with her partner, Andronicus, is applauded as famous among the apostles.[60] The letter also greets two women who, like Junia and Andronicus, seem to operate as a missionary pair (16:12).[61] But this does not mean that the sanctions of gender disappeared. On the contrary, earlier in the letter, Paul uses female homoeroticism as the paradigm of human depravity (1:18–31).[62]

First Corinthians reflects gender conflicts in response to women's spiritual activity.[63] I Corinthians 7 suggests that some of these conflicts stemmed from Paul's concern to be seen as supportive of marriage as a means of sexual and social control. In the wake of the 'family values' campaign of Augustus, intermarriage (especially the conversion of married women) placed Christianity in the vulnerable position of threatening the stability of marriages.[64] In later years, the political philosophy that justified the Roman imperial sexual politics emerged in the household codes of the post-Pauline letters presented in Colossians, Ephesians, I Timothy, and I Peter.[65] Gospel traditions also reflect this trend in the anti-divorce sayings attributed to Jesus in Mark 10:2–12 and Matt. 19:2–12 and 5:27–32.[66] Communal struggles emerge but are more favourably resolved in John 20:1–18, *Gospel of Thomas* Saying 114, and *Gospel of Mary*.[67]

Luke-Acts is an especially significant example of the pattern of gender conflict; this two-volume work increases the number of women included in its narrative over both of its known sources (Mark and Q). But this inclusion of women is governed by a political agenda of control and accommodation to Roman imperial mores that carefully distances the early community from Judaism and from the prophecy of women.[68]

Conclusion

The origins of Christianity and its gender troubles thus appear to have emerged not from Jesus' challenge to Jewish patriarchy but from the deep loyalty and fierce expectation of Jewish women and men who moved out to meet the reign of God in Jesus' company. For them and for at least some of their Jewish and Gentile successors in Christianity, the experience of spiritual power superseded, relativized, or revised the boundaries of gender and the demands of patriarchy. But the 'family values' fostered to support the Roman imperial order produced anxiety in their companions and contemporaries around the empowerment of women. Moral order was identified with subordination in Roman antiquity, and the attempt to claim the moral and political high ground bound later generations of Christians to the hierarchy of gender.

NOTES

1 Among the most problematic of early versions of the argument is Leonard Swidler, *Women in Judaism: The Status of Women in Formative Judaism* (Metuchen, NJ: Scarecrow Press, 1976). The phrasing 'brokerless kingdom' is that of John Dominic Crossan; see *The Historical Jesus: The Life of a Mediterranean Jewish Peasant* (San Francisco: Harper, 1990), 225–416. Crossan explicitly disavows pejorative comparisons with specific tenets of Judaism in areas such as his stress on open commensality, but his claiming that the violation of boundaries was the focus of Jesus' message tends to reinforce such comparisons.

2 Judith Plaskow, 'Anti-Judaism in Christian Feminist Interpretation,' in Elisabeth Schüssler Fiorenza, ed., *Searching the Scriptures, Vol. I, A Feminist Ecumenical Introduction* (New York: Crossroad, 1993), 117–29.

3 Men were initiated into homosocial politics through the *togatus* ceremony (Greeks, through the sexually exclusive gymnasium). I would argue that our own society is but minimally distanced from this most blatant practice of patriarchy.
4 *Lex Iulia de adulteriis* and *Lex Iulia de ordinibus maritandis* appear to have been in force by 17 BCE. The former made adultery a criminal charge and demanded that the erring wife be divorced; the latter imposed penalties on celibacy and childlessness. Though the legislation bears primarily on Roman citizens, and therefore has no direct effect on non-citizens in the provinces, it enshrines Roman attitudes and imperial mores. Hugh Last, 'The Social Program of Augustus,' in S.A. Cook, F.E. Adcock, and M.P. Charlesworth, eds., *Cambridge Ancient History, Vol. X, The Augustan Empire 44 B.C.–A.D. 70* (Cambridge: Cambridge University Press, 1971), 441–56.
5 Gerd Theissen, *Sociology of Early Palestinian Christianity*, trans. John Bowden (Philadelphia: Fortress, 1978), first published in German as *Soziologie der Jesus-bewegung* (München: Kaisar-Verlag, 1977); Wayne A. Meeks, *The Moral World of the First Christians*, Library of Early Christianity (Philadelphia: Westminster, 1986), 96–108. Elisabeth Schüssler Fiorenza has shown the feminist potential of this approach: *In Memory of Her: A Feminist Theological Reconstruction of Christian Origins* (New York: Crossroad, 1983), 105–59. For a critique of Theissen, see Richard A. Horsley, *Sociology and the Jesus Movement* (New York: Crossroad, 1989).
6 Schüssler Fiorenza, *Memory*, 105–59.
7 Ibid.
8 For fuller presentations of the proposal, see Mary R. D'Angelo, 'Re-Membering Jesus: Women, Prophecy and Resistance in the Memory of the Early Churches,' *Horizons: Journal of the College Theology Society*, 19 (fall, 1992), 199–218, and 'The Concrete Foundation of Christianity: Re-Membering Jesus,' in Paul Crowley, ed., *Proceedings of the Catholic Theological Society of America*, Baltimore, 9–12 June 1994, vol. XLIX, 135–46.
9 In Matthew, Jesus promises 'You will sit upon twelve thrones judging the twelve tribes of Israel' (19:28). This promise is directed to the twelve. Luke's version of the saying does not specify the number of thrones, and the promise could be directed to more (or fewer) than twelve. In Luke 22:30, the promise is directed to the twelve. But in Q, it is more likely to have been directed to all of Jesus' followers.
10 On the technical meaning of 'follow' and 'minister' as indicating discipleship, see W.D. Davies, *The Setting of the Sermon on the Mount* (Cambridge: Cambridge University Press, 1964), 422–3. On 'minister,' see also Schüssler Fiorenza, *Memory*, 165–73.

11 In John 6:66–71, the prediction of Jesus' death is addressed to the twelve, and they are warned, 'One of you will betray me.' The reader is informed that this one is Judas Iscariot. In 20:24, the irony of Thomas's doubt is underlined by the author's identifying him as one of the twelve.
12 The word is used only once, in John 13:16, where it seems to apply generically to all disciples; see also 17:18, 20:21; the disciples are sent as Jesus is sent.
13 It is possible that Judas not the Iscariot is the same as Thomas the twin; the Thomas tradition regularly identifies its apostle as Judas Thomas (*Gospel of Thomas, Acts of Judas Thomas*). There are other characters in the story: Nicodemus, the Samaritan woman (4:1–42), the (formerly) blind man (9:1–38), and Mary of Alphaeus (19:25). Mary of Alphaeus is the only real candidate for the twelve among these; Nicodemus is at a distance until the crucifixion (3:1–11, 7:52, 19:39), while the Samaritan woman and the blind man, though they become believers, are unnamed figures who make a single appearance.
14 Bernadette Brooten, '"Junia ... Outstanding among the Apostles" (Romans 16.7),' in L. Swidler and A. Swidler, *Women Priests: A Catholic Commentary on the Vatican Declaration* (New York: Paulist, 1977), 141–4.
15 Perhaps his mother's sister; see John 18:25. Identifying this woman is complicated: Mark refers to her in three different ways in as many verses. She may also appear in Luke's version of the empty tomb (Mary the mother of James, 24:10).
16 Matthew appears to substitute the mother of the sons of Zebedee, a character special to this gospel (cf. 20:20–1).
17 Saying 61; Nag Hammadi Codex (NHC) II, 2, 43, 23–34.
18 Luke removes the special role of female witnesses from the passion story. No women are named at the cross, and not only the unnamed women but also 'all his acquaintances' are said to have watched from afar (23:49). No women are named at the burial (55–6), though the narrative seems to imply that the women named in 24:10 are meant here.
19 *Gospel of Mary*, Berlin Gnostic Papyrus (BG), 7, 9–19; *Gospel of Thomas*, Sayings 21 and 114; NHC II, 2, 36, 34 and 51, 18–27.
20 This work is not actually a gospel in form. NHC II, 3, 59, 1–12, and 63, 31–64-10.
21 NHC III, ,5, 120, 1–147, 23 see especially para. 53, 139, 11–13. See Helmut Koester and Elaine Pagels in James M. Robinson, ed., *The Nag Hammadi Library in English* (San Francisco: Harper, 1988), 245; Antti Marjanen, *The Woman Jesus Loved: Mary Magdalene in the Nag Hammadi Library and Related Documents* (Leiden: E.J. Brill, 1996), 78–93.
22 See Marjanen, *The Woman*, 170–88.

23 Carla Ricci, *Mary Magdalene and Many Others: Women Who followed Jesus* trans. Paul Burns (Minneapolis: Fortress Press, 1994), 192 n. 39.
24 She remains unnamed in Matt. 14:3–12 and Justin Martyr, *Dialogue with Trypho*, 49:4–5; the association seems to have been made through a daughter named Salome referred to by Josephus (*Antiginties*, 18.136).
25 Available in Robert Miller, ed., *The Complete Gospels* (Sonoma, Calif.: Polebridge Press, 1994), 393–4.
26 Adele Reinhartz, 'From Narrative to History: The Resurrection of Mary and Martha,' in Amy-Jill Levine, ed., *'Women Like This': New Perspectives on Jewish Women in the Greco-Roman World* (Atlanta: Scholars Press, 1991), 161–84.
27 Elisabeth Schüssler Fiorenza, 'A Feminist Critical Interpretation for Liberation: Martha and Mary: Luke 10:38–42,' *Religion and Intellectual Life*, 3 (1986), 21–35; Mary R. D'Angelo, 'Women Partners in the New Testament,' *Journal of Feminist Studies in Religion*, 6 (spring 1990), 65–86.
28 To John 12:1–8 compare Mark 14:1–11 and Luke 7:36–50; to John 11:1–44 compare the resurrection of a woman's brother told in *Secret Mark*; see Miller, *Complete Gospels*, 408–11.
29 On the functions of Mary and Martha in Luke 11:38–42, see E. Schüssler Fiorenza, *But She Said: Feminist Practices of Biblical Interpretation* (Boston: Beacon, 1992), 62–7; D'Angelo, 'Women Partners,' 65–86, and 'Women in Luke-Acts: A Redactional View,' *Journal of Biblical Literature* 109 (1990), 441–61.
30 See for example, Marla J. Selvidge, *Woman, Cult and Miracle Recital: A Redactional Critical Investigation on Mark 5:24–34* (Lewisburg, Pa.: Bucknell University Press, 1990), and 'Mark 5:25–34 and Leviticus 15:19–20: A Reaction to Restrictive Purity Regulations,' *Journal of Biblical Literature*, 103 (1984), 619–23; this material is reused in Hisako Kinukawa, *Women and Jesus in Mark* (Maryknoll, NY: Orbis, 1994), 29–30.
31 For instance, Schüssler Fiorenza, *Memory*, 143–5. For a different view of the origin of these sayings and their function, see Mary R. D'Angelo, 'Remarriage and the Divorce Sayings Attributed to Jesus' in William G. Roberts, ed., *Divorce and Remarriage* (Kansas City, Mo.: Sheed and Ward, 1990), 78–106.
32 Robert Hamerton-Kelly, *God the Father: Theology and Patriarchy in the Teaching of Jesus* OBT 4 (Philadelphia: Fortress, 1979), and 'God the Father in the Bible,' in Johannes-Baptist Metz and Edward Schillebeeckx, eds., *God as Father?* English-language editor Marcus Lefébure, *Concilium* 143 (Edinburgh: T&T Clark, and New York: Seabury Press, 1981). Some feminist scholars have accepted Hamerton-Kelly's view that Jesus used 'father' in a non-patriarchal sense and have attempted to subvert the construct itself and to put it to the service of feminist critique of patriarchy and its deities; see Schüssler Fiorenza, *Memory*, 147–51; Sandra Schneiders, *Women and the Word:*

The Gender of God in the New Testament and the Spirituality of Women (New York: Paulist, 1986), 42-9.

For critiques of this position, see Madeline Boucher 'Scriptural Readings: God-Language and Nonsexist Translation,' in Barbara A. Withers, ed., *Language and the Church: Articles and Designs for Workshops* (National Council of Churches of Christ in the U.S.A., 1984), 28-32; Phyllis Trible's review of Hamerton-Kelly's *God the Father, Today*, 37 (1980), 116-19; Shannon Clarkson, Language about God,' *Studies in Religion/Sciences réligieuses*, 18 (1989), 37-49; Mary R. D'Angelo, 'Abba and "Father": Imperial Theology and the Traditions about Jesus,' *Journal of Biblical Literature* 111, no. 4 (1992), 611-30; 'Theology in Mark and Q: Abba and "Father" in Context,' *Harvard Theological Review*, 85 (1992), 149-74.

33 Important exceptions are E. Schüssler Fiorenza, *Memory*, 130-54; *Jesus Miriam's Child Sophia's Prophet* (New York: Continuum, 1994), espeially 88-162; see also Ross Shepard Kraemer, *Her Share of the Blessings: Women's Religions among Pagans, Jews and Christians in the Greco-Roman World* (New York: Oxford University Press, 1992), 128-39; Kraemer makes no attempt to reconstruct Jesus and is solely concerned with the women of the movement.

34 Schüssler Fiorenza, *Memory*, 110-14, 118-40.

35 On the complications involved in estimating the importance of purity rules in the first century, see Shaye Cohen, 'Menstruants and the Sacred,' in Sarah B. Pomeroy ed., *Women's History and Ancient History* (Chapel Hill: University of North Carolina Press, 1991), 273-303; Amy-Jill Levine, 'Discharging Responsibility: Matthean Jesus, Biblical Law and Hemorrhaging Woman,' in David R. Bauer and Mark Allan Powell, eds., *Treasures New and Old: Contributions to Matthean Studies*, Symposium Series 1, Society of Biblical Literature (Atlanta: Scholars Press, 1996), 379-97; Mary R. D'Angelo, 'Gender and Power in the Gospel of Mark: The Daughter of Jairus and the Woman with the Flow of Blood,' in John C. Cavadini, ed., *Aspects of the Miraculous in Jewish and Christian Antiquity* (Notre Dame, Ind.: University of Notre Dame Press, forthcoming).

36 Kraemer, *Blessings*, 93-127; Bernadette Brooten, *Women Leaders in the Ancient Synagogue* (Chico, Calif.: Scholars Press, 1982), and 'Jewish Women's History in the Roman Period: A Task for Christian Theology,' in George W.E. Nickelsburg with George MacRae, SJ, eds., *Christians among Jews and Gentiles* (Philadelphia: Fortress, 1986), 22-30.

37 See, for example, Sanders, *Jesus and Judaism*, 291-2, on the Pharisees. For a study of the characterization of the Jewish leaders in the gospels that takes literary concerns fully into account, see Elizabeth Struthers Malbon, 'The Jewish Leaders in the Gospel of Mark: A Literary Study of Marcan Characterization,' *Journal of Biblical Literature*, 108 (1989), 259-81.

46 Mary Rose D'Angelo

38 These two factors have been forcefully revisited by Elisabeth Schüssler Fiorenza in her recent attempt to present perpetuation of the Christian patriarchal order and of Christian anti-Judaism as the 'right and left hand' of patriarchal christology (*Miriam's Child*, 67–128; for the image see especially 76, 92). It is to be hoped that her considerable influence will get them fuller attention.
39 The high priest's liturgical garments were held in the Roman garrison during Pilate's procuratorship. Josephus, *Antiquities*, 18.90–5.
40 For complete analyses of the trial of Jesus, see Paul Winter, *On the Trial of Jesus*, 2nd ed. rev. and ed. T.A. Burkill and Geza Vermes (Berlin: De Gruyter, 1974), and Haim Cohen, *The Trial and Death of Jesus* (New York: Harper and Row, 1971); see also E.P. Sanders, *Jesus and Judaism* (Philadelphia: Fortress, 1985), 309–18.
41 See also Schüssler Fiorenza, *Memory*, 105.
42 *Jewish War*, 2.8.118; *Antiquities of the Jews*, 18.23–6.
43 See, for instance, Crossan, *The Historical Jesus*, 265–502; John Meier insists that both present and future meanings of God's reign go back to Jesus, but he accepts a division of the sayings of the kingdom into present and future sayings and so exacerbates the focus on this question; see *A Marginal Jew: Rethinking the Historical Jesus*, vol. II (Garden City, NY: Doubleday, 1994), 287–506.
44 On this sentence as a transposition of 'the reign of God has come near,' see C.H. Dodd, *The Parables of the Kingdom* (New York: Charles Scribner's Sons, 1961), 21.
45 Theissen (*Sociology*, 16–22) and Meeks (*Moral World*, 106) attempt to distinguish between the wandering charismatics and more settled groups of sympathizers; Horsley (*Sociology*, 122–8) argues that the settled local communities were the centre of the movement. But it is questionable whether settled groups were a significant feature of the movement before the death of Jesus.
46 *Antiquities*, 20.97–8.
47 Luke also includes the story of a woman anointing Jesus (Luke 7:35–50) but treats her gesture as a deed of love and repentance rather than a prophetic act. See D'Angelo, 'Women in Luke-Acts,' 452.
48 For explorations of this possibility in the case of specific sayings, see E. Boring, *The Continuing Voice of Jesus, Christian Prophecy and the Gospel Tradition* (Louisville, Ky.: Westminster, 1991), 155–84, also Mary R. D'Angelo, 'Remarriage and the Divorce Sayings Attributed to Jesus,' in William G. Roberts, ed., *Divorce and Remarriage* (Kansas City, Mo.: Sheed and Ward, 1990), 78–106. David Aune rejects the possibility of detecting such sayings among

the sayings of Jesus in the gospels; see *Prophecy in Early Christianity and the Ancient Mediterranean* (Grand Rapids, Mich.: Eerdmans, 1983), 233–45.
49 Boring attributes them to the risen Jesus; *Continuing Voice of Jesus*, 192–206.
50 The appearance of the beatitude and response from Jesus in *Gospel of Thomas*, 79 (NHC II, 2, 47, 3–12), suggests that this function is not a creation of Luke.
51 D'Angelo, 'Re-Membering Jesus,' 209–13, and 'The Concrete Foundation of Theology,' 140–2.
52 For a fuller discussion, see D'Angelo, 'Blessed the One Who Reads and They That Hear: The Beatitudes in Their Biblical Contexts,' in F.A. Eigo, OSA, ed., *The Beatitudes: New Perspectives*, Proceedings of the Villanova Theology Institute, (Villanova, Pa.: Villanova University, 1995), 45–92.
53 In the movement led by Theudas, prophecy and exodus traditions also played a role, and, as I suggested above, women may well have been active in that movement also.
54 Female prophets were also a feature of Greek and Roman religion, though their roles were in general more defined by gender than are the Biblical pictures of Deborah and Huldah. For a collection of texts, see Antoinette Clark Wire, *Corinthian Women Prophets* (Philadelphia: Fortress, 1990), 237–40.
55 Carroll Smith-Rosenberg, 'The Cross and the Pedestal: Women, Anti-Ritualism and the Emergence of the American Bourgeoisie,' in her *Disorderly Conduct: Visions of Gender in Victorian America* (New York: Oxford University Press, 1985), 129–64.
56 This distancing could of course never have been as complete for the first three centuries as it was for later generations of readers.
57 But see Steinhauser on Thomas's 'social radicalism' in John Kloppenborg, Marvin W. Meyer, Stephen J. Patterson, and Michael J. Steinhauser, *Q/Thomas Reader* (Sonoma, Calif.: Polebridge Press, 1990), 77–123.
58 See Kraemer, *Blessings*, 174. Kraemer suggests that conflict arose in early Christianity over women's leadership in a way that is not apparent either in Judaism or in the Greek and Roman religions of the period. Graeco-Roman religions provided religious offices for women – but they were largely gender-specific roles. The contested roles in early Christianity appear to have been originally open to both men and women.
59 Schüssler Fiorenza, *Memory*, 168–73, D'Angelo, 'Women Partners,' 72–5.
60 See Brooten, 'Junia,' 141–4.
61 D'Angelo, 'Women Partners,' 72–5.
62 Bernadette Brooten, 'Paul's Views on the Nature of Women and Female Homoeroticism,' in Clarissa W. Atkinson, Constance H. Buchanan, and Margaret R. Miles, eds., *Immaculate and Powerful: The Female in Sacred Image and Social Reality* (Boston: Beacon, 1985), 61–87; *Love between Women: Early Chris-*

tian Responses to Female Homoeroticism (Chicago: University of Chicago Press, 1996), 215–302.

63 Wire, *Corinthian Women Prophets*; also Mary R. D'Angelo 'Veils, Virgins and the Tongues of Men and Angels: Women's Heads as Sexual Members in Ancient Christianity,' in Howard Eilberg-Schwarz and Wendy Doniger, eds., *Off with Her Head! The Denial of Women's Identity in Myth, Religion, and Culture* (Berkeley, Calif.: University of California Press, 1995), 131–64.

64 D'Angelo, 'Remarriage and the Divorce Sayings,' 94–5; Margaret Y. MacDonald, 'Early Christian Women Married to Unbelievers,' *Studies in Religion/Sciences réligieuses*, 19 (1990), 221–34.

65 Col. 3:18–4:1, Eph. 5:22–6:9, I Peter 3:1–8, and I Timothy throughout. See David Balch, *Let Wives Be Submissive: The Domestic Code in I Peter* (Chico, Calif.: Scholars Press, 1981). Schüssler Fiorenza, *Memory*, 243–84; Mary R. D'Angelo, 'Colossians,' in Elisabeth Schüssler Fiorenza, ed., *Searching the Scriptures, vol. II, A Feminist Commentary* (New York: Crossroad, 1994), 313–24.

66 D'Angelo, 'Remarriage and the Divorce Sayings,' 94–5, 98–9.

67 Karen King, 'The Gospel of Mary Magdalene,' *Searching the Scriptures* 2, 601–34, especially 621–5; also Mary R. D'Angelo, 'A Critical Note: John 20:17 and Apocalypse of Moses 31,' *Journal of Theological Studies*, n.s. 41 (Oct. 1990), 529–36.

68 D'Angelo, 'Women in Luke-Acts,' 457–61.

3

The Aesthetics of Paradise: Images of Women in Christian Antiquity

KENNETH B. STEINHAUSER

The aim of this chapter is to discuss images of women in Christian antiquity, the period in history that begins immediately after the composition of the New Testament – the four canonical gospels and probably all but a few of the epistles and other writings. Though some books of the New Testament may have been written during the second century, AD 100 is a convenient starting point. Christian antiquity ends with the beginning of the Middle Ages, which is also difficult to pinpoint. Gregory the Great is a transitional figure, and his death in AD 604 may be considered the end of the period. Gregory was the founder of the medieval papacy, and during his lifetime the focus of western Christianity shifted from the Mediterranean basin to the European continent. Meanwhile, the Byzantine empire manifested signs of separate development, with East and West becoming more isolated from each other. Some scholars may have other favourite dates, but I consider the fall of Rome to Alaric and the Goths in AD 410 too early and the coronation of Charlemagne in AD 800 too late.

The geographical area of Christian antiquity borders the Mediterranean on all sides but also includes the entire Roman empire and its fringes, from Ireland to Ethiopia, from Spain to Persia. Culturally the empire embraces primarily the Greek- and Latin-speaking, world as well as Coptic- and Syriac-speaking peoples in Africa and Asia, respectively.

Method of This Study

Attempting to understand and explain the role, status, and function of women during Christian antiquity is problematic: little information from the period concerns women, and the information available represents, for the most part, the viewpoint of men writing about women. Certainly we would expect to find some diversity in the Christian world through any five hundred–year period, including this one. Therefore we need to find an approach that will allow for diversity while being true to the task at hand.

Today it is generally recognized that the method of any research unavoidably influences the results. In other words, precisely how one goes about studying women during Christian antiquity is crucial for our findings. Many approaches are available, and many have been used in the past. In light of the myriad recent studies[1] on women during this period, another investigation would hardly be justified unless it offered a new and different perspective.

The most common perspective is a political one. To cite but one prominent example, in an article published in 1985 in the *Harvard Theological Review* entitled 'The Politics of Paradise: Augustine's Exegesis of Genesis 1–3 versus That of John Chrysostom,' Elaine Pagels accused Augustine of altering theological tradition to achieve his own political ends.[2] According to Pagels, Augustine emphasized sin and associated sin with sexuality. His attitude towards sex remained a hallmark of Christianity in the West and permanently shaped the sexual mores of Western civilization. In 1988 Pagels repeated this theme even more emphatically in *Adam, Eve, and the Serpent*.[3]

In this study, I would like to shift from politics to aesthetics in looking at gender issues in Christian antiquity. There are a number of reasons for doing so. First, considering gender issues in terms of politics inexorably leads to an analysis in terms of male–female conflict. Politics is based on the *polis*, or city state, which in both classical and Christian antiquity was a male-dominated institution. Furthermore, politics as an institution is fuelled by confrontation and debate. There is therefore an intrinsic bias in any political analysis of ancient society: we know in advance that we are going to find a world of patriarchal oppression.

Second, even from a social point of view, politics is too restrictive. Along with the *polis* in the ancient world, the *oikos*, or household, was central. This point is masterfully made in *Women in Greek Tragedy*, by Synnøve des Bouvrie, who asks why women played such a dominant role in ancient Greek drama at a time when they supposedly had little impact on Athenian society.[4] She responds by focusing on the *oikos* as the basic unit within the *polis*. While men dominated the *polis*, or the public life of ancient Athens, women dominated the *oikos*, or private life in that city state. This social structure and its effects continued well into

Christian antiquity, and so to understand the place of women in society we need to do more than look at their role in politics.

Third, most of the written evidence about the ancient world is literary. We do not have extensive empirical data gathered from sociological surveys such as we might have today. At best, there are spotty bureaucratic records of births, deaths, marriages, and court proceedings, as well as some inscriptions that offer glimpses into the lives of the people of that period. The vast bulk of evidence we possess about personal attitudes and impressions about women and men come to us through the art of writing. Therefore a study based on literature seems to be better suited to the available evidence.

Fourth, an aesthetic approach allows us to investigate all aspects of the literary evidence – the productive, the receptive, and the communicative.[5] One can ask who wrote the text and how it came to be written, for whom it was intended and how it would have been understood at the time, what it reveals of the world that it describes, what it suggests by what it does not discuss, and so on. In other words, aesthetics respects subjectivity without falling into subjectivism. For this reason, too, aesthetics offers a more productive approach because it provides for a diversity and multiplicity of views.

I have therefore carefully chosen as the title of this chapter: 'The Aesthetics of Paradise: Images of Women in Christian Antiquity.' Aesthetics as a principle allows one to consider literary production, its meaning, and its reception. 'Paradise' alludes to the salvific intentionality of Christianity. 'Images' in the plural refers to the variety of pictures available. Christian antiquity is broader than the church, which is restricted to an institution, and includes cultural aspects as well.

From this perspective, and based on the evidence, it seems that we can classify the women of Christian antiquity into three categories, which are not intended to be mutually exclusive: iconic women, symbolic women, and iconoclastic women. Iconic women receive their identities from others. Symbolic women represent idealized identities explicitly linked to a single virtue or vice. Iconoclastic women create their own identities. These terms are intended to be neither pejorative nor laudatory but merely descriptive. At the end, we can consider authority in ministry and orders as an independent issue.

Iconic Women

Iconic women receive their identities from others. In Christian antiquity, as in our own society, women were frequently regarded as icons. The word 'icon' simply means image, but its use in our language has other connotations – namely, a specifically religious image or an object of uncritical devotion. An icon is adored and esteemed by others. Iconic women are created by individuals or by society as images that reflect traditional female roles within the family – wife, mother, and widow. These women are identified by their *stasis* – their status or place. They are recognized through their circumstances – their human context, their roles, or their functions.

While idols, specifically pagan idols, were three-dimensional, the traditional religious icon presented a one-dimensional, or flat image. Iconic women were one-dimensional and were the objects of uncritical veneration, just like the icon. Either women fulfilled certain expected roles that grew out of marriage (for example, wife, mother, and eventually widow), or they took on another acceptable role, renouncing marriage and embracing celibacy.

The role of the woman in marriage was the defining moment for women in antiquity. Let us therefore review some of the evidence that documents early Christian attitudes towards marriage and married women.

One early theological work is the *Divine Institutes* of Lactantius (d. after 317), who viewed sexual desire within marriage as good because it was for the purpose of procreation. Lactantius also argued that adultery was wrong for both men and women. This abrogation of the double standard regarding sexual morality represented a distinctively Christian characteristic and a departure from the pagan Roman view of marriage.

It is difficult, however, to find a distinctively Christian influence on popular customs and imperial legislation even after Constantine's Edict of Milan in 313. Christian funeral inscriptions throughout the period are similar to pagan inscriptions when describing the virtues of the deceased spouse. 'Thorough examination of Constantine's legislation on marriage does not support the often expressed view that his marriage laws clearly reflect Christian teachings and a peculiarly "Christian" spirit.'[6] Only twice can a Christian influence be found – in the prohibition of unilateral divorce and the removal of penalties for remaining unmarried. The concern for female chastity is not a particularly Christian preoccupation. Roman law and literature dwell on the same theme.[7]

Even virginity as the renunciation of marriage was defined in terms of marriage. Tertullian's (d. after 220) *To His Wife* is especially enlightening. In the event that he should die, Tertullian urged his wife not to remarry. One is reminded of *To Marcella*, the letter of the pagan philosopher Porphyry to his wife, which extols honourable widowhood. This and other pagan works such as Iamblichus's *On the Pythagorean Life* suggest that Christian asceticism, particularly the practice of celibacy, may find its roots in Neoplatonic and Pythagorean philosophy rather than the New Testament.[8] For example, Gregory of Nyssa (d. 394), in writing the life of his sister Macrina, praised her for living the philosophical life and for embracing a high level of philosophy, which of course included virginity. Gregory's approach begins with God as a spiritual being separate from creation, and he defines Christianity as an imitation of divine nature. Virginity is claimed to be especially God-like because the Father's generation of the Son is accomplished entirely without sexual relations.

When Jovinian asserted that marriage and virginity were of equal value, Augustine (354–430) responded with *On the Good of Marriage*, presenting his personal views on marriage, which became normative for the later church in the West.[9] According to Augustine, there are three goods of marriage: *proles*, *fides*, and *sacramentum* – offspring, fidelity, and sacramental bond, respectively. Augustine was preoccupied with sex both personally and theologically. Sexual passion was for him the prime example of concupiscence and the means by which original sin was transmitted.

Just how problematic gender was to Augustine is best illustrated by his *One Unfinished Book on the Literal Meaning of Genesis* and the subsequent corresponding note from his *Revisions*, where he catalogued his works towards the end of his life. Augustine wrote that he stopped at the phrase 'Male and female he created them' (Gen. 1:27).[10] Obviously at the time he was stymied and could go no further. This reveals just how problematic sexuality had been in his early life.

Nevertheless, *On the Good of Marriage* presents a positive theology of marriage: offspring are necessary for the continuation of the human race, fidelity exists between the marriage partners, and the *sacramentum* is the bond of permanence. Thus in Augustine one finds both social and personal sides to human sexuality. The socialization of marriage transforms personal, uncontrollable sexual desire into a good.

A statement about marriage is of necessity about women, men, and their relationship to one another. Here and elsewhere Augustine was thoroughly Pauline. He took seriously Paul's description of the relationship of Christ to the church as being analogous with that between husband and wife: Christ is the head, and the husband is the head.

Augustine also accepted Paul's preference for celibacy over marriage as a more perfect state. Nevertheless, he always viewed marriage as a good.

At odds with Augustine in his teaching were the Pelagians, particularly Pelagius himself and Julian of Eclanum, who thought that Augustine's teaching concerning the transmission of original sin through sexual intercourse was a denial of the fundamental goodness of the material world as created by God in the Genesis narrative. The most effective attack of the Pelagians against Augustine involved a hypothetical married couple. Both partners, having been baptized, no longer had original sin. Since through baptism they have been cleansed of original sin, how could they transmit to their offspring what they do not now have? Augustine never satisfactorily countered this argument against hereditary sin. Sex, as the transmitter of original sin, remained permanently tainted in Augustine's thought, though Augustine did develop a distinctively Christian view of marriage, which had been absent from pre-Constantinian writers.

To determine how Augustine's theory worked out in practice, one may consider his reflections on his mother, Monica, contained in both his *Confessions* and his *Dialogues*. Augustine painted a picture of her as a long-suffering spouse married to an impatient husband, who, though a pagan, ultimately converted to Christianity late in life. Monica was also devoted to her son. She interceded with Ambrose, the bishop of Milan; she prayed for her son's conversion, and her prayers were answered. After his dramatic conversion experience in the garden at Milan, Augustine immediately told his mother, who was overjoyed at the news. She was also present at his baptism. Together they shared a mystical experience at the port of Ostia, where she was waiting to depart for Africa. She died in Ostia shortly thereafter and was buried there.

Tradition considers Monica a saintly figure, even though she contributed to the destruction of her son's relationship with his common-law wife, who was the mother of his son, Adeodatus. Monica exhibited a variety of virtues – intelligence, perseverance, loyalty, and hope – all within the context of her position as wife and mother. Nevertheless, Augustine's description in his *Confessions* is realistic. He alluded to his mother's occasional wine-bibbing; he also stated that she was too attached to him. These shortcomings remain entirely unmentioned in an inauthentic letter of Augustine to his sister concerning the life and virtues of their mother: 'Such fear of the Lord occupied her mind that she not only avoided every kind of evil but she also was directed to every good in a spirit of piety.'[11] Subsequent tradition had turned her into an icon.

Jerome's (c. 347–420) view of marriage differed profoundly from Augustine's. In his famous *Letter 22* to Eustochium, he wrote: 'Eve in Paradise was a virgin: it was only after she put on a garment of skins that her married life began. Paradise is your home. Keep therefore as you were born, and say: "Return unto thy rest, O my soul."'[12] Clearly this text is dealing with a primordial state, a fall, and a restoration. Since virginity is natural and marriage came only after the fall, says Jerome, women who embrace virginity return to the state of paradise. Marriage may be a remedy against sin, but virginity represents a restoration to a primitive state lost through the fall. Virginity restores the icon.

No treatment of gender in Christian antiquity would be complete without mention of the *subintroductae*. John Chrysostom (d. 407) wrote two treatises on the practice of syneisaktism – spiritual marriage between male and female ascetics – which was popular and widespread after the second century. Some assert that it represented the solution to a practical problem; since few convents were available until the fourth century, syneisaktism gave female ascetics a place to live without going off into the desert. Others do not wish to lose sight of the fact that this practice did provide men and women celibates with the emotional intimacy and personal satisfaction of association with the opposite sex.[13] Chrysostom argued vehemently against the practice, which he considered scandalous and totally inappropriate. Syneisaktism tarnishes the icon.

Symbolic Women

Symbolic women represent idealized identities explicitly linked to a single virtue or vice. The *passiones* of martyred woman and *vitae* of saintly women express values metaphorically. As there is pictorial narrative, there can also be such a thing as a verbal image. Symbolic women may have been historical figures. However, the symbolic aspect may very well be a fiction or, perhaps better put, a poetic invention, or *poiesis*.

In Christian antiquity there are several idealized images of women that spring from biblical tradition. These images enjoyed tremendous popularity. Essentially the symbols represent extremes diametrically opposed to each other and out of touch with reality. One is based on Eve, the temptress; the other on Mary, the virgin. Eve tempted Adam and convinced him to eat of the tree of good and evil. Mary responded in faith to the call of God through the message of the angel Gabriel. These dialectical symbols presented either a negative type or a positive ideal, and women were categorized under one symbol or the other.

In the New Testament the role of temptress, or whore, is played by Mary Magdalene, even though there is absolutely no evidence that she was a prostitute. Several narratives have been conflated in subsequent interpretations, identifying Mary of Magdala with other women in the gospel narratives. An anonymous sinful woman, Mary Magdalene, Mary of Bethany, Mary who anointed Jesus, Mary at the foot of the cross, and Mary who discovered the empty tomb are frequently treated in Christian tradition as the same person. Thus Mary Magdalene has become a figure of mythic proportions synonymous with repentance.

In Christian tradition, women who are repentant sinners are presented in the tradition of Mary Magdalene. Lives of harlots are preserved in Christian tradition – for example *The Life of Saint Mary of Egypt*, *The Life of Saint Pelagia, the Harlot*, and *The Life of Mary the Harlot*. Most of these *vitae* derive from monastic circles in Egypt and were originally written in Greek. However, in many instances only the Latin translation survives. These stories circulated widely in Europe during the Middle Ages.[14]

Thecla represents another widespread tradition of piety – the tradition of virginity epitomized by Mary, the mother of Jesus. She is a character in the apocryphal *Acts of Paul and Thecla*, which describes her as a virgin from Iconium who broke off her engagement to join Paul in his missionary travels. When, during a period of persecution, she is arrested and cast to the beasts, she is miraculously preserved from death. The cult of Thecla was popular, and a church dedicated to her was built in Seleucia of Isauria in southern Asia Minor, the place of her death. Egeria in the fourth century notes that in visiting the church during a pilgrimage she heard the *Acts of Thecla* read during the liturgy.

The name Thecla occurs frequently in Christian literature. She is one of the virgins in the allegorical *Symposium* of Methodius of Olympus. Obviously influenced by Plato, Methodius has each of his characters describe the merits of chastity. In the treatise, Thecla explains that virginity is being like God: 'Now the word *parthenia* [virginity], merely by changing one letter, becomes *partheia* [godliness], and this is significant of the fact that virginity alone makes divine those who possess her and have been initiated into her pure mysteries.'[15] Gregory of Nyssa notes that his sister Macrina was addressed as Thecla in her infancy to indicate her future life of virginity.

Female martyrs for the most part stand outside the biblical tradition. *The Martyrdom of Saints Perpetua and Felicitas*, reflecting a persecution that took place c. 200, is the most famous of all martyrologies involving women. Clearly the narrative emanates from a Montanist community in North Africa. In this text, Perpetua is reminiscent of the self-sacrificing heroine of classical Greek mythology and drama. In Sophocles' tragedy *Antigone*, the protagonist ultimately must die because she has disobeyed the order of her uncle King Creon and buried the body of her brother, Polynices. She sacrifices her life by placing her obedience to the laws of the gods over the laws of humans. Women had an important place in ancient Greek tragedy and in Christian martyrologies, both of which were ritualistic in character.

In the *Martyrdom*, Perpetua disregards her father's advice to come to her senses and abandon Christianity. Her perseverance earns her the death of a martyr. The ideal presented is that of the self-sacrificing heroine whose actions demonstrate that women could have the masculine characteristic of courage. The 'male woman' was an ideal in both pagan and Christian antiquity: 'When the sensations (the female trait in man) are under the influence and dominance of spirit and reason (the male principle), the male and the female can be harmoniously united in one and the same individual.'[16]

This ideal is especially apparent in Christian apocrypha and in the persons of Thecla, Perpetua, and Macrina. Thecla puts on the clothing of a man when she leaves Myra to join Paul in his preaching. Perpetua becomes a male in a vision when she wrestles with the Egyptian, symbol of the devil. Macrina is praised for her *andreia*, which ironically means both 'courage' and 'manliness.' Women were symbolic of repentance, godliness, and courage.

Iconoclastic Women

Iconoclastic women create their own identities. They may be either heterodox or orthodox. In other words, neither the presence of orthodoxy nor its absence is relevant. The common denominator among them is their departure from traditional roles and expectations. They may be perceived as either iconic, receiving their identity from others, or symbolic, representing a virtue or vice. Iconoclastic women have expanded their horizons and have determined their own identities. Regardless of the consequences, women of this type were bold enough to smash the icon of societal expectations while engaging in social activity.

Macrina (c. 327–379) belonged to one of the most illustrious families in the history of Christianity. The Christian woman Emmelia and her husband, Basil, whose own parents had suffered persecution under the emperor Maximinus, had five sons and five daughters. Of the five sons, three ultimately rose to the episcopacy (Basil of Caesarea, Gregory of Nyssa, and Peter of Sebasteia), one named Naucratius was killed in a hunting accident at age twenty-seven, and another, unnamed son died in infancy. Of the five daughters, only the name of the eldest, Macrina, is known.

Shortly after her death in December 379, her brother Gregory of Nyssa wrote a biography of his dear sister, ostensibly at the behest of the monk Olympius. In his *Life of Saint Macrina*, Gregory paints the portrait of a fascinating lady of great virtue and intelligence. Indeed, he credits her with the intellectual formation of all her brothers, including himself. According to this biography, Macrina chided Basil for taking pride in his rhetorical abilities. She helped her mother raise Naucratius and introduced him to the philosophical life, which he pursued until his untimely death. To her brother Peter she was 'father, teacher, attendant, mother, the counselor of every good, and she held him in check so that, even before his flowering in the tenderness of youth, he was raised to the high goal of philosophy.'[17] Gregory further details the portrait of his sister in his dialogue *On the Soul and the Resurrection*,[18] where his sister instructs him on the nature of the soul and eternal life. She was an intelligent and strong individual and the *éminence grise* behind the Cappadocian Fathers.

Unfortunately, much contemporary research concerning Gregory's pair of 'Macrinian works' is marred by an excessive incredulity about whether a woman like Macrina could have been so learned. An example of this prejudice is the outright refusal to believe that a woman in late antiquity could have been so well educated. Some scholars ask openly, 'Could Macrina really have been such an intellectual figure?'[19] The response to this question is often ambivalent. Regarding *On the Soul and the Resurrection*, Kevin Corrigan concludes that 'we cannot ultimately determine what belongs to Macrina herself and what to Gregory.'[20] Yet he does concede that 'she was at the centre of an intellectual family. I suggest, therefore, that we possess an excellent example in Macrina of the breadth of informal education in the great homes of the fourth century.'[21]

Corrigan's conclusion requires a rather artificial and unhistorical distinction between formal and informal education and tends to diminish the intellectual accomplishments of Macrina herself. Her intellectual achievement is described by her brother Gregory as a genuine contribution to the theological development of this famous family. Macrina was so well educated in the classics that her learning could not have been the result of a so-called informal dabbling in philosophy and literature.

If Macrina's achievement was extraordinary, it was not unique. Palladius, in his *Historia Lausiaca*, described the accomplishments of several learned women, referring to them by name – for example, Eustochium, Melania the Elder, and Juliana.[22] Clearly a woman, particularly a virgin living in a monastic community, could and frequently did acquire an excellent education. Macrina was the epitome of the virtuous ideal presented in the writings of Gregory of Nyssa. Gregory did not hesitate to call her 'the Great' in the same way his brother Basil was called 'the Great.'[23] This is no small matter, because this title was indicative of Macrina's personal accomplishment and gave her a status equal to that of Basil.

Macrina is the perfect embodiment of the philosophical life, or Christian *paideia*. In the literary composition of her story, Gregory has merged a Christian message with a classical Greek genre because in her person she represents the amalgamation of biblical Christianity with classical Greek thought. It would be a mistake to identify this phenomenon with Hellenization, which was the mingling of popular Greek religion and culture with popular oriental religions and cultures, so that one may rightly speak of a Hellenized Judaism even before Christ or of a Hellenized Christianity at its origins.[24] In the Cappadocians, and particularly in Macrina, the mingling takes place on a different level. Here one finds a biblically based theological tradition of Christian thought and practice being combined with a remarkably sophisticated Greek philosophical tradition – not Hellenization, but Christian *paideia*.[25]

Macrina, more than any of her brothers, reflects the cultural syncretism that resulted in the development of an intellectually cultivated Christianity, which could compete with pagan learning on its own grounds. Perhaps because, as a woman, she was unable to become a bishop, her ecclesiastical side is less developed than that of her younger brothers. For that very reason, however, Macrina combines Christian faith with the philosophical life in an almost perfect balance, and she truly embodies Christian *paideia* in its ideal expression. This balance cannot be as evident in Gregory or Basil, who were preoccupied with the practical concerns of theological disputations, ecclesial politics, and pastoral leadership.

In the two works in which Gregory described his sister Macrina, he did not use Christian literary models but rather tried and tested classical forms. Though biblical references and parallels abound,[26] Gregory would not have written of his sister using the classical forms of oration and dialogue if these did not correspond to his personal experience of Macrina as a lettered woman and teacher. The Cappadocian ideal of Christian *paideia* is more perfectly found in Macrina than in any of her siblings, and for this reason Gregory appropriately called her 'Macrina the Great.'

Hypatia[27] (c. 355–415) was a resident of Alexandria from a prominent family. She was a pagan educated in mathematics, astronomy, and philosophy. She entered into the life of the *polis*, giving both private classes and public lectures on various topics. She was especially fond of philosophy. She was a virgin and an esteemed adviser and moral authority in Alexandria, which would have had a somewhat tolerant atmosphere at the time. Furthermore, she certainly would not have been persecuted for her paganism because she was not a practising pagan, and she even sympathized with her Christian students.

Unfortunately, Hypatia was drawn into a conflict between Cyril, the patriarch of Alexandria, and Orestes, the prefect of Egypt. The theological issue was Nestorianism, but the political subplot was the power struggle between church and state. One day in March 415, while she was returning to her home, Hypatia was pulled from her chariot, attacked by a mob, and murdered. Accounts differ regarding the details of her death. But we know that she was stripped of her clothes, she was dragged through the streets, and her body was burned. Hypatia had created her own identity, and it cost her her life.

Theodora[28] (c. 527–548), the wife of Justinian I, is another example of an iconoclastic woman. She was elevated to patrician rank and exercised greater political influence than any empress in antiquity. Because of her support of the monophysite heresy, she was vilified by her biographer Procopius, who stressed her negative characteristics. A famous mosaic of her and her husband may be found in the church of San Vitale in Ravenna.

Ministry, Authority, and Orders

Questions about ministry, authority, and orders in the early church are extremely complex. The New Testament and the Apostolic Fathers present very little evidence about this matter, a fact that often

Images of Women in Christian Antiquity 61

gives free rein to the imagination of scholars attempting to paint a picture of the institutional church during the period.[29] Often they expand a simple noun in a letter of Paul into a faction, party, or community. In other words, polity and ecclesiastical structures during the second century remain obscure. From the third century on, more evidence begins to become available. Inquiring into the place of women in this picture merely adds another puzzle to a problem that is already quite confusing. Finally, when scholars doing the research have personal 'agendas' (as some do) to buttress positions either for or against the ordination of women in the church today, the ambiguous data of history become even more enigmatic when interpreted in contrary ways.

Few would deny that there is at least some evidence that women held the office of both *presbyter* and *episkopos* in the early church. However, there is a fundamental split regarding the interpretation of the data. Though many nuanced arguments have been advanced, essentially there are two opposing theories. The first approach is theological, posing the issue as orthodoxy versus heresy; the second is sociological, framing the question in terms of the charismatic versus the hierarchical.

The theological, or 'traditional,' theory holds that female priests and bishops were to be found only in sectarian or heretical communities.[30] In c. 170, in a remote village of Phrygia, Montanus began to prophesy the immanent return of Jesus Christ. He was soon joined by two female prophets, Maximilla and Priscilla (or Prisca), and quickly gained converts in both East and West. Montanus, Maximilla, and Priscilla proclaimed the impending end of the world. They claimed to speak on behalf of the Holy Spirit, denied all ecclesiastical authority, and urged rigorous asceticism, including both celibacy and fasting. They encouraged martyrdom, and flight from persecution was forbidden. Their oracles, of which only a few are preserved, have antecedents in the pagan Greek oracles at Dodona and Delphi.

Women held positions of authority and roles of leadership in Montanist communities. Epiphanius clearly states that female authority on a par with male authority was a characteristic of Montanism: 'And women are bishops among them, and presbyters, and the other offices, as there is no difference, they say, for "in Christ Jesus there is neither male nor female" (cf. Gal. 3:28).'[31] In the Montanist martyrology, *The Martyrdom of Saints Perpetua and Felicitas*, Perpetua functions as a leader of the jailed Christian community. The Montanist female prophets, Maximilla, Priscilla, and Quintilla, based their teachings on their direct and personal experience of the Holy Spirit. They claimed mystical visions, which provided them with knowledge and authority.

According to the 'traditional' view, these and other aberrations were derived from the role of women in pagan mystery cults and gnostic sects. Female authority in the church finds its roots in pagan practices which infiltrated the church at various times in its history. Several pagan cults allowed women to be religiously active in their communities. The cult of Isis, based on the Egyptian myth of Isis and Osiris, enjoyed popularity in the Graeco-Roman world and was later conflated with the worship of Venus. Women could be priests of the cult and fulfil other liturgical functions. They could also be priests of the Magna Mater in the cult of Cybele.

Orthodox Christians opposed these tendencies. The canons of various councils limited the role of women in society and in the liturgy. Canon 13 of the Council of Gangra (c. 340) barred women from male roles: 'If any woman, under pretence of asceticism, shall change her apparel and, instead of a woman's accustomed clothing, shall put on that of a man, let her be anathema.'[32] The problem here was women wearing the garb of monks. The same council insisted that women could not cut their hair, which was a reminder of their status as a female. Canon 44 of the Synod of Laodicea (c. 430) states: 'Women may not go to the altar.'[33] If women were prohibited from approaching the altar, they could hardly have been allowed to preside over liturgies as priests or bishops. The paradigm of male leadership finds its origin in models inherited from the Old Testament. Both the priests of the temple and the elders of the synagogue were always males, while women were consciously and explicitly excluded.

The sociological or 'feminist' theory holds that women priests and bishops functioned universally in the entire church for a very brief period at the beginning, until they were marginalized by men.[34] This is attested by the importance of women in the teaching and ministry of Jesus, particularly in the gospel of Luke, where women are the first witnesses to his resurrection. Evidence of the role of women in the primitive church is also found in the writings of Paul, particularly in Romans 16, where Paul sends greeting to two apostles, Andronicus and Junias – a couple, one male and the other female. This is a clear indication that there were female apostles in primitive Christianity. As the church became less charismatic and more hierarchical, however, the roles of women were consciously limited by men. Meagre evidence exists today, because the facts were suppressed by males who wished to support and

Images of Women in Christian Antiquity 63

maintain the patriarchal structure that had come into existence. The 'feminist' view is frequently based on a conspiracy theory, whereby men limited the power and authority of women in the early church and subsequently doctored the evidence to accommodate their social goal of oppressing women. Women were eventually marginalized and excluded from all leadership.

A video entitled *Women's Ordination: The Hidden Tradition*[35] advances several pieces of archaeological evidence to demonstrate the existence of female priests and bishops in the church. Two pertain to Christian antiquity: a wall painting in the catacomb of Priscilla in Rome, and funeral inscriptions primarily from southern Italy.[36]

First, regarding the catacomb of Priscilla in Rome, great confusion has surrounded the painting in the so-called Greek chapel. The painting, which depicts seven figures at a meal, has inspired the mosaic in the more recently constructed chapel of the community of Benedictine sisters who care for the catacomb. It is very difficult to determine whether the figures are male or female. Some say only one or perhaps some of the figures are female; others maintain that all seven are female. If all seven are female, and if the figure identified as the celebrant is female, the painting provides physical evidence of women priests in Christian antiquity. The problem is made more complex because the mosaic of the modern chapel, inspired by the painting in the catacomb below, specifically depicts a eucharistic celebration in which some female figures, including the celebrant, have been transformed into male figures to correspond with contemporary practice. Only one figure in the mosaic is female. Debate has centred on the figures in the painting: is this particular figure female or not?

Both sides fail to understand that the whole debate is irrelevant if the original work is not a eucharistic celebration. I maintain that there is absolutely no evidence that the meal depicted in the catacomb itself is a eucharistic celebration. Most probably, the painting depicts not a eucharistic celebration but a *refrigerium*, a commemorative meal at the tombs of the dead, which Christians had inherited from their pagan ancestors.[37] The *Apostolic Constitutions* permitted funeral meals as long as Christians did not engage in excessive drinking and orgiastic behaviour. Both Tertullian and Cyprian condemned the celebration of funeral repasts, while Augustine attempted to reform the custom, which was obviously entrenched in Africa. Archaeological evidence, particularly graffiti, indicates that Christians at Rome also celebrated funeral meals.

Second, inscriptions on graves in southern Italy with the words *pres-*

bytera or *presbyterissa* provide more convincing evidence. These inscriptions have been too lightly dismissed as referring to the wives of priests. Georgio Otranto, professor at the University of Bari, presents a compelling interpretation of the epigraphs. A husband, who was a priest, would certainly not identify his wife as *presbytera* on a formal and permanent inscription without identifying himself as *presbyter*. The wife's title is normally derived from her husband's status, yet here she is identified by title and he is not – in the very same inscription. This does not make sense. These women probably were priests. The discovery of these kinds of inscriptions in a limited geographical area may indicate either a local custom or sectarian practice.

No one disputes the presence of deaconesses in the early church. Several passages of the New Testament are pertinent. The most important is the word *gunaikas* at I Tim. 3:11, where the qualifications of ministers are listed. Some translations prefer ambiguity and render the word 'women.' Others translate the passage as 'the wives of the deacons,' and yet others, 'female deacons.' Initially the use of the word 'women' in the text may appear ambiguous, but, when one recalls that there is no feminine form of the word 'deacon' in Greek, the translation 'female deacons' in this context is perfectly logical. Furthermore, Clement of Alexandria, a native of Athens whose mother tongue was Greek, interpreted the passage as referring to female deacons.[38]

The fourth-century *Didascalia Apostolorum* presented extensive evidence concerning female deacons and their activities in the community. They had various liturgical functions, especially during the rite of baptism. Candidates were baptized by immersion. They were naked when they entered the water and were then clothed in a white garment after they came up out of the water, symbolizing the resurrection. Deaconesses assisted female candidates. Deaconesses also visited the sick.

The discussion of ministry, authority, and orders in the early church would not be complete without mention of widows. The *Didascalia Apostolorum* indicates that a widow had to be at least fifty years of age to enroll officially in the order of widows. They were sustained by donations from the community and were expected to spend considerable time in prayer. Some widows also participated in ministry, and the *Testimonium Domini* includes these widows, who have been specially designated for ministry, among the clergy. Bonnie Thurston advances the hypothesis of a conflict between the widows, representing an earlier, charismatic ministry, and the deaconesses, representing a later, hierarchical ministry. The deaconesses ultimately won out because their office allowed them to administer the donations that sustained the widows.[39]

Conclusion

Most of the information that we have about women in Christian antiquity has been communicated to us in verbal images. Images need to be approached within a hermeneutic of perception – an aesthetic interpretation that allows one to deal with each individual image as it functions on a single plain or on a variety of plains. Furthermore, the hermeneutic of perception permits the data to be appropriated differently by various individuals and groups of individuals without invalidating other perceptions.

At one point in his *Vorlesungen über die Ästhetik*, G.W.F. Hegel explained the relationship between the content of art and its external expression.[40] The image is the expression of the spirit and carries with it meaning. For example, the images of women, which we have seen, are expressive of meaning. According to Hegel, art faces a crisis when the expression and meaning are disunited and become separated from one another. Hegel perceived the rift between the spirit and its articulation as the major factor contributing to the crisis in art that existed in the nineteenth century.

In my opinion, a separation or rift on the level of the spirit and its articulation did not exist in Christian antiquity. Meaning and expression were not distinguished from each other in art, literature, and culture. Different meanings found different expressions. The production of images took place in three areas. Images were expressive of place, symbol, and action – *stasis, poiesis,* and *praxis,* respectively – and as such gave meaning either to society as a whole or to individuals within it. Iconic women were identified by their relationships, symbolic women by their meanings, and iconoclastic women by their achievements.

In addition to having a secondary reception, or an 'afterlife,' for us today, these images were immediately received by the communities that produced them. The primary reception of these images took place on two levels. Reception by means of memory (*anamnesis*) and imitation (*mimesis*) expressed two central aspects of Christian morality and Christian spirituality, namely, *contemplatio* and *imitatio*. Hence the images are of interest to people today. Though no dichotomy existed between the images and their meanings, there was definitely a dichotomy between their production and their reception. The hermeneutic of perception allows one to identify this dichotomy. The production of verbal and visual images of women in Christian antiquity took place in a pagan world, while their reception was essentially Christian.

Herein lies the dichotomy. On one hand, the images of women in Christian antiquity grew out of an ancient and esteemed pagan society, where an infant Christian culture was attempting to assert itself. Christian marriage is described in terms no different from pagan marriage. Christian virginity finds its roots in pagan asceticism. Christian female martyrs are similar to the heroines of Greek tragedy. On the other hand, the images were immediately received and interpreted as distinctively Christian by the very same society that created them.

NOTES

1 These studies include Jean LaPorte, *The Role of Women in Early Christianity*, Studies in Women and Religion 7 (New York: Edwin Mellen, 1982); Elizabeth A. Clark, *Women in the Early Church*, Message of the Fathers of the Church 13 (Wilmington, Del.: Michael Glazier, 1983); Elisabeth Schüssler Fiorenza, *In Memory of Her: A Feminist Theological Reconstruction of Christian Origins* (New York: Crossroad, 1983); Mary R. Lefkowitz, *Women in Greek Myth* (London: Duckworth, 1986); Ben Witherington, *Women in the Earliest Churches*, Society for New Testament Studies Monograph Series 58 (New York: Cambridge University Press, 1988); Susanne Heine, *Women and Early Christianity: A Reappraisal* (Minneapolis: Augsburg, 1988); Elaine Fantham et al., *Women in the Classical World: Image and Text* (New York: Oxford University Press, 1994); Gillian Clark, *Women in Late Antiquity: Pagan and Christian Life-styles* (New York: Oxford University Press, 1994); Ross Shepard Kraemer, *Her Share of the Blessings: Women's Religions among Pagans, Jews, and Christians in the Greco-Roman World* (New York: Oxford University Press, 1994); and Sue Blundell, *Women in Ancient Greece* (Cambridge: Harvard University Press, 1995).
2 See Elaine Pagels, 'The Politics of Paradise: Augustine's Exegesis of Genesis 1-3 versus That of John Chrysostom,' *Harvard Theological Review*, 78 (1985), 67-100.
3 See Elaine Pagels, *Adam, Eve, and the Serpent* (New York: Random House, 1988).
4 See Synnøve des Bouvrie, *Women in Greek Tragedy: An Anthropological Approach*, Symbolae Osloenses Fasc. Suppl. 27 (Oslo: Norwegian University Press, 1990), 39-45.
5 See Hans Robert Jauss, *Ästhetische Erfahrung und literarische Hermeneutik* (Frankfurt: Suhrkamp, 1984), 103-91.

6 Judith Evans Grubbs, *Law and Family in Late Antiquity: The Emperor Constantine's Marriage Legislation* (New York: Oxford University Press, 1995), 317.
7 See Gunhild Vidén, *Women in Roman Literature: Attitudes of Authors under the Early Empire*, Studia Graeca et Latina Gothoburgensia 57 (Göteborg: Acta Universitatis Gothoburgensis, 1993), 174–9.
8 See Griet Petersen-Szemerédy, *Zwischen Weltstadt und Wüste: Römische Asketinnen in der Spätantike: Eine Studie zu Motivation und Gestaltung der Askese christlicher Frauen Roms auf dem Hintergrund ihrer Zeit*, Forschungen zur Kirchen- und Dogmengeschichte 54 (Göttingen: Vandenhoeck & Ruprecht, 1993); Susanna Elm, *'Virgins of God': The Making of Asceticism in Late Antiquity* (New York: Oxford University Press, 1994); James A. Francis, *Subversive Virtue: Asceticism and Authority in the Second-Century Pagan World* (University Park: Pennsylvania State University Press, 1995); Vincent L. Wimbush and Richard Valantasis, eds., *Asceticism* (New York: Oxford University Press, 1995).
9 See Emile Schmitt, *Le marriage chrétien dans l'oeuvre de saint Augustin: une théologie baptismale de la vie conjugale* (Paris: Études Augustiniennes, 1983); David G. Hunter, ed., *Marriage in the Early Church* (Minneapolis: Fortress, 1992), 20–5.
10 See *Retractationes*, 1, 17, trans. Mary Inez Bogan, Fathers of the Church 60 (Washington, DC: Catholic University of America Press, 1968), 77.
11 *Epistola, sub nomine S. Augustini ad sororem scribentis, edita de vita & virtutibus S. Monicae*, Acta Sanctorum Maii 1:481, my translation: *Tantum timor Domini mentem ejus occupaverat, quod non solum ab omni specie mali sibi cavebat, sed spiritu pietatis ad omne bonum prona erat*.
12 Jerome, *Epistola* 22, ed. and trans. F.A. Wright, Loeb Classical Library 262 (Cambridge, Mass.: Harvard University Press, 1991), 93.
13 See Elizabeth A. Clark, *Jerome, Chrysostom, and Friends: Essays and Translations*, Studies in Women and Religion 1 (New York: Edwin Mellen, 1979), 158–63.
14 See Benedicta Ward, *Harlots of the Desert. A Study of Repentance in Early Monastic Sources*, Cistercian Studies Series 106 (Kalamazoo, Mich.: Cistercian Publications, 1987), 1–9.
15 Methodius of Olympus, *Symposium*, 8, 1, ed. Herbert A. Musurillo, Sources chrétiennes 95 (Paris: Éditions du Cerf, 1963), 200–2, trans. Herbert A. Musurillo, Ancient Christian Writers 27 (Westminster, Md.: Newman Press, 1958), 105.
16 Kerstin Aspegren, *The Male Woman: A Feminine Ideal in the Early Church*, Acta Universitatis Upsaliensis A4 (Stockholm: Almqvist & Wiksell, 1990), 143; see also Clementina Mazzucco, *'E fui fatta maschio': La donna nel cristianesimo*

primitivo (secoli I–III) (Florence: Casa Editrice Le Lettere, 1989); Verna E.F. Harrison, 'Male and Female in Cappadocian Theology,' *Journal of Theological Studies*, 41 (1990), 441–71; Gillian Cloke, *This Female Man of God: Female Spirituality and the Church Fathers in Late Antiquity* (New York: Routledge, 1995).

17 *Vita s. Macrinae*, trans. Virginia Woods Callahan, Fathers of the Church 58 (Washington, DC: Catholic University of America Press, 1967), 172.

18 *De anima et resurrectione*, trans. Virginia Woods Callahan, Fathers of the Church 58 (Washington, DC: Catholic University of America Press, 1967), 193–272.

19 Kevin Corrigan, *The Life of Saint Macrina*, Peregrina Translations Series 10 (Toronto: Peregrina, 1989), 21.

20 Ibid., 22.

21 Ibid., 23.

22 See Palladius, *Historia Lausiaca*, 41, 54, and 64, trans. Robert T. Meyer, Ancient Christian Writers 34 (Westminster, Md.: Newman Press, 1965), 118, 134–6, 145–6.

23 *Gregorii Nysseni Opera*, ed. Virginia Woods Callahan (Leiden: E.J. Brill, 1952), VIII, 1: 380,17; 388,3; 389,19 (referring to Basil); 392,19; 394,4 (alternate reading in Codex Marcianus Venetus Graecus 69 and PG 46); 394,8; 404,23; 411,22.

24 See Martin Hengel, *Judaism and Hellenism: Studies in Their Encounter in Palestine during the Early Hellenistic Period* (Philadelphia: Fortress Press, 1981).

25 See R. Dostálová, 'Christentum und Hellenismus: Zur Herausbildung einer neuen kulturellen Identität im vierten Jahrhundert,' *Byzantinoslavica*, 44 (1983), 1–12; Werner Jaeger, 'Paideia Christi,' *Zeitschrift für neutestamentliche Wissenschaft und die Kunde der Älteren Kirche*, 50 (1959), 1–14; Werner Jaeger, *Early Christianity and Greek Paideia* (Cambridge, Mass.: Belknap Press, 1961).

26 See Eugenio Marotta, 'La base biblica della *Vita s. Macrinae* di Gregorio di Nissa,' *Vetera Christianorum*, 5 (1968), 73–88; Elena Giannarelli, *La vita di s. Macrina*, Letture cristiane del primo millennio 4 (Milan: Edizioni Paoline, 1988), 13–73.

27 See Maria Dzielska, *Hypatia of Alexandria*, Revealing Antiquity 8 (Cambridge, Mass.: Harvard University Press, 1995).

28 See Robert Browning, *Justinian and Theodora* (New York: Thames & Hudson, 1987).

29 See, for example, James S. Jeffers, *Conflict at Rome: Social Order and Hierarchy in Early Christianity* (Minneapolis: Fortress Press, 1991).

30 See LaPorte, *Role of Women*, 109–32, and Roger Gryson, *The Ministry of Women in the Early Church* (Collegeville, Minn.: Liturgical Press, 1976), 112.

31 Epiphanius, *Panarion*, 49.2, *The Montanist Oracles and Testimonia*, ed. and

trans. Ronald E. Heine, Patristic Monograph Series 14 (Macon, Ga.: Mercer University Press, 1989), 134–5.
32 Nicene and Post-Nicene Fathers, Second Series 14 (Grand Rapids, Mich.: Eerdmans, 1983), 97.
33 Nicene and Post-Nicene Fathers, Second Series 14, 153.
34 Arthur Frederick Ide, *Women as Priest, Bishop and Laity in the Early Catholic Church to 440 A.D.*, Woman in History 9b (Mesquite, Texas: Ide House, 1984); Anne Jensen, *Gottes selbstbewusste Töchter: Frauenemanzipation im frühen Christentum?* (Freiburg: Herder, 1992); Karen Jo Torjesen, *When Women Were Priests: Women's Leadership in the Early Church and the Scandal of Their Subordination in the Rise of Christianity* (San Francisco: Harper, 1993).
35 *Women's Ordination: The Hidden Tradition*, 58 min., British Broadcasting Corporation, 1992, videocassette.
36 A third item is the mosaic from the ninth century in the church of Santa Prassida in Rome depicting four figures: the Blessed Virgin Mary, St Praxidis, St Prudentia, and 'Theodora Episcopa.' 'Theodora Episcopa' is portrayed with a square halo, indicating that she was alive at the time when the mosaic was made. The question is whether 'Theodora Episcopa' is a female bishop or the mother of the pope. Since the ninth century is outside the period of the present investigation, I have no judgment on this piece of evidence one way or the other.
37 See Heikki Kotila, *Memoria Mortuorum: Commemoration of the Departed in Augustine*, Studia Ephemeridis 'Augustinianum' 38 (Rome: Institutum Patristicum 'Augustinianum,' 1992), 62–77.
38 Clement of Alexandria, *Stromata* 3, 6, 53, trans. Henry Chadwick, *Alexandrian Christianity* (Philadelphia: Westminster, 1954), 65.
39 See Bonnie Bowman Thurston, *The Widows: A Women's Ministry in the Early Church* (Minneapolis: Fortress Press, 1989), 104–5.
40 G.W.F. Hegel, *Vorlesungen über die Ästhetik*, Werke 13 (Frankfurt: Suhrkamp, 1973), 1:316–62.

4

Excluded by the Logic of Control: Women in Medieval Society and Scholastic Theology

MARIE ANNE MAYESKI

Introduction

Even as Constantine was legitimizing Christianity in the Roman empire, forces were at work that eventually transformed the Mediterranean world, brought an end to Roman political dominance, and reshaped the goals and the structure of the church itself. Vast movements of peoples and a great shift in political and military power forced Christian leaders to pay attention to the new inhabitants of Europe. Once again, the church had to focus its energies on the evangelization of pagans, but this time in a new cultural context. Such changes affected the situation of women and the church's attitude towards them.

In the fluid situation created by the contact between Christian missionaries and the Germanic peoples of the north, some new opportunities opened up for women, but at the same time patriarchal tendencies in these cultures accepted and reinforced many of the church's restrictions on them. It is not possible here to draw with a fine brush the many distinctions among ethnic and regional cultures, nor to trace all the contexts within which women lived their Christian life. But even a broad overview can suggest the complexity that marked the history of European women during the early Middle Ages.

In this chapter, we survey historical evidence to become acquainted with the lives of real women, and this leads us to some general ideas about the opportunities for and accomplishments of women in the Middle Ages. We also look at some connections between opportunity and social status, between accomplishment and life choices at that time. Then we examine statements on women found in various types of church documents and religious writings. This dialogue between real lives and written documents may help us to understand the historical setting for some theological opinions about women that later came to be looked on as universal truths.

This essay rests on two historical assumptions. The first is that during the early Middle Ages (roughly the fifth through the eleventh centuries) the social, political, and economic situation was fluid enough to allow at least some women to make an impact on ecclesiastical and social life, but beginning in the twelfth century a new stability led to a decline in opportunities for even the most extraordinary women. The second assumption is that, in those same early medieval centuries, church teachings were concerned primarily with pastoral matters and were formulated without much regard for the philosophical systems and doctrinal developments of the first four centuries. Church leaders and theologians tended to rely heavily on biblical texts and to decide practical problems in light of them. The theology and traditions of the earlier centuries were not ignored, but they were not always known or known very well. As a consequence, the historical context of the time seems to have had a greater influence on church teachings than would later be the case. These two assumptions involve some oversimplifying, but the picture of women's lives and church teachings that emerge from them is essentially sound.

Transition to the Middle Ages

By the end of the fourth century, the freedom and opportunity that may have marked the first generations of Christian women[1] were for the most part a thing of the past. The church had long since adapted itself to the social expectations of the classical world, and women's roles within the church were shaped, with some exceptions, by their sociopolitical status in society at large. As they were prohibited from cultic roles, women's sphere of action was generally domestic life. But the church's official regard for the state of virginity did permit virgins and those widows who chose not to remarry certain religious opportunities, though every effort was made to control even permitted activity.

Wealthy matrons, widows, and virgins had the leisure and economic resources to devote themselves to intellectual life at a time when the intellectual study of scriptures and doctrine was central to the life of the church. The lives of Macrina,[2] sister to the Cappadocian bishops Basil and Gregory, and of Paula,[3] friend and companion to Jerome, show that women of means could aspire to be involved in the intellectual understanding of the Christian mysteries, though they took no part in the great debates of their time and left no writing by which their theological gifts can be evaluated. Each of these women, and others, founded monastic communities, where women of like means and like minds could live apart from the social and economic constraints of marriage and child-rearing and devote themselves to the life of the mind and the spirit. Women also took up the ascetical ideals that flourished in the third century and afterward. Rich women such as Paula implemented those ideals within their own affluent contexts, while others, such as Mary of the Desert, sought the same solitude and discipline as men did in the desert places of Syria and Egypt.[4]

Denied virtually all official standing and function within the growing church hierarchy, women in Christian antiquity none the less made places for themselves within the movements that were at the centre of the church's action and attention. This pattern remained as the church was slowly transformed into a European and medieval institution. Social and economic status determined women's ecclesiastical opportunities; virginity, when officially recognized and controlled, offered some possibilities; exclusion from all clerical functions was still strictly maintained. But women also continued to make a place for themselves within the church's intellectual life and within the strategies for evangelization that more and more preoccupied church leaders as the situation in Europe evolved.

Women in the Early Middle Ages

From the sixth to the tenth century, that period generally referred to as the 'Dark Ages,'[5] there is a surprisingly large body of evidence that speaks to the significant activity of women. We review some of that evidence by focusing on three matters: the marriages of aristocratic Christian women to pagan princes and what they did to Christianize those princedoms, the foundation by aristocratic women of female monastic communities, and the gradual curtailment of women's power and status in ecclesiastical institutions.

Medieval Christian Women and Marriage

With the baptism of Clovis in the year 496, the penetration of the church into the Germanic kingdoms of Europe began. The story of this conversion is told by Gregory of Tours in his *History of the Franks*.[6] Gregory gives credit to Clotilde, Clovis's Christian wife from Burgundy, for having attempted to bring Clovis to the faith, but his narrative attributes the conversion itself to divine intervention and to Remi, bishop of Reims. However, in a letter written c. 560, Nicetus of Treve urges Clotsinda, one of Clotilde's granddaughters, to imitate her illustrious ancestor in bringing her own husband from Arianism to orthodox faith. In the interpretation of Nicetus, closer in time to the events than is Gregory's, Clotilde is understood as the primary instrument of God's grace to Clovis.[7]

Similarly, in *A History of the English Church and People*,[8] Bede narrates the stories of Bertha, who came as a Christian bride to Ethelbert, the pagan king of Kent, and of Ethelberga, who married the royal pagan Edwin of Northumbria. Though Bede likewise attributes the definitive role in the two subsequent conversions to the missionary bishops Augustine and Paulinus, he also includes a letter from Pope Boniface to Ethelberga, which exhorts her to bring about the conversion of her husband and quotes Paul to strengthen his request: 'The unbelieving husband shall be saved by his believing wife,' (I Cor. 7:14).[9]

In both cases, that of Gregory and that of Bede, official ecclesiastical historians do not attribute an evangelical function to the Christian women who marry pagans. But in both cases also, alternative opinions (even from bishops and popes!) are available.[10]

This pattern of marriage and mission was to be repeated in many situations in different parts of Europe: Theodolinda brought the faith as dowry to Bavaria, Dumbrawa to Poland, and Elizabeth to Hungary, to name only three of the missionary queens. We have, unfortunately, no access to the motivation of these women who left not only their own families but their own lands, culture, and religion to marry the pagan scions of other princely families. Perhaps they were only passive pawns in the political marriage game, but some popes and bishops seemed to interpret their actions as part of the evangelical mission of the church.

By the Carolingian period, it was the institution of marriage itself that was seriously debated by civil and church leaders. In these debates the conflicts and compromises brought on by the meeting of Roman Christianity and Germanic culture are quite apparent. Marriage was integral to such royal political projects as validating a dubious dynasty, diluting the power of other noble families, and promoting the image of the kingdom of the Franks as a Christian nation. Already under the two Pepins and Charles Martel, marriage issues important to the church (such as consanguinity, indissolubility, and sexual fidelity) were debated, affirmed, or rejected by the kings, according to their political strategies.

Throughout the century-long discussion, various church leaders had attempted to maintain certain policies that honoured the full personhood of women, especially the equal rights of women in the marriage bed and in the consequences of separation and divorce. From Boniface in the mid-eighth century to Hincmar of Rheims in the mid-ninth, church officials worked to remove the burden of the double sexual and legal standard from women, though their attempt was not always successful. Through shifts in policy and many compromises made by church leadership in the name of cultural accommodation, and in spite of the wide discrepancy that remained between theory and practice, by the end of the Carolingian period marriage had become an institution structured to reflect both ecclesiastical and dynastic concerns. It was binding for life, required the consent of both parties[11] (or their lawful guardians), and involved the descent of property among the upper classes. The growing political significance of marriage had positive consequences for at least upper-class women.

Perhaps the most notable of these consequences was a new status given to marriage as a vocation in which women could both achieve holiness and further the spread of the gospel. During the ninth century, the emphasis on the superiority of virginity diminished, while the Carolingian church promoted the idea that married people constituted a true *order* within the church, equal to that of the celibates.[12] At least one cleric, Haimo of Auxerre, believed that a married woman could be as pleasing to God as a consecrated virgin.[13] The role of the noble wife within the extensive household of her family gave her many opportunities to exercise her Christian influence.

Most important, the wife's role in the education of her children had the weight of a religious obligation; to ready her children for life involved teaching them the doctrines and obligations of the life of faith. There is evidence that many noble women, including the Empress Judith and her daughter Gisela, took this responsibility seriously.[14] The only text written by a woman during the early Middle Ages, the *Liber manualis* of Dhuoda of Septimania (fl. 840),[15] was composed to accomplish the religious and ethical formation of her distant sons.

Because of a noble wife's central position as the administrator of her husband's property and household, however, her influence and Christian obligation extended beyond her children. Jonas of Orleans, in the *De institutione laicali*, promoted the idea that lay nobles had a truly *pastoral office* in regard to all the members of their household. He spoke specifically of the wife who is responsible to God for the spiritual well-being of those under her care (though, rather typically for the time, he also warned her of the spiritual dangers of her role as a married woman).[16]

With the dissolution of the central and unifying power of the Carolingian dynasty, the social and political situation of western Europe became, once again in the tenth and eleventh centuries, more fluid and more conflictual and also more malleable to the desires and ambitions of women. Married women remained active in the church's work of evangelization (which often meant the Christian formation of those already baptized); by political marriages, they continued to extend the church's sphere of influence. For instance, Mathilda of Tuscany played a part, if only a small one, in the struggle between pope and emperor during the investiture controversy of the eleventh century. Aristocratic women also continued to gain access to the power of their husbands; many exercised the full range of administrative rights and privileges pertaining to the rank and position of a spouse[17] who spent his life – and often lost it prematurely – in military campaigns. As Wemple says, 'A growing number of tenth-century wives became castellans, mistresses of landed property, proprietors of churches, participants of secular and ecclesiastical assemblies, and exercisers of military command and attendant right of justice.'[18] By the beginning of the twelfth century, a powerful noblewoman such as Eleanor of Aquitaine could influence dynastic and territorial claims even while she helped to shape cultural and religious developments.

Women and Monastic Life

Gregory of Tours, Bede, and other early historians left stories of aristocratic women who renounced the possibilities of a dynastic marriage. Instead they founded or joined monastic communities of women, helping to carve out space for the pursuit of spiritual and intellectual careers. Some, such as Etheldreda, whose story Bede narrates,[19] and Radegunde, whose life was preserved by both the poet Fortunatus and one of her own nuns, Baldonivia,[20] consented to a political marriage (in fact, Etheldreda married twice) but either refused to consummate the marriage or removed themselves from their husbands' beds and courts after a certain period. Others, such as the Anglo-Saxon Hilda, never married, and used their riches and political influence for the benefit of other women.[21]

Various patterns emerge from their stories. There is the pursuit of study as exemplified by Hilda's life. She became the abbess of a double monastery in Northumbria, and so noteworthy did her establishment become for its superior curriculum that, as Bede narrates, several bishops were named from that community. She also recognized the gift of the simple peasant Caedmon and became his patron, giving Britain the first of its illustrious poets.

Radegunde, a Thuringian princess wed to a Frankish prince, did not relinquish the political power of her rank, though she tried to modify its use. Remaining involved in the political struggles of her day, she engaged in an ongoing attempt to make peace among the warring Frankish factions, ever concerned about the effect of warfare on the lives of ordinary people.[22] At the same time, she founded a monastery in Poitier where aristocratic and peasant women alike could pursue an independent life. She brought relics to Poitier and made her city a pilgrimage centre, with economic and spiritual benefits for its citizens. Baldonivia reports that the church she built to house the relics of the Holy Cross became a centre of healing, especially for women, and at Radegunde's death the lay sisters of her community (those not aristocratic by birth) led her bier to the burial with rites that seem at least semi–liturgical. Clearly Radegunde's monastery was a place where women experienced some access to power.[23]

This kind of power allowed monastic women from the seventh to the tenth century important and acknowledged roles in the mission of the church. Leoba, an English nun, became part of Boniface's missionary project to the Saxons of Germany. Her life was preserved by Rudolph of Fulda, who lived about three generations after her death.[24] In his *Vita*, Rudolph emphasized the superior understanding of the scriptures to which Leoba arrived by her own study as well as by the grace of God. Called personally by Boniface to found a monastery for women in Saxony, she oversaw the spiritual formation of indigenous women who aspired to the monastic life and, as the abbess of a large monastery, influenced life in the villages that grew up around that institution. Sometimes she arbitrated their conflicts; at other times, she protected them by her apparent power over nature. In Rudolph's view, such authority and power as Leoba possessed came from her intellectual acuity, which she always placed in the service of practicality as described in the wisdom books of the Old Testament.

During the Carolingian period, as noted above, political and social attention focused on marriage. Stories of powerful and influential nuns are virtually non-existent, replaced by a few narratives about significant aristocratic laywomen. But by the tenth century, monastic life for women flourished again, especially under the Ottonian regime, and a number of monasteries rose to a prominence that allowed their abbesses to become virtual rulers of small kingdoms, with jurisdiction over an army and a court, the right to mint coins, and representation in the imperial assembly.[25] The opportunity for education and for all the crafts associated with scholarship (such as scribal transcription and illumination) expanded within these monastic settings, and at least one female author from a tenth-century monastery is mentioned in history books. Hrotswitha of Gandersheim was a prolific writer of plays and poetry 'discovered' and widely translated in the sixteenth century,[26] undoubtedly because her imitation of classical models seemed a hint of the Renaissance to come.

What this summary reveals is the broad outline of the social and ecclesial situation of early medieval women. They remained narrowly confined within the boundaries of social class and gender roles. Aristocratic women, through potential or actual marriages, were factors in the shifting equations of political power. There is some suggestion in the textual evidence that their marriageability was viewed, by some church leaders and possibly by themselves, as an opportunity to further the church's mission. Whether this was simply another way in which women were exploited, or whether it allowed them to transform traditional roles remains open to debate.

Women with adequate financial resources and with the power or temperament to fight against the grain had also the possibility of life in monastic community. Some modern historians see the convents as dumping grounds where still-passive aristocratic females were, more or less respectably, disposed of. But the texts of the times (in one case at least written by a woman) suggest that the noble women who sought monastic life were motivated by a desire for some sort of autonomy and power. In the convent, they were free from the social and physical obligations of marriage. If we remember that married women were virtually the property of their husbands and that child-bearing was a life-threatening condition, we can perhaps understand the sense of freedom that could be experienced in monastic life. In the convent, women also had access to learning. Education is always a source of power; in the world where it was rare and yet absolutely necessary for political and ecclesiastical activity, education could be even more a source of authority than would later be the case.

With the conversion of the Germanic tribes, the church administered not only a religious heritage but also the cultural heritage of the Roman empire, with its emphasis on law and its rich tradition of texts, to which the inhabitants of medieval Europe continued to aspire. To be Roman (or to aspire to be so) was to live in a world of the written word. Then, too, Christianity was from the beginning a learned religious tradition (as was Judaism and later Islam); to be able to read and understand the sacred books was to stand in the centre of religious power. Perhaps most important, the education that women received in monasteries, based on the study of the seven liberal arts and oriented to full literacy, was not in any way different from that available to men (a fact that would change in the twelfth century). Though education for women would always be of limited availability, though educated women would often be suspect, though restrictions on their use of their education would continue, when women did become educated they were to some extent able to enter into the conversations of their day.[27]

Finally, in the convent, women had access to the full means of holiness. We can be tempted today to undervalue holiness, for the medieval world identified itself as Christian and honoured the values of the gospel, at least rhetorically, in courts as much as in pulpits. Genuine holiness gave women the power to influence both ordinary people and the politically powerful, as the lives of women from Leoba in the eighth century to Catherine of Siena in the fourteenth testify. Convents were places where various kinds of power were available, at least to noble women, and sometimes to women from lower social backgrounds.

But restrictions remained for aristocratic and ordinary women, for monastic women, and for those who married. In the fluid social world of the early Middle Ages, however, restrictions on women were not at the centre of the church's attention, and the social and cultural patterns shifted regularly as systems of culture and power changed and interacted. In such a world, women with unusual determination and/or unusual opportunities were able to push against the walls imposed on them. Radegunde and Etheldreda refused the full weight of obligations imposed by royal marriage. Leoba, from a simple land-owning family, became extraordinarily learned, an abbess and a missionary. Hilda trained bishops. Radegunde negotiated for the possession of the church's most important relic and supervised the construction of a church to house it.

We do not know what their actions cost them; we do not know exactly what motivated them. We know their lives almost exclusively through the stories of male historians, whose view, even when laudatory, usually neglects those questions. But the success of these few women (and those whose stories have not survived) may be partially assessed through the ecclesiastical pronouncements and policies that they provoked.

Women in Theology and Discipline

The medieval church inherited the misogynist ideology of the writers of the first four centuries. In the great synthesis forged between biblical revelation and the principles of Neoplatonism, writers such as Origen, Tertullian, Jerome, Chrysostom, and Augustine had used a Platonic understanding of woman's 'nature' as an interpretive grid to explicate biblical texts such as the creation narratives, the menstrual taboo in Leviticus, and Paul's apparent teaching that excluded women from various public roles.

This synthesis resulted in a two-fold indictment of women. First, women were considered as subordinate in nature because they were created second (in the Yahwist creation story) and were under the domination of their bodies (a Neoplatonic premise). Second, they were understood to be intensely susceptible to sin (because of the Neoplatonic understanding of bodiliness) and indeed the very gateway through which sin entered and still enters the world (interpretation of the Yahwist's story of the sin of the first humans). This was a commonplace of the understanding of women by the end of the late classical period and was the rationale for (though not necessarily the cause of) almost all the restrictions imposed.

Sundry church documents reiterated that women were not to teach because they were inferior beings and so subject to error and sinfulness that they were not trustworthy interpreters of the truth. The same documents restricted opportunities for widows and virgins to function in the public forum because they were especially vulnerable to sexual temptation and potent in their ability to seduce men. The canons from the many synods, small and large, that took place between the third and the seventh centuries[28] reveal this double bias. Women were seen as threats to clerical establishments as well as to the general holiness of the church.

The misogynous themes of the early writers were repeated, with little that was new, during the early Middle Ages. Eve's supposed responsibility for the sin of the world remained a popular theme in the poetry and letters of Bishops Avitus of Vienne and Desidarius of Cahors during the Gallo-Roman period. The essentially sinful nature of woman was maintained by Bishop Caesarius of Arles, even though he is generally more sympathetic to women than other clerics of his day. One of the important grammarians of the seventh century, the monk known as the Defensor Grammaticus, wrote: 'A woman's reputation of modesty is so fragile that it quickly languishes at the slightest suggestion, as if it were a flower that would wither at the lightest breeze, especially when her age inclines her to vice and she is not ruled by a husband.'[29]

In truth, however, the misogynist ideology of the early church does not seem to have been as significant in the early Middle Ages as it once had been and would be again. As discussed above, the social and political situations that presented themselves from the fifth to the eleventh century were new and ever-changing. While church leaders were avid in preserving the teaching of earlier centuries, they were not themselves scholars, and, when they questioned the scriptures and read what patristic treatises they had available, their questions were different and their concerns more practical. In their interpretation of the scriptures, people such as Bede addressed urgent pastoral needs; they appreciated practical applications of the scriptural texts more than philosophically grounded teaching. Perhaps, too, they so much regarded church restrictions on women as 'given,' as proven doctrine, that they felt no need to elaborate on them. However, as women continued to take advantage of their few opportunities and indeed to create new ones for themselves, church teaching and legislation began to reflect new ecclesiastical anxieties. It is on the practical level, that of decree and prohibition, that we find the church's response to women during the early Middle Ages.

During the fifth and sixth centuries, the decrees of councils and bishops give evidence of concern about the connection of women to the sacramental life of the church. Marriage was not yet seen as an impediment to the ordination of men, but, as the policy of clerical celibacy grew stronger and more universal, decrees were promulgated to control the wives of deacons, priests, and bishops. Some decrees, generally the earlier ones, were designed to protect the mutuality of the marriage contract and required that the wife agree to her husband's ordination and share his religious conversion by a vow of her own; thus did the Council of Agde argue in 506, and Pope Gregory I agreed.[30]

Later legislation allowed a man to choose ordination or the monastic life without his wife's consent (though the wife was not given the same freedom), and decrees from later in the sixth century manifest great concern to restrict any contact between clerics and their former wives. Thus the Council of Orléans (541) required priests and deacons to have rooms separate from their wives, the Council of Tours (567) ordained that bishops should provide a separate residence for theirs, and the Council of Lyons (583) forbade priests and deacons even to see their wives on a daily basis.[31] Such legislation was, of course, punitive to wives, who fell more and more into general suspicion, had no fixed place in the social hierarchy, and were generally reduced to isolated, often useless, lives.

At the same time, the diaconate order, open to women on a limited basis from the early days, began to be closed off. Though scholars continue to debate what opportunities the diaconate really offered to women in various regions of the church, it seems that in the west (the Gallo-Roman region), attempts to limit women's ordination to the diaconate began in the late fourth century; by the Council of Orange (441), there was an official prohibition. None the less, the issue continued to be debated in later documents and councils, suggesting that Frankish women did not cooperate with the efforts to banish them from the ranks of the ordained.[32] By the late sixth and early seventh centuries, however, the ban against women in the altar precincts was both sweeping and extreme; at the Synod of Auxerre women were forbidden to receive the Eucharist in their hands or touch the altar cloths or any sacred vessel and were required to be veiled in the presence of the sacrament and when at prayer. By 829, at the Council of Paris, women were excluded even from the area around the altar.[33]

This growing body of legislation argues that the women of the early Middle Ages did not go gently from the sacramental and public life of the church. While the narratives we have, mostly written by male clerics, give us many pictures of women active within the more acceptable venues of home and cloister, the laws and decrees suggest that they also sought a more active and prominent place within the liturgical actions of the church, from which they were more and more forcefully excluded on the basis of their supposed impurity.

Even within the home and the cloister, church laws sought to control women's activity. Though they originally had a fair degree of autonomy, especially under the rule written by Caesarius Arles, monasteries of women were to be drawn more completely under episcopal control throughout the eighth and ninth centuries. With increasing frequency and rigidity, the decrees promulgated by the councils of Verneuil (755), Frankfurt (796), Chalons (813), and Paris (829) limited the freedom of nuns in contrast to that of their monastic brothers, erased the distinctions between nuns and canonesses (originally a freer gathering of religious women who had some clerical status), forbade the foundation of new and smaller communities, mandated the clothing of cloistered women, restricted their access to the world, and imposed monastic community and rules on any woman who desired to remain unmarried for religious reasons by the taking of a private vow. Rich widows who had taken the veil no longer could remain at home; they had to join some religious house that was under episcopal control. It is not to be wondered at that enthusiasm for the cloistered life waned by the ninth century. There are no stories comparable to those of Radegunde and Leoba to be found in the late Carolingian period.

The energy and commitment to education that many women manifested during the early Middle Ages seem to have prompted at least one important cleric to speak out on their behalf. In the ninth century, Rabanus Maurus, abbot of Fulda and later archbishop of Mainz, composed a commentary on the Book of Judges in which he put together bits and pieces of allegorical interpretations borrowed from earlier writers. Suddenly, in commenting on the story of Deborah, he shifts from allegory and makes the following, obviously personal, comment: 'First, let this idea itself be set forth anew: that although there were many men who were judges in Israel, of none of them is it said, as it is said of Deborah, that he is a prophet. In this issue, even the literal meaning [of the text] offers no small encouragement to the sex of women and it challenges them not to despair because of the weakness of their sex, since they are able to become capable of the gift of prophecy. Let them know and believe that this grace is given according to the purity of mind rather than according to the differentiation of the sexes.'[34]

An investigation of what Rabanus could have meant by the role of prophet reveals that by his day exegetes had come to interpret the title 'prophet,' as given by Paul in his lists of charisms, to mean one who is gifted to interpret the scriptures with pastoral efficacy. Elsewhere Rabanus even suggests that one may prepare actively to receive this gift by assiduous study of the seven liberal arts and of the sacred text. It is highly likely that he was moved to depart from his sources and his allegory here by his knowledge of a real woman's accomplishments.

Earlier in his life, he had asked Rudolph to write the life of Leoba, whose remains rested within the monastery at Fulda. Rudolph's *Life* stresses Leoba's unusually strong commitment to studying the scriptures, her skills in interpreting them, and the pastoral efficacy of her biblical wisdom. Leoba's influence seems to have triumphed, in the mind of Rabanus at least, over traditional misogynist ideology and legislation. Evidence cited above in the discussion of Carolingian marriage further suggests that aristocratic women of Rabanus's day assumed responsibility for the Christian formation of their children and households; Rabanus's affirmation shows that he was ready to recognize their work by naming it a prophetic gift.

A very slender body of legislation and theological opinion emerges, then, from the early Middle Ages and, such as it is, it reflects the ambiguities and internal contradictions that have consistently marked the church's thinking about women. There is the definitive exclusion of women from the sacramental life of the church and a relentless increase of legislation designed to control the freedom of women in monasteries or in the single life. However, women must have continued to press for acceptance and expanded opportunities, and the powerful bishop of Mainz, Rabanus Maurus, is concerned that repeated rebuffs have discouraged them to the point of 'despair.' Based on the achievements of some, he conceded the possibility that women could be prophets, a ministerial function never completely separated from the official structure of the church.

In marriage legislation there was consistent ecclesiastical pressure to ensure some measure of mutuality and equality of rights and privileges. Regular acquiescence of the church to patriarchal and aristocratic demands, however, prevented marriage from being a vocation that promoted equal dignity and autonomy for women. Officially, women were still excluded from the altar and its activity, feared as a source of moral contamination, and restricted to convents in which ecclesiastically approved rules governed even the smallest details of their lives or to church-sanctioned marriages, equally controlled by ecclesiastical law.

But church policy generally depended for its implementation on the power and acquiescence of the civil authority, which ebbed and flowed during the tenth and eleventh centuries in such a way as to allow some women at least to develop their gifts for leadership, learning, and the stewardship of both worldly and spiritual goods.

Women from the Twelfth Century On

The twelfth century was a period of significant change in western Europe, which altered the situation of women for many centuries to come. The social order experienced a major increase in population and a migration of peasants to newly created towns with their opportunities for artisanship and small businesses. Though research has been limited, town records as well as the records of the guilds that grew up in urban artisan circles have begun to reveal the contributions of women, both as entrepreneurs and as skilled workers, who laboured side by side with fathers and husbands in what were essentially family enterprises. Politically, smaller units of power were once again brought under the control of kings, whose authority went beyond the local; France and England began to look like the dominant kingdoms they would soon become.

The church, centralized by the development of the Roman Curia, began to extend a more widespread influence. The call for the first crusade in 1098 reinforced papal claims to universal authority, and the promulgation of canon law, codified by Gratian c. 1150, further strengthened that central authority. In the debates that again arose over the nature and sacramentality of marriage, the discussion of the free consent required of both parties renewed ecclesiastical support for the legal status of a marrying woman.[35] At the same time, there is no doubt that by collecting all the ancient prohibitions about women, now removed from their original context and formulated as universal laws, Gratian dealt a comprehensive blow to the activities and aspirations of all women, regardless of status. Before Gratian, women could (through social or political status, education, or sheer force of will) forge out a space in which they might pursue ecclesiastical and pastoral purposes. After Gratian, all women would be subject to the universal decrees that kept them outside the altar precincts and confined within the domestic hearth or the cloister.

Women participated equally with men in the religious revivals early in the twelfth century. The followers of Robert of Arbrissel (fl. 1096) who abandoned their homes and essayed a radically 'apostolic life' were from both sexes, though eventually he had to place his women followers in strict enclosure.[36] Fontevrault, his initial foundation, was originally a double monastery, led by the abbess. Women were as inspired by the ideals of Citeaux as were men; when the existence of Cistercian nuns finally came to the attention of the monks (c. 1190), the male order made continued, if ultimately ineffective, efforts to limit and control them.[37] Cistercian nunneries continued to proliferate, though always on the fringe of the men's congregations. Similarly, the women who followed the ascetic reform of St Norbert at Premontre (c. 1121) were permitted only limited participation in the liturgical life of the community, were obliged to do most of the domestic work, and were subject to the abbot, never given their own community and autonomy.

As late as the early thirteenth century, the mendicant experiment found women eager to be involved in the new apostolic spirituality. But their zeal was given short shrift; by 1245, the Dominican nuns were strictly controlled in number, forbidden to preach or beg alms, and obliged to very strict enclosure within which they were to 'spiritualize' the apostolic zeal and poverty that were the hallmarks of the order. Likewise, the women who followed St Francis, in spite of the exceptional character and intense spirituality of St Clare, were never permitted to practise the absolute poverty and itinerant ministry of the founder.[38]

In most of the above cases, the disapproval of Roman authorities, at the height of their political power, squelched the zealous courage of the women (as in the case of Arbissel) or prevented charismatic founders from even considering new possibilities for the women whom they inspired. Though the twelfth and thirteenth centuries saw no diminution of fervour, religious energy, and enthusiasm on the part of women, there came to be fewer and fewer channels through which that energy could be expended.

Medieval intellectual life saw the reintroduction of the works of Aristotle (long forgotten in the West, but recently rediscovered through renewed contact with the East) into the organization of knowledge, as well as the creation of the university, a new venue set aside exclusively for learning. The growing organization of regional kingdoms and the ubiquitous church required a body of lawyers, bureaucrats, and clerical staff, and this need in turn spurred the growth of the universities, which were more or less designed to prepare men for positions in civil and ecclesiastical administration.

Thomas à Becket is an epitome of these developments: born to a merchant family in London (which had immigrated from Normandy), he had a wealthy patron, who sent him to the University of Paris, where he attracted the attention of Theobald, archibishop of Canterbury. He did further legal studies at Auxerre and Bologna and then came to the notice of Henry II. First chancellor of England and later archbishop of Canterbury, he exercised enormous influence over ecclesiastical matters and issues of English statehood. His rise in status was a direct result of his university education which fitted him for the changing needs of king and church.

It may well be that Fulbert, canon of the Cathedral of Notre Dame in Paris, had similar ambitions for his niece Heloïse, whose striking educational accomplishments were well known. Why else would he have brought her to Paris and arranged for her to be tutored by Peter

Abélard, the rising star of the new city classrooms? If so, it was not just her own destiny that was altered by her passion and the ethos of university men such as Abélard. Indeed, the development of the universities seems to have had its most enduring influence both on the concrete situation of women in church and society and on the theories and legislation that were eventually developed to validate that situation.

The curriculum of the universities quickly became different from the traditional liberal arts curriculum followed in monastic and cathedral schools. Emphasis shifted from those literary skills that enabled clerics to interpret biblical texts for pastoral and personal purposes to the dialectical method (founded in Aristotelian logic) that prepared students for legal and philosophical debate. Up to the twelfth century, the education of both men and women was substantially the same, enabling women with access to a monastic or cathedral education (or even to good tutors at home) to converse on equal footing with educated men. After the twelfth century, men could receive a university education (from which women were legally barred) that fitted them for the new positions in church and state. Schoolmen also developed a new system of philosophy and law within a world set apart from actual women, their questions, and their concerns. The stage was set for the full development of the scholastic movement, a sea change in Catholic theology. Though early scholastics (such as Abélard) were most exercised by the dialectical method founded on Aristotle's logic, the Greek philosopher's metaphysics made its presence felt everywhere by the thirteenth century and shaped the teaching of the great scholastic theologians.

Thomas Aquinas on Women

In the writings of Thomas Aquinas, a Dominican theologian at the University of Paris in the mid-thirteenth century, we find all the major theological arguments that have determined the thinking of the Roman Catholic church about women down to the present time. Aquinas is selected here not because his influence on subsequent Catholic theology was substantial (indeed, until the so-called Thomistic revival from the end of the nineteenth century to the middle of the twentieth, he was often thought of as a synthesizer rather than as an original thinker) but because it is representative not only of medieval thought but also of later Catholic thought, which remained in a scholastic mould until the Second Vatican Council (and, in some quarters, even afterward).

In Part I, Question 92, of the *Summa theologiae*,[39] Aquinas reveals his conviction that there is something distinct about the nature of woman, some essential questions that are not answered when he considers human nature as a whole, and therefore he introduces a series of hypotheses to discuss 'the production of woman.' This methodological move is not without theological significance: for Aquinas, there is a separateness about woman's nature, a quality or qualities that make his general conclusions about human nature inappropriate or in need of exception. Anyone who reads recent ecclesiastical documents can see his enduring influence here, for the question of a separateness of nature (as distinct from the practical separation of functions) still forms part of the debate on women's roles in church life.

Here in the *Summa theologiae*, Aquinas considers three major issues pertinent to the 'distinct nature of women.' He asks whether woman was necessary to the divine plan of creation from the beginning (i.e., before there was sin in the world), whether it was appropriate that woman be made from man, and whether the 'fact' that God used Adam's rib in creating woman has any essential significance. The way in which he develops his arguments allows us to see the tension between Aristotle and earlier church teaching within his theology, as well as the determinative role of his philosophy.

Aquinas argues that the sexual distinction between male and female is part of the divine will from the beginning. He believes that the noble human activity for which the male is designed – the use of his intellect for ordering human activity and society – requires a certain freedom from the purely physical business of procreation. This freedom is obtained, according to Aquinas, by the separation of the active and passive powers in human generation (the male and female principle, respectively). Aquinas notes that such biological separation exists in all 'perfect animals' (plant life often contains the male and female components together), allowing sometimes the male, sometimes the female, to be freed from the continual burden of reproduction for some more 'noble' animal purpose (which he does not define).

Male humans, however, have an even nobler purpose than other animals: their purpose is the exercise of intellection, which requires them to be biologically separate from the female for all activities except 'carnal generation.' It is clear that Aquinas saw this separation not as freeing the woman, nor does he note any comparable noble purpose that might be hers. She is determined by her reproductive function, while the male is 'freed' from that function to serve higher ends. Woman therefore is *by nature* subject to the male, as physical functions are naturally subject to spiritual ones.

Aquinas furnishes two arguments to establish the natural subjection of woman. The first he takes from biology: individual women are biologically 'misbegotten' because they are produced by some defect in the act of generation. Aquinas's thought here is determined by Aristotelian biology, which held that semen, the only element in conception visible to the naked eye, contained everything necessary to reproduce itself and ought therefore always to produce a male child. When it did not do so, when a female resulted from the act of conception, the 'seed' had malfunctioned because of some 'material indisposition' (i.e., the seed was defective) or some 'external influence' (such as the blowing of a moist east wind during the act of coition).

The second argument he bases on Aristotelian metaphysics: it affirms that women are naturally subject because 'in man the discretion of reason predominates.' This is a reprise of the old Platonic dualism, equally prevalent in Aristotle, which understood women as primarily body while men are predominantly soul and therefore in possession of reason to a significantly greater degree. In this argument we can hear one of the many notes of tension between philosophical conclusions and the propositions of revealed faith: Aquinas recognizes the church's position that women have their own, if secondary, place in the divine creation (even though they are the principal occasion of sin to men), and he attempts to reconcile that position with their natural subordination. Women are to be tolerated, he concludes, because the common good requires the separation of the passive force of procreation from the active, and the resultant social freedom of the male gives female passivity a higher purpose.

In the second article, Aquinas asks whether it was appropriate for the woman to be made from the man. In affirming the appropriateness of what he believed to be revealed, Aquinas gives a rather strange combination of reasons; they reveal, I think, the painful ambivalence that has consistently been at the heart of this whole question (of woman's nature) within the Catholic tradition. On the one hand, such a creation for woman clearly subjects her to the man, whose dignity consists in his being very like God, the single 'head' of creation. As God is the creative principle of the whole universe, so the man is the creative principle, both biologically and intellectually, in humanity. On the other hand, this unique and intimate creation of woman enables the man to love her faithfully in a life-long commitment, since human reproduction requires not just a biological act but the foundation of a permanent domestic life, in which woman has her particular, if subordinate, duties. The positive side of woman's place vis-à-vis the male is what gives her the power to represent the church symbolically (as the male does Christ).

Aquinas uses a similar argument in defence of God's use of Adam's rib: it signifies the social union of man and woman, in which woman is neither in authority over man nor subject to his contempt and enslavement. Reading biblical revelation through the prism of Aristotle, he assumes that nature (and therefore the divine will) is the foundation of all the social subordination in the medieval world. Yet that same biblical revelation reveals to him that woman is capable of a symbolic representation of the church as bride of Christ, and he knows the consistent tradition that makes her place in the marriage partnership sacred. His discussions about Adam's rib lead him almost to the point of affirming the equality of woman; yet his acceptance of Aristotle's explanation of nature and of the common patriarchal presuppositions requires that he continue to affirm subordination.

Happily (because it enables us to make a comparison), Thomas Aquinas revisited the question of the possibility of women as prophets, which we have seen Rabanus discuss. Persuaded anew by the arguments of Aristotle that woman was inferior by nature, Aquinas reworked Rabanus's thought and further revealed the way in which philosophy conditioned both his reading of biblical texts and his appropriation of the earlier tradition.

In the *Summa theologiae*, Part II, Section II, Question 177, Article 2,[40] Aquinas sets up the question in his usual way, giving the counterarguments first: 'But prophecy is granted to women, as we read of Deborah, of Hulda the prophetess, wife of Selnor, and of the four daughters of Philip. Even St Paul speaks of "every woman prophesying or praying."' Note that he takes seriously the historical existence and the prophetic title of these biblical women; he also acknowledges, as did Rabanus (and in words that sound suspiciously like literary dependence), that the gift of prophecy is given in respect to the capacity of the mind and not to the differentiation of the body. But against the historical evidence of the texts from both the Jewish scriptures and the Christian testament, Thomas quotes Paul (considered the author of I Timothy) against himself: 'St Paul says that "women should keep silence in the churches," and "I permit no woman to teach or to have authority over men."'

Aquinas is here forced to make an overly fine distinction between the gift of prophecy that women can use 'privately, to one or a few, in familiar conversation' and that which is proclaimed 'publicly, addressing oneself to the whole church. This is not conceded to women.' Though he purports to be dependent on the text of I Timothy, Aquinas's argument draws its force from the Aristotelian understanding of 'the condition of the female sex, which must be subject to man, according to Genesis.' Again, though Aquinas cites the biblical text, his reading of it is Aristotelian. It is a question of the categories of authority and submission and whether these are intrinsic to human nature or conditioned by historical and social circumstance. Having settled these issues to his satisfaction in an earlier part of the *Summa*, Aquinas demonstrates clearly that Aristotelian philosophy is determinative in his understanding.

Even more telling perhaps is his argument in Part III (Supplement), Question 39.[41] There the issue is whether being female constitutes an impediment to the sacrament of ordination,[42] and he cites arguments in opposition to this view from scripture and from the historical accomplishments of women. The arguments of his opponents (real or hypothetical, as they may have been) affirm a parallelism between prophets and priests (both stand as mediators between God and the people) and note that women's reception of the gift of prophecy was established both historically and biblically. They further argue that religious authority had been granted not only by God to Deborah and other women but also by the church itself to the women who exercised authority in religious life. And still further, the counterarguments continue, since the ability to perform priestly acts, like the ability to prophesy, is a gift of the soul and not the body, gender cannot be an impediment to that sacrament.

Against all these points, which seem quite persuasive today, Aquinas affirms that woman is properly impeded from the sacrament of holy orders because she lacks the essential capacity to signify 'eminence of degree,' because she 'is in a state of subjection' (a position derived from Aristotelian biology and metaphysics). His argument, that the one who presides over liturgical assemblies must resemble Christ in some unique way because of the symbolic nature of Christian sacramental worship, sounds quite familiar to those who are acquainted with recent Vatican pronouncements on this matter. For Aquinas, such resemblance consists in the 'eminence' granted to the male in the natural order of things. Since Christ is head of the body that is his church, so must the one who presides over the church assembly be naturally and visibly capable of headship (control, excellence, dominance), a capacity that he believes intrinsic and exclusive to the male sex.[43] Finally, Aquinas concludes that the argument from prophecy does not apply because prophecy is a gift and not a sacrament, while the authority exercised by women prophets and abbesses is not ordinary authority but authority delegated to them (in the latter case) 'on account of the danger of men and women living together.'

Thus the arguments that persuaded Rabanus Maurus in the ninth century that women can receive the gift of prophecy – namely, the force of biblical texts and the actual accomplishments of women – are in Aquinas (and the other scholastics) subverted by the teaching of Aristotle. Aquinas and his contemporaries believed that the Philosopher (as Aquinas always refers to him) had adequately explained the reality of human nature and that God, the author of all nature, could not possibly contradict in the revelations of scripture what had already been revealed in the act of creation.

In many of the tensions that they discovered between the two revelations, the scholastics gave to Aristotelian philosophy the determinative, if not the last, word. And since they found echoes of Aristotle's positions on women in writings of the fathers of the church who had a bias towards Neoplatonism, they expressed their misogyny with confidence.

Conclusion

After Aquinas and the other scholastics, the situation for women in the Christian world was permanently altered. In the centuries to come, individual women such as Catherine of Siena might find that their personal holiness could give them access to power in a world that subscribed to the Christian myth even when worldly Christians did not live up to it, but they would be the exception. Women's deep involvement in the spiritual and mystical life of the church might flourish; indeed, the eras of the great mystics would follow the scholastic period. The monastery of Helfta, the English and Rhineland mystics of the fourteenth century, and the great Spanish mystics of the Catholic Reformation remind us that limits can never be set on prayer, asceticism, and grace. The enduring strength and contributions of the mystical tradition form a legacy of which Christian women may be justly proud.

Yet not all are called to this path, and women would continue to struggle against the narrow limits within which their lives would be circumscribed by ecclesiastical decrees; thus would the Beguines, for instance, attempt to carve out for themselves a way of living an apostolic, spiritual life in the world as single women.[44] Some women would fight their way into the university and receive philosophical and medical degrees. Nuns, with the support of apostolically zealous men such as Francis de Sales and Vincent de Paul, would work their way out of the cloister and transform themselves into 'sisters' of all those deprived of work, education, familial support, and spiritual guidance.

The theological approach of the scholastics, however, institutionally separated from scholarly women who could have brought an alternative point of view and counterarguments to the discussion, would remain the *philosophia perennis* of Catholicism. Philosophically connected to an impressive body of systematic theological teaching and invested with a kind of universal and absolute validity, scholastic positions survived the many social and historical changes that followed. Indeed, they survive even today in the minds of those who believe that women's nature is somehow different from – and usually subordinate to – men's, in areas of family and church leadership.

NOTES

1 See Elisabeth Schüssler Fiorenza, *In Memory of Her: A Feminist Theological Reconstruction of Christian Origins* (New York: Crossroad, 1983), for the possibility of reconstructing the participation of women from the meagre evidence in New Testament texts.
2 St Gregory of Nyssa, 'Life of St. Macrina,' in *Ascetical Works, Fathers of the Church*, vol. LVIII (Washington, DC: Catholic University of America Press, 1967).
3 See Jerome, 'Letter to Eustochium, Memorials of Her Mother Paula,' in *A Select Library of Nicene and Post-Nicene Fathers of the Christian Church*, vol XVI (New York: Christian Literature Co., 1893), 195–210.
4 See Benedicta Ward, SLG, *Harlots of the Desert* (Kalamazoo, Mich.: Cistercian Publications, 1987).
5 The use of this in contrast to the actual accomplishments of women suggests the rightness of Gerda Lerner's observation that we would assess the relative importance of various historical periods differently if women's experience were considered. See *The Majority Finds Its Past: Placing Women in History* (New York: Oxford University Press, 1970).
6 Trans. O.M. Dalton (Oxford: Clarendon Press, 1927).
7 Felice Lifshitz, 'Des femmes missionnaires: l'éxemple de la Gaule franque,' *Revue d'histoire écclésiastique*, 83 (1988), 5–33.
8 Bede, *A History of the English Church and People*, trans. Leo Sherley-Price (New York: Barnes and Noble Books, 1993), vol. I, 25, 69.
9 Book II, 11, 120–2.

10 In his commentary on the Gospel of Mark, Bede gives a telling interpretation of the story of the gentile woman who petitions Jesus on behalf of her daughter. Bede calls her an 'evangelist,' who leaves everything – home, family, and culture – in order to take the faith to pagan lands. Bede may well be thinking of Bertha and Etheldreda here; *In Marci evangelium exposito*, ed. D. Hurst, *Corpus Christianorum*, vol. CXX (Turnholt: Brepols, 1960), 523–5.
11 Though the church had long championed the right of the woman to give or withhold free consent to the marriage contract, in practice the force of social expectations that a young girl would marry whomever her parents wished was often given added strength through the pressure of influential churchmen. See, in this regard, *The Life of Christina of Markyate: A Twelfth Century Recluse*, ed. and trans. C.H. Talbot (Oxford: Clarendon Press, 1959), 62–3.
12 Janet L. Nelson, 'Les femmes et l'évangelisation au IXè siècle,' *Revue du Nord*, 68, no. 269 (April–June, 1986), 475.
13 Suzanne Wemple, 'Women from the Fifth to the Tenth Century' in Christiane Klapish-Zuber, ed., *A History of Women in the West*, vol II, *Silences of the Middle Ages* (Cambridge, Mass.: Belknap Press of Harvard University Press, 1992), 107.
14 Nelson, 'Les femmes,' 475.
15 The English version of this text is *Handbook for William: A Carolingian Woman's Counsel for Her Son*, trans. Carol Neel (Lincoln: University of Nebraska Press, 1991). For a study of Dhuoda's theology, see Marie Anne Mayeski, *Dhuoda: Ninth Century Mother and Theologian* (Scranton, Pa.: University of Scranton Press, 1995).
16 Nelson, 'Les femmes,' 476.
17 See, for instance, the discussion of coins bearing the name of a ruling woman in Alan M. Stahl, 'Coinage in the Name of Medieval Women,' Joel T. Rosenthal, ed., *Medieval Women and the Sources of Medieval History* (Athens: University of Georgia Press, 1990), 321–41.
18 Wemple, 'Women from the Fifth to the Tenth Century,' 184.
19 Bede, *A History*, IV, 19–20, 238–42.
20 A translation of Radegunde's life by both authors is to be found in *Sainted Women of the Dark Ages*, ed. and trans. Jo Ann McNamara and John E. Halborg (Durham: Duke University Press, 1992), 60–105. A translation of the life by Baldonivia, done by Jane Crawford, and an essay giving a feminist interpretation of that life by Marie Anne Mayeski are forthcoming from City University of New York Press.
21 Bede, *A History*, III, 24–5, 184–7; IV, 23–4, 245–52. See also Janemarie Luecke, 'The Unique Experience of Anglo-Saxon Nuns,' in Lillian Thomas Shank and

John A. Nichols, eds., *Peaceweavers: Medieval Religious Women*, vol. II (Kalamazoo, Mich.: Cistercian Publishers, 1987), 55–65.

22 The French government made her feast a national holiday in 1921, fulfilling a vow taken during the First World War, and thus reclaimed the political implications of her life in a new story. See JoAnn McNamara et al., *Sainted Women of the Dark Ages* (Durham, NC: Duke University Press, 1992), 93 n 102.

23 For the specific connection between holiness and power in the medieval world, see Eleanor McLoughlin, 'Women, Power and the Pursuit of Holiness in Medieval Christianity,' in Ann Loades, ed., *Feminist Theology: A Reader* (London: SPCK Press, 1990), 99–120.

24 Critical edition is in *Monumenta Germaniae historica, scriptores*, ed. Waitz (Hannover, 1887), vol. XV, 127–31. An English translation by C.H. Talbot is to be found in *The Anglo-Saxon missionaries in Germany* (London: Sheed and Ward, 1954), 205–26.

25 Wemple, 'Women from the Fifth to the Tenth Century,' 193.

26 Ibid., 199.

27 In *Writing a Woman's Life* (New York: Ballantine Books, 1988), Carolyn Heilbrun defines power as 'the ability to take one's place in whatever discourse is essential to action and to have that place matter,' 20.

28 As found in C.J. Hefele, *A History of the Councils of the Church* (Edinburgh: T. & T. Clark, 1896).

29 This quote is given by Suzanne Fonay Wemple in *Women in Frankish Society* (Philadelphia: University of Pennsylvania Press, 1981), 30. The Defensor's book was an important school text and therefore influential in the intellectual formation of young men and women for several centuries. The preceding examples of the three Gallo-Roman bishops are also from Wemple, who points out that occasionally a church council or synod settled a theological issue in a way that maintained the early church's insistence on the full salvation of women. Thus the Council of Macon (586) decided that 'the designation *homo* in the [Vulgate] bible included both males and females, an important point in the dispute over whether or not God intended to save women,' 30.

30 See, for instance, the Decrees of the Council of Agde (506), *Corpus Christanorum Series Latina*, vol. CXLVIII, 201, and the letters of Gregory the Great, *Registrum epistularum* 11.30; *Monumenta Germaniae historica, epistulae*, vol. II, 301.

31 All these examples are from Wemple, *Frankish Society*, 133–4.

32 Fortunatus's life of St Radegunde included an account of her being made a deacon by a rite of veiling that included the laying on of hands. This story remained popular and seems to have been used as evidence in the argument in favor of women deacons. See ibid., 140.

33 Cited in Janet L. Nelson, 'Les femmes et l'évangelisation,' 472. According to Nelson, the bishop of Basle himself made the ban more precise for his own diocese: 'It is forbidden for women to approach the altar. If the altar linen needs to be washed, it must be taken off the altar by the priests and given to the women in the chancel area.'
34 Migne, *Patrologia latine*, 108, 1154 cd. The translation is my own, though a generous colleague, Dr Matt Dillon, checked it for accuracy.
35 See James A. Brundage, 'Sexual Equality in Medieval Canon Law,' in Joel T. Rosenthal ed., *Medieval Women and the Sources of Medieval History* (Athens: University of Georgia Press, 1990), 66–79.
36 J. Smith, 'Robert of Arbrissel's Relations with Women,' in Derek Baker, ed., *Medieval Women* (Oxford: Basil Blackwell, 1978), 175–84.
37 S. Thompson, 'The Problem of the Cistercian Nuns in the Twelfth and Early Thirteenth Centuries,' in Derek Baker, ed., *Medieval Women* (Oxford: Basil Blackwell, 1978), 227–52.
38 See Fidelis Hart, 'Following in the Foot Prints of the Poor Christ: Clare's Spirituality,' in Lillian Thomas Shank and John A. Nichols, eds., *Peaceweavers: Medieval Religious Women*, vol. II (Kalamazoo, Mich.: Cistercian Publishers, 1987), 175–95.
39 Translated by the Fathers of the English Dominican Province (London, 1922) and reproduced in Martha Lee Osborne, ed., *Women in Western Thought* (New York: Random House, 1979), 68–72.
40 *Summa theologiae*, vol. XLV, trans. Roland Potter (New York: Blackfriars, 1969), 133–5.
41 Given in Osborne, *Women in Western Thought*, 74–5.
42 A more complete discussion of Aquinas on women's ordination can be found in two articles by Dennis Michael Ferrara: 'Representation or Self-Effacement: The Axiom *In Persona Christi* in St. Thomas and the Magisterium,' *Theological Studies*, 55, no. 2 (June 1994), 195–224, and 'The Ordination of Women: Tradition and Meaning,' *Theological Studies*, 55, no. 4 (Dec. 1994), 706–19.
43 Once the church moves away from a philosophy that supports that natural 'eminence,' it is forced to find the natural signification of the liturgical presider in something else that males alone possess – namely, the very gender of the male. But see Ferrara, 'Representation.'
44 C. Neel, 'The Origins of the Beguines,' *Signs: Journal of Women in Culture and Society*, 14, no. 2 (1989), 321–41; E.A. Petroff, 'A New Feminine spirituality: The Beguines and Their Writings in Medieval Europe,' *Body and Soul: Essays on Medieval Women and Mysticism* (New York: Oxford University Press, 1994), 51–65.

5

Ave Virginia, Regina Terræ: The Power of Culture and the Culture of Power in Renaissance England

WILLIAM H. SWATOS, JR

The title of this chapter reflects an academic game I have played with comparative-religion students. By the time I have them to the seventeenth century of our era, they have learned about Alexander and Alexandria, Constantine and Constantinople, and they are now getting to James and Jamestown. But for whom, I ask, is Virginia named? The answers I get are mixed, but never yet have I had the correct one: Elizabeth I, the Virgin Queen, whose forty-five year reign, from 1558 to 1603, was one of the longest and most momentous in English history.[1] During this era, Shakespeare began writing, the Spanish Armada was defeated, the New World began to open to serious English exploration, and 'Puritan' became a meaningful term in Western civilization. Under Elizabeth as well, a stable, 'reformed Catholic' Church of England took shape in an ecclesiastical arrangement that was to have profound effects on the way all Anglo-American Christendom was to conceive itself thereafter, for better or worse.

Unlike my students, the early University of Chicago sociologist Albion Small did know that Elizabeth was termed 'the Virgin Queen,' but he also remarked in an essay that whether or not she was experientially a virgin mattered little to the meaning of her reign 'as an index of the effect of previous conjunctions of social forces, and as a cause of further rearrangements of social relations.'[2] There is some truth to this. What exactly her anatomy might betray is certainly irrelevant to the course of subsequent social and historical developments as we now

---

Leslie Fairfield and Mary Hampson offered a wealth of suggestions for this chapter, which were enormously helpful; no responsibility should be attached to them for any defects that remain.

Ave Virginia, Regina Terrae 97

receive them. On the other hand, the fact that she chose to be and was *perceived* to be the Virgin Queen is of considerable importance – or at least that is part of the thesis I am advancing.

Looking to another early Chicago sociologist, W.I. Thomas, I would argue that the 'definition of the situation' theorem is fully applicable here: a situation *is* what it is defined to be by the participants in an action system, and what is perceived as real in society *is* real in its consequences.[3] In social science today this view is often referred to as 'constructionist' – the notion that 'reality' is the result of the social processes in which people externalize, objectify, and internalize their experiences in interaction with others in the world around them.[4] Elizabeth, her ministers, and her people created an image of her that influenced the development of English civilization in perhaps its most crucial period until the even longer reign of Queen Victoria in the nineteenth century.[5]

What I want to illustrate by focusing on the reign of Elizabeth is *the power of culture to create a culture of power*. Elizabeth, in order to reign effectively, had to conform to a set of cultural norms that could not be altered simply because she was queen. That is, she could not, because she was queen, decree that gender-role expectations for men and women in English society would change and thus make it be so. Indeed, quite to the contrary, she reigned effectively precisely because she caught particularly well the strong central currents of her era and rode them out vigorously. I pose this thesis against an alternative view that power is a relatively independent variable, which is to say that, given the power of rulership, Elizabeth could have altered gender relations in her society however she wanted. Rather, I would argue that she accomplished what she did as queen because she accepted existing gender relations and used them to channel her energies, and her society's, in other directions.

Portions of this argument have already been developed in Carole Levin's book *'The Heart and Stomach of a King': Elizabeth I and the Politics of Sex and Power* – the title based on words allegedly spoken by Elizabeth to the British troops at Tilbury on the eve of the anticipated invasion of the Armada: 'I may have the body of a weak and feeble woman, but I have the heart and stomach of a king.'[6] This one sentence encapsulates the dynamics of culture and power that I wish to illustrate; Elizabeth embraces the dominant worldview of womanhood to enhance her rulership. By admitting the weakness of her outward female frame, she is enabled to assert her inner fortitude, hence her right not only to reign but to command as well. Throughout her tenure, Elizabeth sought to demonstrate that she was no figurehead, but a 'working monarch,' very much in control of her realm.

The Elizabethan Settlement

Elizabeth was the last of the monarchs of the House of Tudor, which came to power in England at the end of the fifteenth century by the victory of Henry Tudor at the battle of Bosworth Field, whereby he became Henry VII. His intended heir, Arthur, Prince of Wales, predeceased him, hence his second son followed him to the throne, as Henry VIII. Henry VIII, unable to conceive a son with Arthur's widow, Katherine of Aragon, whom he had married to continue to solidify a Spanish–English alliance engineered by his father, began a process of divorce that not only ended his marriage but led to the separation of the church in England from Rome. Elizabeth was the last of three children from Henry to succeed to the throne, and she inherited a religious mess.

Norman Cantor says: 'Henry VIII was no more Protestant than the Pope,' and he may well be right, but the effect of the separation of the English church from Rome and the Royal Supremacy that followed from it (that is, the claim that the monarch was 'Supreme Head' of the Church in England) was to create fertile soil for Protestant seeds.[7] They sprang up fast during the reign of the boy-king Edward VI, who succeeded his father at age ten, under the tutelage of Protestant sympathizers. What Henry apparently also did not see (or perhaps simply did not care about) was that the royal supremacy could take England right back to Rome, as it did next in the reign of Edward's eldest sister, 'Bloody Mary' Tudor. Edward and Mary each died after a reign of about five years, and neither produced a new heir. Elizabeth's reign brought a period of relative compromise and toleration in religious matters, generally through a plan of 'comprehension' termed the Elizabethan Settlement.

Historians have debated the role that Elizabeth played in effecting the settlement. This kind of question arises in virtually any rulership. Did Henry VIII or Thomas More, for example, write the critique that earned Henry the title Defender of the Faith from the pope in Henry's younger years, before the divorce issue arose? Though Winthrop Hudson has, for example, made a good case for the view that Elizabeth helped create the settlement that bears her name, what really matters is that she was *perceived* to be involved.[8] From the public to the pope, Elizabeth was seen as putting forth a specific shape for English religion. It was probably more Protestant than Catholic, but it was quite different from any other form of Protestantism, because it strove towards compromise and toleration – within limits. Those limits were nothing other than the Royal Supremacy, and it was this more than anything else that headed Elizabeth on a collision course with both Rome and the Puritans. 'In the interests of the State,' the settlement meant that Elizabeth 'executed Catholic and Puritan impartially,' if either one crossed her politics.[9]

The settlement was devised 'for the according and uniting' of all English subjects 'into a uniform order of Religion,' with two principal intentions. As regards Roman Catholicism, the plan was 'that nothing be advised or done which anyway in continuance of time were likely to breed or nourish any kind of Idolatry or Superstition.' As for Protestant extremism, however, the intention was 'that by no Licentious or loose handling any manner of Occasion be given, whereby any contempt or irreverent behaviour towards God and Godly things, or any spice of irreligion, might creep in or be conceived.'[10] Rational orderliness was the *summum bonum* of Elizabethan religion; this view receives no higher expression than Richard Hooker's magisterial apologetical text *Of the Laws of Ecclesiastical Polity*, written near the end of Elizabeth's reign.

The intended comprehensiveness of the settlement was based on Elizabeth's tolerance of varying theological 'opinions.' In her view, theological differences should be accepted for the sake of political accommodation. This is epitomized in the famous joining of the words of administration from the more Catholic (1549) and more Protestant (1552) Prayer Books in her book of 1559, to create perhaps the longest sentence of administration in Christian history.

David Hume (among others) observed there was no 'regular plan of liberty' in a constitutional sense during Elizabeth's reign, but there was theological toleration.[11] Personal beliefs about God and God's activity were not to be examined or to be the cause of censure; neither were personal religious practices. Elizabeth made this clear by her own decision to maintain crucifix and candles in her private chapel, to the horror of Protestant partisans. If one were to try to define her theology, the phrase 'Christian humanist' would probably best fit. Yet precisely because the new state religion combined what would today be called Catholic and Protestant elements, it is difficult to categorize the Anglicanism that began in her reign.

The Royal Supremacy, however, was made into a *conditio sine qua non* for legitimate participation in English society; ironically, it was a virtually infallible dogma. This, too, was consistent with Renaissance humanism, which was rather absolutist.[12] The institutional church as a geographical expression of English religion was completely in Elizabeth's hands. Though she sidestepped the title 'Supreme Head,' which her father had taken and the presbyterian reformer John Calvin had called blasphemous, for 'Supreme Governor,' there was no question that her government was supreme. John Whitgift, one her archbishops of Canterbury, held that the decision to have bishops, for example, was entirely Elizabeth's; if she had wanted 'no bishops at all, we could not have complained justly of any defect in our church.' He claimed that Elizabeth, if she chose to, could have ordained priests herself. Indeed, as J.T. Tomlinson observes, 'According to her own notions,' Elizabeth 'succeeded to the powers formerly wielded by the Pope' and directly altered Prayer Book rubrics, the Articles of Religion, and the *Homilies* before their publication. This led to a position that made both Puritans and Papists unhappy: the church would tolerate theological differences but demand organizational uniformity.[13]

A practical outcome of this attitude that caused no little problem over time was Elizabeth's general rejection of preaching, that is to say, of an ordained minister delivering a sermon of his own composition. Less than two months after she ascended the throne, and prior to her coronation, she prohibited all preaching until the service of the church could be regularized. Even after the necessary acts of Supremacy and Uniformity had been passed by Parliament, free preaching was narrowly circumscribed. As Wallace MacCaffrey comments: 'the very notion of a preaching clergy cut across the grain of Elizabeth's conception [of the English religious order]. The Minister's task was to teach, not to preach, to instruct a docile and passive audience in habits of obedience to a received body of wisdom, not to exhort them to a more strenuous and demanding spiritual life.'

The immediate public consequence of this policy was a worship service based on the reading of fixed texts known as the *Homilies*, about which more below. The more relaxed attitude of Edmund Grindal, archbishop of Canterbury before Whitgift, towards free preaching – known as 'prophesying' – and his admonishing the queen about her own view on the subject led to Grindal's 'sequestration,' a status close to house arrest that removed from him all of his administrative powers for his last seven years. But, as MacCaffrey notes, 'the prophesyings were subtly subverting the whole hierarchic structure envisaged by the Queen's programme,' and over time, religious affairs became the forum of conflict between Protestant partisans and the royal prerogative.[14]

The Virgin Queen

Elizabeth had watched a succession of women among royalty come to unhappy ends, directly or indirectly through what had seemed to be politically advantageous marriages. Her own mother, Anne Boleyn, had been executed, as had stepmother Catherine Howard. She had seen two of her stepmothers and Mary Tudor die from what seemed to be physical side-effects of the birth process. She also eventually, reluctantly, signed the death warrant for Mary, Queen of Scots, who had effected a tolerable religious settlement with Scottish Protestant partisans before she became entangled in marital woes. Elizabeth struggled against being both the daughter of Anne Boleyn and the sister of Mary Tudor.[15] The latter's reign, in particular, had created a flurry of propaganda – most viciously in John Knox's *First Blast of the Trumpet against the Monstrous Regiment of Women*, written shortly before Elizabeth came to the throne and quickly banned by her – against women monarchs, some composed by those very Protestants with whom Elizabeth would like to have made league upon her accession.

Writing over a hundred years ago, the historian James Froude claimed: 'Marriage, under all forms, was disagreeable to her.'[16] Not quite; she chose instead to adopt the fascinating posture of being a political nun: she married England. When her councillors would become too urgent about marriage, she would take the coronation ring from her finger and declare that she was 'already bound unto a husband which is the Kingdom of England.'[17] Elizabeth 'progressed' around the southern portion of the country, especially in summer, rarely spending more than six months at a time in any one place. She generally endeared herself to her subjects, but she also paid a price: even in her decision not to marry, she accepted the cultural mores that required singlehood and putative celibacy ('virginity') as the alternative to marriage and children. She particularly had to accept thereby the ending of the house of Tudor – the very thing that her father claimed to be saving when he began his first divorce.

That Elizabeth could have married is beyond doubt. She had suitors from her teens. She was by all accounts pretty – an attribute she obtained from her father, rather than her mother. She also was well educated, at times sharing tutors with her half-brother, Edward. She spoke and wrote fluently in French, Italian, and Latin; one of her tutors claimed: 'She readeth more Greek every day than some Prebendaries of this Church do in a whole week.'[18] She could be flirtatious; one of the powerful dynamics of the 'Virgin Queen' image was her apparent delight in the engaging, sometimes intimate, companionship of men. Even in the 1590s, Henry IV of France could joke that 'whether Queen Elizabeth was a maid or no' was one of the great imponderables of history.[19] Pope Sixtus V (1585–90) enormously admired her leadership ability and fantasized that if but he and she could have married, 'Our children would have ruled the whole world.'[20]

Despite her decision about her own life, however, her reign established the context for clerical marriage in the Church of England, and in Anglo-American society, up well into the twentieth century. Despite the married state of most Anglican clergy today, the Henrican reformation was not sympathetic to clerical marriage; in fact, clerical celibacy was mandated both by royal proclamation in 1538 and in the Act of Six Articles of 1539. Clerical marriage was decriminalized during the reign of Edward VI by the repeal of the Act of Six Articles and given grudging tolerance (as better behaviour than clerical fornication) by a 1548 act of Parliament. Needless to say, the return to Catholicism under Mary brought a sudden if brief end to this weak acceptance of clerical marriage, and during her reign all married priests were deprived of their parishes or other livings.[21]

Strictly speaking, clerical marriage was not part of the Elizabethan Settlement, as the queen removed from the final version a provision for clerical marriage approved by Parliament in the second supremacy bill. Nevertheless, the Royal Visitation injunctions of 1559 'explicitly affirmed the lawfulness of clerical marriage,' and 'by 1563, ... clerical marriage was a secure and unchallengeable feature of the Elizabethan church,' incorporated in the Articles of Religion, still printed in most versions of the Anglican *Book of Common Prayer*, and the closest thing to an Anglican statement of faith. The Articles became statutory law in 1571, following the ill-fated bull *Regnans in excelsis* of Pope Pius V in 1570, by which he sought to topple Elizabeth, and all Church of England clergy were required to subscribe to them.[22]

The injunctions of 1559, however, are especially instructive with respect to clerical marriage in relation to sexism and Christianity, since their primary purpose seems to have been to regulate the women whom the clergy might marry. The injunctions in effect required that the potential bride's character be certified to the bishop in one of several ways. A variety of suits and divorces, including clerical remarriage after divorce (even a bishop, Thornborough of Limerick, with the queen's explicit permission), indicate that the injunctions were hardly successful and that wise bishops looked into the character of the clergy-*man* as well.

As Eric Josef Carlson notes, however, Elizabeth's conduct of the affairs of the church shows that she wanted to protect her own position not only as Supreme Governor of the church but as *Her* Majesty. To that end, she wanted to ensure that the character of the wives of parish clergy in particular – the agents of the state most directly involved in the day-to-day lives of her subjects – was not going to bring into question her governance of the church or her right to rule. Elizabeth, Carlson writes, was

> deeply agitated by the possibility of scandal in the church ... It was imperative, in the queen's view, that the new church settlement be allowed to establish its credibility with a laity for the most part either hostile to or skeptical of it. Any scandal at the parochial level by the representatives of the Establishment undermined the credibility of the church ... Moreover, at a time when the pulpit was used to transmit not only doctrine and ethics but also political ideas and information, undercutting loyalty to the occupant of the pulpit was ultimately undercutting loyalty to the queen herself.[23]

The ideal 'clergy wife' in Anglo-American thought reflected Elizabeth's idea of how a woman ought to act for the good of the state.

From this we may also understand why Elizabeth chose not to marry and often discouraged, prohibited, or prosecuted marriage by women in her court.[24] She believed strongly that order in human social relations was divinely ordained. God had intentionally created hierarchy in all social institutions; marriage was no different in this respect from political or ecclesiastical life. Some people were in charge of other people by virtue of a combination of the gifts that God gave them and how they chose to use them. No social institution could continue to function without hierarchy. In marriage, men were heads over women; this is what God ordained. Though they put different slants on their interpretations, both Catholic and Protestant theologians affirmed this point. When Elizabeth said, 'I will have here but one mistress, and no master,' she was speaking about both domestic and political life. If she were married, she would have to obey her husband, because her whole theory of her own monarchy rested on the principle of divinely ordained hierarchy. She could not be simultaneously *under* a husband and *over* England. To free women from their husbands was, in Elizabethan politics, to license anarchy.

Texts

The advent of the printing press in the mid-fifteenth century had an effect on Western Christianity that can never be overestimated. The printed word, more than anything else, gave shape to the Protestant Reformation as we have received it. This was certainly true in England, where a series of critical texts has directly or indirectly shaped subsequent Anglo-American ideas.

The Prayer Book and the Articles of Religion

The *Book of Common Prayer* is the distinctive religious expression of the Church of England; there is nothing directly comparable to it outside Anglicanism. The Elizabethan prayer book of 1559, though superseded by the *Book of Common Prayer* of 1662, is the core of the later volume. The 1559 version is the normative book of Anglicanism. It was that to which the Puritans in the Stuart reigns objected (as they did in Elizabeth's, but less stridently), and one of the grievances of the Great Rebellion of 1641. The 1662 text made only minor accommodations to Puritan sensibilities. The 1559 version was closer to the Protestant book of 1552 than to the Catholic one of 1549, but it was precisely the most stridently Protestant elements that the 1559 book altered.

Though Elizabeth formulated specific changes in the 1559 book, the marriage service was generally left unchanged until 1662. The text of that year dropped the requirement that the newly married couple receive the Eucharist 'the same day' as their wedding – a formal concession to the Puritans, but perhaps as well a recognition of actual practice, since the nuptial Eucharist seems widely to have fallen into disuse. The official English books have always treated marriage as a single-ring ceremony, in which the wife, having vowed to 'obey' her husband, is 'endowed' with all his 'worldly goods,' of which the ring is representative.[25]

The sacramental character of the marriage ceremony within Anglican theology seems to have been in flux throughout this period, but the purpose of marriage was quite clear: it was pre-eminently regulatory. In the statement of 'the causes for which matrimony was ordained' by God, marriage both ensures that children will be 'brought up in the fear and nurture of the Lord,' and serves as 'a remedy against sin, and to avoid fornication, that such persons as have not the gift of continency might marry, and keep themselves undefiled members of Christ's body.' In the public world of Elizabethan religion, all marriages were essentially political acts, intended for a purpose well beyond the mutual satisfaction of the couple, or even their immediate families.

The Elizabethan marriage ceremony reflected both newly awakened Protestant sentiments and aspects of civil law. The woman's vow of obedience and service was intended to transfer her from one form of guardianship to another; it was connected to her being 'given away.' As A.J. Stephens wrote, 'The weaker sex is always supposed to be under the tuition of a father or guardian.' This view was considered to be consistent not only with biblical injunctions (for example, Eph. 5:22–4; Col. 3:18; Titus 2:5; I Peter 3:1–5), but with ancient Roman law as well. Stephens also commented that the man is addressed first in the ceremony, because a woman's seeking of a husband would not 'very well suit the modesty of this sex.'[26]

Indeed, the issue of 'modesty' was one to which the reform impetus was particularly sensitive. The words 'to love, cherish, and obey' were inserted beginning with the 1549 rite as a substitute for the Sarum (Salisbury) rite, which had held sway in England for almost 500 years. The older text did not speak of obedience: rather, the wife promised 'to be bonair and buxom in bed and at board,' which the reformers considered capable of 'wanton meaning.'[27] In the reformers' eyes, this change raised the status of both women and marriage. The husband's promised endowment in turn not only was an acceptance of the guardianship transferred from the bride's father or father-surrogate, but also legitimated her children as heirs – again affirming marriage as a politico-legal state.

The *Articles of Religion*, as mentioned above, continue to be reproduced in Anglican prayer books and form the basis of the orientations of other bodies that derive from Church of England auspices, including Methodism (though it specifically repudiated the Articles as a doctrinal 'test'). Article XXXII, *Of the Marriage of Priests*, reads, 'Bishops, Priests, and Deacons, are not commanded by God's Law, either to vow the estate of single life, or to abstain from marriage: therefore it is lawful for them, as for all other Christian men, to marry at their own discretion, as they shall judge the same to serve better to godliness.'[28] This is probably the most liberal statement on clerical marriage produced during the Elizabethan period, as it allows the clergy to marry 'at their own discretion,' even though in fact sanction from their bishop was supposed to be obtained. (There is no article on marriage in general.)

The Books of Homilies

Books of Homilies were authorized in the reigns of both Edward VI and Elizabeth to be read in the churches, and they were formally recognized in the Thirty-nine Articles as containing 'a godly and wholesome Doctrine.'[29] In Anglicanism, reading aloud these composed sermons was the norm well into the eighteenth century. (This is why Church of England priest John Wesley, who would preach from his heart practically anywhere, got into so much trouble – and ultimately why the Methodist church was founded.) The dominant pattern of Anglican worship was a service that was read or sung and a homily that was also read. Few members of the clergy actually preached in the modern sense, which required a licence above and beyond ordination. The *Homilies* were intended to 'be repeated and read againe' through the year, year after year, 'in such order as they stand in the Book.' As such, they constituted, other than the Prayer Book itself, 'the one body of doctrine familiar to every Anglican from the time of Edward VI on.'[30] Further evidence for this practice again is provided by the Puritan objection that the Church of England failed to provide a 'preaching ministry.'

Homily 18 of the Elizabethan series, 'Of the state of Matrimonie,' is crucial to our study, though it is well coupled with the Edwardian homily 'Against Adulterie' (also entitled 'Against Whoredome and Uncleannesse'), which was reauthorized in Elizabeth's reign. The homily against adultery was written by the reform divine Thomas Becon, sometime chaplain to Thomas Cranmer, who fled to the continent during Mary Tudor's reign but returned to accept a living again once Elizabeth came to the throne. The English composition of the homily on matrimony has never been firmly established, but it 'is taken partly from a homily by [the fourth century patriarch of Constantinople, St. John] Chrysostom, and partly translated from an address by Veit Dietrich, a Lutheran, of Nuremberg.'[31]

The decision-making processes that led to the topics selected for homilies are generally unknown. The most careful historical scholarship has centred on those of either great theological (idolatry, fasting, and sacraments) or political (disobedience and wilful rebellion) significance. Nevertheless, certain things can be said about the homilies on adultery and matrimony even in their present state. First, Elizabeth reviewed the entire 'Second Book' of homilies (i.e., those first published in her reign) and did alter some texts. Thus we can say that the homily on matrimony was in accord with her own views. Second, though the Prayer Book itself provided a homily to be read at weddings when there was no sermon preached, the words seem clearly directed towards marrying couples. If not written by Becon, they clearly betray his influence, but also that of the reform tradition of the age. The homily begins by reminding the hearers that one of the purposes of marriage is 'to avoid fornication' and specifically that 'God hath straightly forbidden all whoredome and uncleannesse, and hath from time to time taken grievous punishment of this inordinate lust' – the very words and tone of the homily against adultery.

Similarly, several things about the relationship of the sexes and the status of marriage in this period can be read from the texts. The homily on matrimony condemns wife beating, which from both the quantity and quality of the discussion, makes it clear that wife beating was a common occurrence that the reformers opposed. (A man fined for thrashing a servant too severely complained that, if a man might not thus 'correct' his servant, 'the day would soon come when a man might not beat his own wife!'[32])

The reformers' specific complaint about wife beating was that the couple should pray together to effect such a spiritual union as St Paul had said should reflect that between Christ and his church, and people who are at enmity are indisposed to mutual prayer. Elizabeth intervened to dismiss a Puritan plan to make adultery a capital offense. The homily against adultery, by contrast, blames it for 'a great part of the divorces which (nowadays) be so commonly accustomed,' suggesting that Tudor marriages were hardly ideal.

Hooker and Spenser

Among works that would be considered somewhat religious today was Richard Hooker's *Of the Laws of Ecclesiastical Polity*, a brilliant philosophical statement of the Elizabethan point of view on church and state. Though not a bishop, Hooker was the complete apologist for the policies of Archbishop Whitgift, hence of Elizabeth herself, in regard to the prayer book and episcopal government. In the Fifth Book of the *Laws*, Hooker takes up the celebration of matrimony, strongly defending the use of the nuptial Eucharist; yet he also shows that the practice is not fully 'put in use.' The *Laws* as a whole assert royal prerogative as the basis for proper church government, justifying both the settlement and royal supremacy.

An additional text worth noting is Edmund Spenser's *The Faerie Queene*. Spenser, the leading poet of his era, obtained Elizabeth's favour. His great work celebrates the spirit of the age. Gamaliel Bradford writes that Spenser took delight in 'ladies of a pure and almost unearthly loveliness ... To Spenser's ladies their chastity, nay, an ideal purity, is the very essence of their charm.' One of his evil women, Duessa, becomes allegorically interpreted alternately as the 'Scarlet Lady' of Rome in general, and Mary, Queen of Scots, in particular. In contrast, the Virgin Queen 'receives every now and then some peerless and noble tribute of chivalric adoration.'[33] Of course this is an idealization of Elizabeth, but it represents the intensity with which the high culture of the era approached the monarch: '[T]he worship of Queen Elizabeth, Gloriana, Belphoebe, Sweet Cynthia, Deborah, the "beauteous Queen of Second Troy," the Virgin Queen, Astraea, the goddess who dwelt on earth and was metamorphosed into the that of the Virgin Mary, a cult dedicated to "a Monarch maiden Queen, whose like on earth was never seen" the "second Maid," the "second sun."'[34] *The Faerie Queene* remained important enough in the seventeenth century to be one of the works Charles I kept with him as he was awaiting execution.

Conclusion

Histories are always perspectival. This realization makes a constructivist approach both powerful and weak at the same time. On the one hand, we can recognize that what is received as historical 'truth' is a definition of the situation made by someone for some purpose; on the other hand, our own perception is equally situational. What can we say with any certainty about the world of gender relations in the church of the English Renaissance?

Probably the best estimate of Elizabeth's world can be gained from the reactions against it by both Puritans and Papists. That it was acceptable to neither is certain. How much the opposition centred around political motives, how much on religious questions, is less clear. There was a long-standing resistance on the part of the English to foreign intervention in their affairs. Over two centuries before Henry VIII effected the formal separation, the English had taken steps to curtail Roman ecclesiastical jurisdiction in their land. However, the Puritans had little to gain directly from their opposition to Elizabeth's policies. That they continued to oppose her even in her finest hours strongly suggests that the Elizabethan Settlement was a genuinely powerful cultural dynamic in English life.

This does not mean that English people necessarily lived the ideal religious life envisioned in the settlement. Indeed, the Act of Uniformity, which established the Prayer Book of 1559, spends far more time on consequences for those who did not use it than would be the case if its authors believed that it was a popular solution. Puritans regularly produced alternative books, some formally rejected, others informally adopted.[35] The *Homilies* were often apparently ignored, and required attendance at Sunday parish worship was most obviously observed in the breach. Northern England continued to use Catholic ceremonial. Church properties were expropriated to the point that even Whitgift complained, and episcopal sees were not filled for long periods. Complacency and neglect in religion were punished far less than was zeal.

What then do we make of Elizabeth's putative virginity, her intervention in religious matters on both minor and major points in all the major ecclesiastical documents of her era, and the marriage service as we receive it?

It is clear from the way in which she treated her maids and others that Elizabeth was not enthused about the married state, nor did she view sexual impropriety lightly. However, she made no move to alter the marriage rite or to change significantly the status of women in English society. She viewed order as divinely given, and her rulership as such a gift, for she saw her accession to the throne as God's rescuing her from death at her own sister's hands. Though impatient with professional theologians, Elizabeth was inclined to theologize much of her experience. Though not inclined towards the Puritans, she shared with them a Protestant reverence for the scriptures as the Word of God. To have altered the nature of marriage or the status of women as related to marriage and family would have too much undermined the 'firm foundation' on which she based her claim to be a 'true Prince.'

NOTES

1 Virginia was the name given by Elizabeth when the colony was presented to her. In the Latin Christian (Roman Catholic) tradition, there are devotions said to the Blessed Virgin Mary that include the *Ave Maria*, or 'Hail Mary,' and the *Regina Coeli*, 'Heavenly Queen.' The former adapts the biblical salu-

tation of the angel Gabriel found in Luke 1:28; the latter, one of the titles that the Church has bestowed on Mary, 'Queen of Heaven.' My title plays off both these ascriptions.
2 Albion E. Small, 'The Sociological Stage in the Evolution of the Social Sciences,' *American Journal of Sociology*, 15 (1910), 691.
3 Thomas's theoretical work is scattered across empirical studies. The most significant of these for our purposes are W.I. Thomas and Florian Znaniecki, *The Polish Peasant in Europe and America*, vol. I (Chicago: University of Chicago Press, 1918), and W.I. Thomas, *The Unadjusted Girl* (Boston: Little, Brown, 1923).
4 The core text for this point of view is Peter L. Berger and Thomas Luckmann, *The Social Construction of Reality* (Garden City, NY: Doubleday, 1967).
5 Though exploring it in detail goes well beyond the scope of this chapter, the Victorian period was formative for Anglo-American Christianity, particularly as it is received today. Much of the way in which we think about Puritan sexual conduct and public morality, associating it with the Elizabethan period, actually derives from the time of Victoria.
6 Carole Levin, *'The Heart and Stomach of a King': Elizabeth I and the Politics of Sex and Power* (Philadelphia: University of Pennsylvania Press, 1994), 1.
7 Norman F. Cantor, *The English* (New York: Simon and Schuster, 1967), 306; more generally, see Herman Israel, 'Some Religious Factors in the Emergence of Industrial Society in England,' *American Sociological Review*, 31 (1966), 589–99; David Little, *Religion, Order, and Law* (New York: Harper & Row, 1969); Frederick M. Powicke, *The Reformation in England* (London: Oxford University Press, 1942); William H. Swatos, Jr, *Into Denominationalism: The Anglican Metamorphosis* (Storrs, Conn.: Society for the Scientific Study of Religion, 1979), 17–20.
8 Winthrop Hudson, *The Cambridge Connection and the Elizabethan Settlement* (Durham, NC: Duke University Press, 1980).
9 Michael Foss, *Tudor Portraits: Success and Failure of an Age* (London: Harrap, 1973), 151.
10 From the speech of Lord Keeper Nicholas Bacon at the opening of Parliament, 25 January 1559; cited in Francis Procter and Walter Howard Frere, *A New History of the Book of Common Prayer* (London: Macmillan, 1965), 97.
11 David Hume, *History of England*, vol. I (New York: Harper, 1854), x; Elizabeth's reign is dealt with in detail in volume III.
12 The literature on this point, with specific application to the Elizabethan period, is succinctly summarized in Little, *Religion, Order, and Law*, 247–8. In the Enlightenment, in contrast, such notions as the 'rights of man' and 'individual liberty' gained primacy of place in political theory.

13 Whitgift himself, whom Elizabeth called her 'little black husband,' is an interesting case in point. Theologically he was a Calvinist, but he rejected Calvin's ecclesiology – and the system of church government that proceeded from it in Geneva – as utterly wrong-headed. He took this point of view, ironically, not out of a particular belief in episcopal polity, but because he considered polity an 'indifferent matter' (*adiaphora*) to the church's mission – while the Puritans held that polity was *de jure divino*. His formulation of a 'high' doctrine of royal prerogative with regard to Holy Orders repudiated Puritan claims to the contrary, a point further reinforced by the work of Richard Hooker. Despite later divisions between presbyterian and congregational sectors within the Puritan movement (each of whom held its form to be what God in fact had ordained), they certainly agreed that God had not ordained monarchial episcopacy. See Christopher Hibbert, *The Virgin Queen: Elizabeth I, Genius of the Golden Age* (Reading, Mass.: Addison-Wesley, 1991), 96; Swatos, *Into Denominationalism*, 22; J.T. Tomlinson, *The Prayer Book Articles and Homilies* (London: Church Association, 1897), 246.

14 Wallace MacCaffrey, *Elizabeth I* (London: Arnold, 1993), 322; see Patrick Collinson, 'The Downfall of Archbishop Grindal and Its Place in Elizabethan Political and Ecclesiastical History,' in Peter Clark, Alan G.R. Smith, and Nicholas Tyacke, eds., *The English Commonwealth 1547–1640* (Leicester: Leicester University Press, 1979), 39–57. Many North Americans automatically associate 'freedom of religion' and 'freedom of speech,' but there is no inherent connection: one may well be entitled to believe whatever one wishes, even practice this in private, but not to publicize one's convictions. What perhaps makes the Elizabethan system so surprising is that this restriction was generally imposed even on the clergy; yet the clergy were not in any sense 'building congregations.' They were rather servants of the state, and the congregation was under obedience to hear them broadcast the official policy of the Supreme Governor.

15 See Christopher Haigh, *Elizabeth I* (London: Longmans, 1988), where this dynamic may be overinterpreted but is clearly documented.

16 James Froude, *History of England from the Fall of Wolsey to the Death of Elizabeth*, vol. IX (New York: Scribner, 1895), 383.

17 Hibbert, *Virgin Queen*, 78.

18 Elizabeth had her father's features rather than her mother's. Of the young Henry VIII's 'very beautiful' face it was said 'that it would have become a pretty woman' – so Hibbert, *Virgin Queen*, 4; on Elizabeth's learning and intellect, 26–7.

19 Levin, *Heart and Stomach*, 66.

20 Hibbert, *Virgin Queen*, 80.

21 While much is legitimately made of the persecution of reform-minded ('Protestant') bishops and other clergy under Mary, a chapter on sexism should also record that many of the people she burned were women of humble birth; so Hibbert, *Virgin Queen*, 54. (This is true as well of some of the Catholic sympathizers martyred during Elizabeth's reign – for example, Margaret of Clitherow.) Though the martyrs in both reigns certainly did end up equally dead, and often cruelly so, there is also a difference between the two reigns, in that the reformers were formally martyred for their religion by Mary Tudor, whereas during Elizabeth's reign the martyrdoms were technically on the grounds of 'treason' – i.e., refusing to accept the Royal Supremacy in itself.

22 Eric Josef Carlson, 'Clerical marriage and the English Reformation,' *Journal of British Studies*, 31 (1992), 1–31. Subscription to the Thirty-nine Articles has been required of Church of England clergy into the twentieth century, though the exact form of subscription changed several times; see E.J. Bicknell, *A Theological Introduction to the Thirty-Nine Articles of the Church of England*, 3rd ed. (London: Longmans, 1955), 20–1.

23 Carlson, 'Clerical marriage,' 20.

24 See Hibbert, *Virgin Queen*, 71–85, 123–31.

25 The 1549 book specified that the ring be 'gold and silver'; from 1552 onwards no particular composition was required.

26 Archibald John Stephens, *The Book of Common Prayer: With Notes, Legal and Historical* (London: Ecclesiastical History Society, 1854), 1603–4.

27 Ibid., 1608.

28 Note the use of the word 'men' ('all Christian men'); this is the *English* version of the article, printed over and over again in a language 'understanded of the people' (article 24). The Latin simply uses the word *Christianis*, which could be equally well translated 'Christians' as 'Christian men.' Latin editions of the *Book of Common Prayer* were in regular use at English universities at least into the nineteenth century, on the presumption that it was the language of 'learned men,' but the Latin versions never entered into common use either in Great Britain or in the United States, nor were they necessarily completely faithful reproductions of the 1559 book. The Latin version was used – ironically, for the 'unlearned' (those who could not read English) – in Ireland up to 1608, when an Irish version finally appeared. See Procter and Frere, *New History*, 116–25

29 The First *Book of Homilies* was issued during the reign of Edward VI, the Second during the reign of Elizabeth.

30 *Certain Sermons or Homilies Appointed to be Read in Churches In the Time of Queen Elizabeth I* (Gainesville, Fla.: Scholars' Facsimiles & Reprints, 1968), xi,

[a3–4]. There is general agreement that the Homilies were unpopular among partisan clergy, both Puritan and Papist, hence were read unintelligibly; thus the article requires that they be read 'diligently and distinctly' (see Bicknell, *Thirty-nine Articles*, 319–20).

31 Tomlinson, *Articles and Homilies*, 245.
32 Hibbert, *Virgin Queen*, 66.
33 Gamaliel Bradford, *Elizabethan Women*, first pub. 1936 (Freeport, NY: Books for Libraries, 1969) 209, 213, and *passim*.
34 Hibbert, *Virgin Queen*, 67.
35 See Procter and Frere, *New History*, 131–5.

6

Separation of the Sexes: The Development of Gender Roles in Modern Catholicism

ELLEN M. LEONARD

All academic disciplines, including history and theology, have traditionally viewed women from an androcentric perspective as subordinate and auxiliary to men. The emergence of women's history and gender studies is shifting the focus from the study of dominant males to a much wider study of the everyday lives of men and women. Women are presented as subjects of history, active and creative agents in society. The focus in this chapter is not on exceptional women, but on how Catholic women from different classes lived their lives in families and in religious orders or congregations.[1]

How did the Catholic church's position on women during the modern period affect the lives of women? As a member of a religious congregation of women founded in seventeenth-century France, I bring to this study a particular interest and question. Did religious orders and congregations of women help to shape gender roles, or did they simply fulfill the role assigned to them by church and society?

The primary source for Catholic teaching during the modern period (1550–1950) was the Council of Trent (1545–1563), which both responded to what it considered the 'errors' of the Protestant Reformation and inspired a Catholic Reformation. The council's statements formed the bases for the Catholic church's catechetical teaching and preaching for the next four hundred years. These teachings shaped how women were officially perceived within the Catholic tradition, but they do not indicate how women saw themselves. The answer to that question cannot be fully recovered. Historians are finding hints in women's diaries, letters, and other writings. But what of the countless women who were unable to write and whose stories remain hidden? Much more work needs to be done in order that we may catch even a glimpse into their lives.

Throughout history, religion has been both liberating and oppressive for women. This was certainly true in the period between 1550 and 1950. Religion opened up opportunities for service where women had some autonomy and were able to use their gifts. It also provided meaning in lives that were often extremely difficult. At the same time, religion imposed stereotypes on women that severely limited their opportunities. Women were distinguished by their marital status as nuns, wives, widows, and single women, whereas men were identified by their occupation and class. Based on a dual anthropology, which saw women as complementary to men, the Catholic position emphasized woman's vocation as motherhood, in either the physical or the spiritual sense. The image of Mary, virgin and mother, was used to exemplify and to reinforce this view of woman's vocation.

This chapter looks at women in Europe, particularly in France, but includes references to missionary activity, which extended the Catholic understanding of gender roles to the Americas, as well as to other parts of the world.

The Impact of the Reformation on Women

The reformers viewed marriage as part of the natural order and considered it to be the vocation of most Christians, especially women. They rejected celibacy as a mandatory discipline for clergy and taught that marriage was preferable to celibacy. Following the traditional view of marriage as the means of procreation and as a way to deal with human lust, they also recognized it as a noble vocation, though not a sacrament. The reformers' teaching on marriage has been largely seen as effecting a positive change in the status of women. But recent studies note that their positive valuation of marriage and family was set within a patriarchal model of domesticity, which actually reduced opportunities for women.[2] Public and private spheres became more sharply delineated; women were confined to the private sphere of the family, while men belonged to the public sphere, returning home to the family for physical and emotional support. For Luther, the virtuous woman was the wife who remains at home, sits still, keeps house, and bears and rears children.

Based on a positive appreciation of marriage and a desire to correct abuses among clergy, the reformers encouraged clergymen to marry. Unlike the priest's mistress, who had neither legal status nor respect, the minister's wife received a special position of honour within the community.

Members of religious orders were also encouraged to marry, for marriage was presented as woman's true vocation. Women were created by God to be wives and mothers, but what of the relatively high number of spinsters and widows? The elevation of the role of wife and mother in the teachings of Luther and Calvin resulted in the removal of the virgin life of the monastery as an option for women. While elevating the vocation of the married woman, Protestantism brought a new sort of restraint, the restraint to marry and be subject to a husband. Women who were not married were abused and feared in an emerging social climate that placed marriage and motherhood at the top of the moral ladder to God. The vocation of the nun was seen as violating the spirit of reform, and convents were viewed as destructive of the family. The reformers also disapproved of the responsibilities that the abbesses had exercised. Former priests and monks could become Protestant pastors, but there was no place in the new church structure for nuns.

As a result of the Reformation, women lost what had been their centres of culture and learning. Since they had not been admitted to the universities, monasteries and convents had provided educational opportunities for some women, usually from the upper class. The Reformation, which forbade female confraternities, cut off women's opportunities for expressing their spirituality in an all-female environment.[3] Whereas men belonged to guilds and city councils, women had no opportunities for group action. Convents had provided the one exception to this rule, serving as spheres of female power and autonomy. In areas where the state supported the Reformation, convents were expropriated and the nuns were sent away. Some nunneries were turned into male colleges of higher learning – for example, the convent of St Radegund in Cambridge became Jesus College.[4] A number of convents fought the religious changes that were being thrust on them, which included closing of their homes and negating of the value of their lives.

What happened to the nuns whose convents were taken over and who were 'freed' by the Reformation? Some continued to live together in unrecognized, informal groups.[5] A few orders were able to relocate in areas that had remained Catholic.[6] Other nuns found themselves scattered in a world that was hostile to unattached women. Those who took dispensations were given a small sum of money to support themselves until they could settle down and marry. Some, like Katherine von Bora, who married Luther, left the convent voluntarily and were able to enter wholeheartedly into their new vocation as wife and mother. Others, unfamiliar with the ways of the world after leading a secluded life for many years, drifted in a world where they would never really belong.

Like other women who were unattached to men, they were considered 'out of order' or 'loose women' and were looked on with suspicion. As a result of their lack of social, economic, and political rights, single women often found themselves with no means of support. Women, particularly widows and single women, formed the majority of indigent persons.[7] Many former nuns were added to that number.

Women and the Catholic Reformation

The Council of Trent, which met in three phases from 1545 to 1563, reacted in its final phase against the teachings of the reformers concerning marriage and celibacy. Women were not present at the council and had no say in decisions that would affect their lives and the lives of future generations of women.[8] The pope and the council fathers understood women according to the teaching of Aquinas, based on Aristotle, as 'defective males,' who were therefore in need of protection. All women were expected to be 'chaste, silent and obedient,' a view that was shared by the reformers.

One of the major concerns of the council fathers was priestly celibacy. With the Reformers, the Fathers realized that the discipline of celibacy was often not observed. Their concern about clerical celibacy influenced their teaching on marriage and on the higher value they placed on virginity and celibacy. They insisted that marriage was not simply a holy sign, but one of the seven sacraments and therefore under the authority of the church. In the past, the church had recognized secret or clandestine marriages, based on the belief that mutual consent creates a marriage. At Trent the council took a firm stand against these unions, decreeing that henceforth all marriages of Catholics had to be witnessed by the parish priest or his designate and two or three witnesses in order to be valid. This insistence on canonical form for validity was a response to what had become a serious social problem – namely, the seduction and/or abduction of young girls. It also ensured that men would no longer be able to marry secretly and later become priests. Canonical form helped to correct a number of abuses but raised other difficulties. The Catholic church's insistence on regulating marriages was particularly problematic in situations of marriage between a Catholic and a Protestant.

Reacting to Luther's elevation of marriage and derogation of celibacy, the council proclaimed in canon 10: 'If anyone says that the married state excels the state of virginity or celibacy, and that it is better and happier to be united in matrimony than to remain in virginity or celibacy, let him be anathema.'[9] This insistence on celibacy as a higher state had profound effects on how women were viewed by celibate clergymen as well as on how women understood themselves as sexual beings. Women were perceived as temptresses who would all too easily lead men astray. The teaching of the council led to a hardening of attitudes towards sexuality, and towards women who were identified with the body.

One of the most effective measures for reform initiated by Trent was the establishment of seminaries to educate clerics. Young boys were removed from the influence of their families and educated in an all-male environment, where women were perceived as dangerous to the priestly vocation. In order to uphold clerical celibacy, seminarians and priests were warned against women as a source of temptation. All women were identified with Eve, a theme that found expression in preaching that placed the burden of sin on women, with the notable exception of Mary. This negative image of woman as temptress was deeply engraved on the conscience and the unconscious of both men and women.

By its affirmation of virginity and celibacy, the council encouraged religious life and thus continued to provide a respectable alternative to marriage for Catholic women. At the same time, it recognized the need to reform convents and monasteries, which had in some instances become 'a convenient repository for superfluous daughters of the aristocracy and wealthy urban classes.'[10] The reform envisaged was a return to the idealized version of religious life as it had developed in the Middle Ages. This was the monastic life, with its solemn vows of poverty, chastity, and obedience and its strict rules of enclosure, or *clausura*, for women. The term referred to both the living space reserved for religious, which they were forbidden to leave and others to enter, defined by walls and grills, and the law that so constrained religious and others. The council reaffirmed *clausura*, forbidding nuns to leave the grounds of their monastery without the expressed approval of the bishop, their spiritual father. The same restrictions were not imposed on religious orders of men. This male control of nuns reflected the view of society that women required either a husband or a cloister, *aut maritus, aut murus*. The Protestant reformers insisted on a husband, while the Catholic reformers insisted on the cloister or, for those who did not receive this superior call, a husband.

Pope Pius V, continuing the reform of religious life in the spirit of

Separation of the Sexes in Modern Catholicism 119

Trent, issued two documents, *Circa pastoralis* (1566) and *Lubricum vitae genus* (1568), which commanded all forms of religion to accept solemn vows and full monastic discipline or be dispersed. There was to be no intermediary state between the wholly secular and the wholly religious. This insistence on the monastic form of religious life for women continued throughout the centuries until Pope Leo XIII in 1901 officially recognized non-cloistered women as 'true religious.'

Nuns and Sisters

At the same time that the pope and the council fathers were insisting on the monastic model of religious life, groups of women, inspired by the social and religious needs around them, and especially the needs of women, were seeking new expressions of religious commitment. Women, who in the past would not have been able to join a religious order because they lacked the required dowry, were joining with other women in caring for the sick and the needy or in the work of teaching. Since by custom and by law women were considered too weak to live alone, they formed communities.[11] The Ursulines had already received approval from Pope Paul III in 1544 as a confraternity, with some privileges of a religious order, but after the council restrictions were placed on them. In France they were required to make solemn vows and to accept a modified *clausura*, which allowed girls to enter the convent for instruction but forbade the sisters to go out to teach. Women, however, were beginning to see the need not only to instruct those who came to them but to go out to those requiring assistance of various kinds.

In the early seventeenth century, Mary Ward in England envisioned a society of women, comparable to the recently formed male Society of Jesus, who would work for the Catholic cause. In spite of Ward's best efforts, the English Ladies were disbanded in 1631. The Bull of Suppression stated among the reasons for this action: 'They went freely everywhere, without submitting to the laws of *clausura*, under the pretext of working for the salvation of souls; they undertook and exercised many other works unsuitable to their sex and their capacity, their feminine modesty, and above all, their virginal shame.'[12] The official Catholic church was not yet ready to accept female apostles.

Catholic families often did not support their daughters who wished to join groups who were not 'real religious,' that is orders with solemn vows and *clausura*. Aristocratic families wanted their unmarried daughters to take solemn vows, a practice which meant that these daughters were considered legally dead, with no right to inheritance. The monastic vocation provided greater stability than the new communities that were springing up, composed mainly of women of lower social status who would not have had an adequate dowry to join a monastery. These women made simple vows or promises, from which they could be released. They were able to go where they were needed and wanted, and they could leave a place when they were no longer needed. Unlike the monasteries, where women spent their entire lives in the same location with the same sisters, these new groupings were flexible and consequently were seen as unstable.

One of the needs that motivated seventeenth-century women to band together, and that eventually brought them official recognition in the church and society, was the education of young girls. The Catholic church opposed coeducation but gradually recognized the need for institutions to educate girls. In the spirit of the Counter-Reformation, which was anti-Protestant, the concern to reach women led to female institutions analogous to the male colleges.

The reformers had insisted on the importance of religious instruction and had drawn up catechisms as a means of presenting the teaching of the Reformation. Though Trent had legislated that Catholic priests were to catechize both children and adults and Catholic catechisms had been drawn up, there was a crying need for the rechristianization of the people and the elimination of heresy. Many women were attracted to the reformed religion. Education, especially of mothers, was necessary if the Catholic faith was to be preserved and handed on to future generations. Wealthy girls might attend monastery schools, often as boarders, but there were no schools for poor girls. The nuns in their monastery classrooms, double-locked so as not to violate *clausura*, showed that the education of girls was desirable. It was seen as a way to influence families, for girls would become wives and mothers. Schooling was perceived as a means of regenerating society. Educated women would become more effective and more virtuous mothers.

Though teaching was a male profession and considered an unsuitable task for a nun, one that would be a threat to her chastity, dedicated Catholic women gradually broke down resistance to female teachers by providing an essential service in the community. Besides, schoolmistresses were less costly than schoolmasters, and the new congregations did not charge their students; the sisters supported themselves and their schools by their handwork. There was even stronger resistance to women catechizing – a task that belonged to the clergy – but the needs were so great that eventually the schoolmistresses won a place within both church and society.

Education for girls was seen as a preparation for motherhood and home management, and so the curriculum emphasized subjects that would prepare them for these tasks. To seek learning for its own sake was considered unfeminine and dangerous. Religious instruction was central, but reading was also taught, as 'an instrument of salvation,' since it allowed access to the word of God. Fewer girls learned to write, which required tools and facilities. Some moralists saw writing as a dangerous skill for women, which would enable them to carry on underhanded liaisons. Handwork was also taught, considered useful for girls of all social classes. Such work provided a way in which all women could avoid the evil of idleness, and working-class and poor girls learned manual skills, which enabled them to support themselves. Girls usually stayed in school for only two or three years, until they received their first communion at the age of ten or twelve.

In order to achieve recognition, the new congregations of women required the approval of their bishop and the sanction of the civil authorities. Often they had priests who encouraged them and wealthy women who supported their cause, but it was the generosity and determination of the women themselves that created a new form of religious life, which contributed to a reformed Catholicism by its education of girls. Not only did these women have to convince others of their usefulness, but they had to resist the temptation to become 'real religious' by taking solemn vows and submitting to *clausura*.

The contemplative life of the monasteries, which aimed at personal perfection, was seen by the church as a higher form of religious life than that of the active groups, which had simple vows and no enclosure and whose purpose was either care of the sick poor or education. Some groups succumbed to pressure from parents and ecclesiastical superiors to become 'real religious' but most saw their own form of life as one that met the needs of the church and society in their day. It took the official church much longer to recognize these congregations. The service that they provided became indispensable. In France, when religious congregations were disbanded during the Revolution, no one was able to replace the sisters, and Napoleon had to invite them back.

Despite their good work, the official church viewed the new congregations with suspicion and sought to control them. More restrictions were imposed on them than on congregations of men. Within them, as well as in church and society, strict hierarchy existed. 'A community is nothing but a Tower of Babel if obedience does not rule and order all things.'[13] Obedience to authority was the cornerstone of post-Reformation Catholicism, as well as a civic virtue.

These groups of women, who were in many ways secular, continued to flourish, especially in France, where they were called *Filles séculières*. They did not wear a religious habit but wore the dress of their class. Lower-class women wore brown or grey, and schoolmistresses wore black, which characterized widows' garb. They lived simply in small groups organized around their work. These new congregations became instruments in the rechristianization of society in Europe and pioneers in the New World, where they exercised a powerful influence on Catholics and Protestants through their work in hospitals and schools.[14] Though members' lives were often difficult, they enjoyed opportunities open to few other women of their time.

In 1917 the Code of Canon Law regularized all religious congregations so that they lost their individual flavour and were defined according to law.[15] The code once again equated the religious life with the monastic life and restricted the autonomy of religious congregations of women. It was not until 1947 that Pius XII recognized secular institutes, which did not require common life and stressed service in the world, as an approved form of religious community.

The Catholic church today recognizes the 'canonical status' of women in religious orders and congregations, but women have no official voice within the ecclesiastical order and hence no power in determining policy and making decisions. They are dependent on the male hierarchy for canonical recognition and on the male clergy for the sacraments. Within their own houses and institutions they have considerable scope for creative activity, but within the larger church they remain dependent on male authority.

Married Women

Many women of the Catholic Reformation seem to have sought relief from marriage. Young women were sometimes encouraged by priests to disobey their parents and enter convents in order to escape from an arranged marriage. Pious women often vowed their widowhood to God, even before the deaths of their husbands. Catholic preachers promoted virginity as the holiest and happiest of all conditions and presented marriage as causing nothing but pain. Nevertheless, marriage was the path that most women followed. The church spoke on behalf of the value of family but supported the superior position of the male, imposing stronger moral sanctions on women than on men. Women were expected to practise the 'lady-like virtues' of piety, purity, submission, and domesticity.

Obedience was required of all women, based on the view that women were inherently inferior. Even the concessions granted to women by medieval jurisprudence were negated in the seventeenth century. Wives were reduced to something very close to perpetual minority and could be corrected, even imprisoned, at their husband's will. Subordination of wives to husbands was the accepted norm. Clerical literature warned against female independence and encouraged the development of a distinctly housewifely ethic. Married women were called to 'modesty, silence, keeping the house, and obedience.'[16] Fénelon described the ideal: 'The strong woman spins, she stays in her house, she is silent, she believes, and she obeys.'[17]

Society's view of women, supported by the Catholic church, may be seen in the Code Napoléon of 1804, which classified married women with children, along with the insane and criminals, as politically incompetent. Married women were economically and legally subject to their husbands. It was almost impossible for women to attain economic self-sufficiency. In nineteenth-century England, husband and wife were viewed as one person, and that person was the husband. The 'Victorian feminine ideal' was that of the proper, passive, home-oriented 'lady.' The subordination of wives to their husbands lasted into the twentieth century.

Women belonged to the family and not to public life. Their lives were often difficult, characterized by numerous pregnancies. Their babies often died, and they themselves risked dying in childbirth. Educational opportunities were inadequate or non-existent. The education that women did receive was geared to their roles as wives and mothers, for this was their vocation.

The Code of Canon Law (1917) reiterated traditional Catholic teaching concerning marriage, insisting that its primary end was the procreation and nurture of children, while the secondary end was mutual help and the remedying of concupiscence.[18] The love of the couple and the growth of their mutual relationship were not seen as essential for marriage. If the couple granted each other the right to have sexual intercourse for the purpose of having children, a marriage existed. Since the secondary purposes of marriage served the primary, the mutual union of the couple was not an end by itself, but it helped make a better marital environment in which the couple could have and raise their children. Contraception was forbidden, since it went against the main purpose of marriage.

Catholic teaching on marriage was reinforced not only in religious instruction, particularly marriage instructions and in sermons, but in papal encyclicals. Pope Pius XI, in *Casti conubii* (On Christian Marriage, 1930), maintained that the husband was the head of the family and the wife, the heart. He urged women to an obedience of the heart. The pope recognized husband and wife as equal in dignity of human souls and in rights proper to the marriage contract, but in other things he insisted on a certain inequality for the right ordering and unity and stability of home life. Women's efforts for social, economic, and psychological equality were condemned as 'debasing and unnatural.' The role of the married woman was circumscribed, but within her family she was encouraged to act as a domestic missionary, instructing her children and supporting her husband by her example and prayers.

Not only were women seen as subordinate to and dependent on men, but Catholic teaching and preaching continued to present marriage as inferior to celibacy. Catholics had to wait until Vatican II (1965) for some changes in the teachings concerning marriage and celibacy set forth at Trent. While official teaching presented the role of the married woman in narrow terms, the ways in which women actually lived their lives in family and community varied greatly and cannot be neatly delineated.

Mary, Virgin and Mother

The place of Mary within Catholic devotional life both exemplified and reinforced the Catholic teaching on women. In reaction to the Protestant Reformation, which had removed the feasts of Mary and the saints from the worship and piety of the people, the Catholic church had retained and even intensified its emphasis on devotion to Mary and the saints. Feast days and processions added colour to the lives of ordinary people. However, the images of female saints, particularly Mary, were highly ambiguous. On the one hand, powerful female images served as a corrective to the pervasive male imagery in Christianity, and their retention was empowering for women. On the other hand, these images were used in ways that were oppressive for women. Mary was often presented as a passive vessel; to be like Mary, the virgin mother, was an impossible ideal.

Women were exhorted to imitate Mary, 'the handmaid of the Lord,' by leading a morally pure and selfless life. Preachers portrayed Mary, the new Eve, as the immaculate virgin, whereas all other women were seen as the daughters of Eve, tempting men to sin by immodest dress and use of jewellry and cosmetics. For the celibate clergy, Mary was a spiritual mother. Though the clergy used Mary to preach women's submission, women, especially mothers, saw in Mary a woman who understood a mother's pain. Virgins also claimed her as their powerful patron and protector.

Devotion to Mary continued throughout the modern period, taking different forms. During the nineteenth century a number of apparitions of Mary, often to poor women and children, were reported, and shrines were subsequently erected in honour of Mary, the most famous at Lourdes. The church attempted to control these popular expressions of Marian devotion while curbing what it considered excesses. It also solemnly defined two Marian dogmas – the Immaculate Conception in 1854 and the Assumption of Mary in 1950. While the reported apparitions brought Mary closer to ordinary men and women in their daily struggles, the dogmas removed Mary from other human beings. She alone of all humans, in virtue of her position as Mother of God, was conceived without original sin and assumed body and soul into heaven.

The role of Mary, presented as parallel, but always subordinate, to that of her son Jesus, supports the Catholic position, which sees women as having their distinctive gifts, to be used under the supervision of males, be they husbands or sons, bishops or priests.

Conclusion

Tridentine (post-Trent) Catholicism taught the superiority of the celibate over the married life, encouraged the cult of Mary and the saints, emphasized 'deeds' or works towards perfection, and insisted on the church as intermediary between God and humankind. Religious congregations of women reflected these elements in their constitutions and in their lives. Within convents women had a special world of their own and enjoyed respect and status as the chosen 'brides of Christ.' Catholic married women accepted their role as wife and mother, perhaps hoping and praying that one of their sons might become a priest and one of their daughters a nun.

Catholic women in families and in religious orders and congregations were a powerful force in the Catholic Reformation in Europe. Their influence in carrying Tridentine Catholicism to other parts of the world was great and has often been overlooked by historical scholarship, which has focused on male leaders.[19]

Male–female relationships have evolved differently in Protestant and Catholic societies. Mainline Protestant societies have tended to be 'assimilationist.' Based on a single anthropology, which emphasizes the same human nature in both men and women, they have gradually admitted women to all levels of ecclesiastical decision-making as well as all church offices.[20] Catholic societies, in contrast, have been more 'pluralistic.' This pluralism has been attributed to the choice offered to Catholic women between marriage and the religious and single life.[21] Catholic societies have also been 'separatist,' maintaining separate spheres for men and women in civil and ecclesiastical life. Girls were educated separately from boys, a situation made possible by the female congregations, which often had their own Catholic colleges providing specific female education for their sisters as well as for other women. Segregation of the sexes was based on the view that men and women have distinct natures, with different gifts and responsibilities, and distinct gender roles, a view that supports Catholic teaching that men and women are complementary rather than equal. This dual anthropology was exemplified and taught by members of religious congregations of women. By maintaining a separate space for women, these congregations provided a sphere for female spirituality and autonomy. Nevertheless, they continued to be dependent on male clerics, who acted as their confessors and ecclesiastical superiors.

Women religious and their impact on education, both in Europe and in the New World, influenced the development of gender roles for both women and men. The sisters incarnated in their lives a view of male and female roles as separate and distinct. Through their teaching, they helped to shape how Catholic men and women understood themselves and their respective roles well into the twentieth century.

NOTES

1 The options and roles available to women depended on social class.
2 See the studies in Sherrin Marshall, ed., *Women in Reformation and Counter-Reformation Europe: Public and Private Worlds* (Bloomington, Ind.: University Press, 1989).
3 Merry E. Wiesner, 'Nuns, Wives, and Mothers: Women and the Reformation in Germany,' in Sherrin Marshall, ed., *Women in Reformation and Counter-*

Reformation Europe: Public and Private Worlds (Bloomington, Ind.: University Press, 1989), 8–28.
4 Janice G. Raymond, *A Passion for Friends: Toward a Philosophy of Female Affection* (Boston: Beacon Press, 1986), 105.
5 These groups are described by Sherrin Marshall in 'Protestant, Catholic, and Jewish Women in the Early Modern Netherlands,' in Sherrin Marshall, ed., *Women in Reformation and Counter-Reformation Europe: Public and Private Worlds* (Bloomington, Ind.: University Press, 1989), 128–32.
6 Jeanne de Jussie, nun of the order of St Claire, chronicles the events of the years 1526–35 in her journal, *The Leaven of Calvinism, Or the Beginning of the Heresy of Geneva*. She describes the persecution of the nuns who finally left Geneva and settled in Annecy. See June Dempsey Douglas, 'Women and the Continental Reformation,' in Rosemary Radford Ruether, ed., *Religion and Sexism: Images of Women in the Jewish and Christian Traditions* (New York: Simon and Schuster, 1974), 292–318, especially 309.
7 In Italy there were special refuges for women at risk. See Sherrin Cohen, 'Asylums for Women in Counter-Reformation Italy,' in Sherrin Marshall, ed., *Women in Reformation and Counter-Reformation Europe: Public and Private Worlds* (Bloomington, Ind.: University Press, 1989), 166–88.
8 *The Canons and Decrees of the Council of Trent*, trans. H.J. Schroeder (Rockford, Ill.: Tan Books and Publishers, 1941), has only one entry for 'women' in the index, a reference to penitent women.
9 Ibid., 182.
10 Sherrin Marshall Wyntjes, 'Women in the Reformation Era,' in Renate Bridenthal and Claudia Koonz, eds., *Becoming Visible: Women in European History* (Boston: Houghton Mifflin Co., 1977), 168.
11 Women could not travel alone. Innkeepers were forbidden to take in any woman travelling on her own.
12 Elizabeth Rapley, *The Dévotes: Women and Church in Seventeenth-Century France* (Montreal: McGill-Queen's University Press, 1990), 32–3.
13 Ibid., 183; quotation from Union Chrétienne, *Constitutions* (1673).
14 See Mary Ewens, 'Leadership of Nuns in Immigrant Catholicism,' in Rosemary Radford Ruether and Rosemary Skinner Keller, eds., *Women and Religion in America*, vol. I, *The Nineteenth Century* (San Francisco: Harper & Row, 1981), 101–7; Asuncion Lavrin, 'Women and Religion in Spanish America,' and Christine Allen, 'Women in Colonial French America,' in *Women and Religion in America*, vol. II, *The Colonial and Revolutionary Periods* (San Francisco: Harper & Row, 1983), 42–50 and 79–86, respectively.
15 See Lucy Vazquez, 'The Position of Women According to the [1917] Code,' in Michael W. Higgins and Douglas R. Letson, eds., *Women and the Church: A*

Source Book (Toronto: Griffin House, 1986), 111–23. The imposition of the Code of Canon Law is an example of men's power to define women and their place. Is it a coincidence that these restrictions were imposed on congregations of women at the same time women were seeking the vote?
16 Rapley, *The Dévotes*, 18.
17 Ibid., 163.
18 Vazquez, in 'The Position of Women,' 123, points out that the code portrays women as being less than full adults, on a par with men. 'They are to be protected, separated, observed, supervised, and, at least on occasion, even mistrusted.'
19 See Mary Jo Weaver, *New Catholic Women: A Contemporary Challenge to Traditional Religious Authority* (San Francisco: Harper & Row, 1985), for ways in which Catholic scholarship has overlooked women; also James J. Kenneally, 'Eve, Mary and the Historians: American Catholicism and Women,' in Janet Wilson James, ed., *Women in American Religion* (Philadelphia: University of Pennsylvania Press, 1980), 191–206.
20 See Wendy Fletcher-Marsh, chapter 7, below, especially 139–40.
21 Rapley, *The Devotées*, 9.

7

Towards a Single Anthropology: Developments in Modern Protestantism

WENDY FLETCHER-MARSH

As all of Christianity, Protestantism has inherited a tradition of religious thought and practise that bears the scars of androcentrism. In Protestantism, however, this androcentricity has been relieved by the gradual evolution of a single anthropology. At least in theory, many branches of Protestantism are in the process of healing the dualistic anthropology that they inherited from earlier Christian centuries and that separated men and women into rigidly distinct spheres, which in turn were placed in hierarchical relation to each other, with the female realm inferior. The Protestant reformers, though obviously patriarchal in their worldview, introduced ideas that opened up the possibility of eliminating gender-based discrimination from Christian theology and social practice. Building on the perhaps-unintentional contributions of the early reformers, Protestantism from the sixteenth to the twentieth century moved slowly towards a unified anthropology, which could provide a new, normative framework for the theory and practise of Christian life and ministry.

Since I comment below on Protestantism in a general way, we have to be aware that Protestantism is not homogeneous and that we can generalize only with the greatest of caution. Diversity and complexity are the defining characteristics of that Christian family, which has generated by recent count over twenty thousand denominations. While it is clear that many denominations and groups do not work out of a unified anthropology, much of mainline Protestantism has slowly moved to an inclusive polity, allowing women and men full and equal participation in all forms of organizational ministry. Our discussion cannot embrace the totality of Protestantism, and so I limit my analysis to representative illustrations from Europe and North America.

I trace the gradual evolution towards a unified anthropology from its

Reformation roots, in the teaching and practice of key reformers such as Martin Luther, John Calvin, and the Anabaptists. We then look at the teaching and practise of atypical groups, which served as an early model of what eventually became standard teaching on gender in most mainline Protestant churches. Moving to the eighteenth century and beyond, we discuss first the Great Awakening and holiness movements in North America and the rise of voluntary associations, and then five developments specifically related to women – the office of deaconess, the advent of the paid professional church worker, the woman missionary and preacher, the enfranchisement of women in ecclesiastical polities, and finally the ordained woman as leader of local communities. This journey through centuries and across denominations can illuminate the process by which a single anthropology became normative in much of Protestantism.

Present and Past

At a recent international ecumenical gathering, I witnessed an exchange that reveals the tension within Christianity between a dual and single anthropology vis-à-vis gender. A Protestant theologian was discussing the implicit and explicit sexism that prevents women from being ordained in some branches of Christianity. An Orthodox theologian responded hotly that the label of sexism obliterates rather fundamental theological differences that separate their traditions on gender issues. He contended that referring to the exclusion of women from orders as sexism missed the point that women in the Orthodox tradition are definitely not seen as inferior. Rather, he argued, women are perceived as complementing men, with a different function in life and in the community, which is not less important but simply different. He was claiming, in other words, that a dual anthropology does not imply sexism.

Here we see in stark relief the line that divides Christian understandings of men and women. Both sides view their positions as fundamentally faithful to scriptural teaching and the tradition of Christian practise. The first reflects a single, or unified anthropology, and the second, a dual or dualistic anthropology.

Dual Anthropology

For many centuries, a dualistic anthropology was normative in Christian circles. Born into the male-dominated Graeco-Roman world as a descendant of male-biased Judaism, Christianity quickly became patriarchal itself. On the basis of biological difference, Greek philosophy taught that being female was essentially different from being male. Woman's nature was defined by her biology as child-bearer and suckler. In societies built on the principles of a patriarchal household structure, this view restricted a woman's function to domestic life, whereby she became the guardian of the hearth and the nurturer within the family and societal unit.

Superimposing nascent Christian beliefs and practices on this model of the patriarchal household, early Christian thinkers quickly moved to limit the role of women within the faith community. Rather than simply adopting a theology of complementarity in difference of function, however, Christians thinkers began to develop an anthropology (a doctrine of humanity in relation to God and salvation) that attributed a difference to women that went beyond the practical. Within a few short centuries of Jesus' lifetime, theologians were arguing that the female soul is as different from the male's as the female body is from the male's. In 584, for example, at the Council of Macon in Lyons, France, the nature of women's humanity was debated by elders of the church. The debate asked, 'Do women have souls?' What was at issue was whether or not women should be considered as human or as something less than human. Ultimately the church fathers determined that indeed women did have souls and were therefore human. The issue was decided, however, by only one vote.

Obviously the ancient church was not of a common mind about the nature of women's humanity. It is clear, moreover, that in the view of many early Christian thinkers women's nature was different from men's, and not only on a physical level. From such evidence, we can trace the theoretical genesis and practical implementation of a dual anthropology within Christianity.

This dualism was not limited to a male–female split, however, for that dichotomy was often viewed as symbolic of a deeper division between matter and spirit. Though Christians have in theory always rejected this type of gnostic dualism, their practices and teachings have often modelled it. Given woman's perceived connection to things physical through menstruation and the bearing and nurture of children, the classical Christian schema relegated her to association with matter, which the gnostics despised, and man to intellect and reason, the elements of mind or spirit that the gnostics most valued. Traditional Christian theology theoretically viewed all humanity as equally impaired by original sin, but in practice women were more impaired because it was their nature to be less logical and less rational. Woman's deprivation because of sin was therefore equated with depravity, and many church fathers echoed the teaching of Tertullian, who stressed that man should beware of woman, for she is the devil's gateway.[1]

Dualism of this sort persists into the twentieth century, as we have seen, in the debate over the ordination of women. Liturgical churches such as the Orthodox and the Roman Catholic emphasize the notion that the priest in leading public worship is an icon of Christ. Moreover, since Christ was male, they argue, a woman could never truly represent Christ in the liturgy. The contention that a woman, given her particular nature, cannot represent the divine invokes a dualistic anthropology either explicitly or implicitly.

Martin Luther

Much of Protestantism has rejected traditional dualism in favour of a teaching and practice which holds that even though men and women may be different physically, they are all essentially one in Christ Jesus. This fundamentally Pauline doctrine was first taught and lived in the early modern era by Martin Luther.

When Luther worked to 'liberate' nuns from convents, he did not do so with equality in mind, and so any thought that he was a feminist cannot be seriously entertained. His theology, however, did sow the seeds for fuller participation of women in Christian communities and positions of leadership, as did the thought of some of his contemporaries.

Luther devoted considerable energy to 'freeing' women in monastic vocations from their cloistered lives, motivated in large measure by his belief that the Catholic church was wrong when it celebrated virginity and asceticism as the highest state of perfection for women. He argued that the normative state of a woman was wife and child-bearer. Therefore he encouraged women in monastic vocations to leave their lives of prayer, learning, and work with other women to become housewives and mothers in traditional, patriarchal households.

Nothing here leads in the direction of healing the Christian tradition of androcentricity. Luther's efforts led, in the worst of cases, to destitute women vagabonds roaming the European countryside with no means of support and few affiliations to the larger social fabric.[2] In the best of cases, former nuns married (often former monks) and began a new life as wives and mothers, subject to the direction and probable domination of their husbands. In either situation, the positive options available to Protestant women became fewer than those available to their Roman Catholic sisters, who could still choose singlehood in community with other women.

Luther never advocated equality for women within the household or society. In his *Commentaries on the Book of Genesis* he maintained a view of Eve's role in original sin at least compatible with the Catholic view. He noted that Eve's share of the sin committed by the first human parents was greater than Adam's because she offered the forbidden fruit to her husband. For her sin, Luther claimed, Eve was condemned to a life as Adam's inferior partner, subject to his domination.[3] All women after her were thus subject to the domination of their husbands as well.

This account does little to support any claim that Luther challenged Christianity's dual anthropology, but his attempt to exalt the vocation of woman as wife and mother eventually bore fruit. By challenging the centuries-old assumption that a woman who denied her female sexuality as a nun was more holy and valued than her married and procreating sisters, Luther opened the door for an eventual rethinking of Christianity's veneration of asexuality.

The possibility of pursuing holiness as a sexually active woman became the norm within Protestant circles. Luther made acceptable and even desirable a new and different form of piety for women. Moreover, by establishing the ground for integrating body and spirit in a holy life, he helped promote a non-dualistic spirituality.

The Minister's Wife

If we consider Christian married life as modelled by Luther and his wife, Katherine Von Bora (one of the nuns whom he 'liberated' from the convents), we discover a striking paradox. In his writings on marriage, Luther made it clear that the primary function of a woman was to be a subordinate partner to her husband and a bearer of children: 'Take women from their housewifery and they are good for nothing ... If women get tired and die of bearing there is no harm in that; let them die as long as they bear; they are made for that ... Men have broad shoulders and narrow hips, and accordingly they possess intelligence. Woman have narrow shoulders and broad hips. Women ought to stay at home; the way they were created indicates this for they have broad hips and a wide fundament to sit upon, keep house and bear and raise children.[4]

In other writings, however, Luther often referred to the partnership in ministry that he enjoyed with Katherine. On more than one occasion he identified her as his partner and as the pre-eminent preacher of their household.[5] She was an active participant in his ministry, providing hospitality, and in the theological exchanges carried on at their dinner table. Thus to some extent what Luther said about women's role in the household was at odds with his practice.

Katherine and many of her contemporaries were models of a new form of ministry by women – the pastor's wife. While some may dismiss the idea of pastor's wife being a ministry, anyone who knows or has studied such women can see the logic of calling their contribution to the life of the church a ministry – and indeed a ministry not unlike that practised by many women of the New Testament period. Hospitality was a primary form of ministry; pastor's wives provided food and lodging for refugees and travellers, as well as for members of the newly forming Protestant communities. As Luther noted about his own wife, these woman also actively engaged in extensive theological discussion and debate with guests.

Most outspoken among them was Katherine Zell, wife of Matthew Zell, a former Catholic priest turned Protestant pastor. She eagerly expressed her theological views both inside her own home and publicly. When some sought to silence her, arguing that her public 'preaching' was inappropriate for a woman, she argued, citing Paul and Joel: 'You remind me that the Apostle Paul told women to be silent in church. I would remind you of the word of this same apostle that in Christ there is no longer male nor female and of the prophecy of Joel: "I will pour out my spirit on all flesh and your sons and your daughters will prophecy."'[6]

At no time did Katherine or any of her contemporaries argue for the equality of women. However, by their work and example they made a defiant statement against the norms of the old dualistic anthropology, which would have had them remain silent and unthinking. Instead they practised ministry by proclaiming and theologizing as well as by serving others. When challenged, they referred, as Zell did, to the passages of scripture that became foundational for the Protestant development of a single anthropology.

Other Early Developments

The male leaders of the Reformation in no way advocated equal leadership for women. For the most part, Luther maintained the Pauline admonition against women's public participation in ministry. However, he did allow that women could preach and baptize if no 'competent male' was available. Perhaps more important, he emphasized Paul's theology of justification by faith and the priesthood of all believers. In other words, he did not distinguish between men and women with regard to salvation. According to Luther, all are equally unworthy and thereby equally justified or redeemed by faith alone; neither men nor women can do anything to earn their salvation, which is God's free gift. As a community of disciples equally unworthy but also freely redeemed by Christ's atoning work, men and women participate fully in the priesthood of all believers.[7]

This emphasis on the priesthood of all believers led Luther to articulate progressive views on the education of women. Since all Christians were to serve God in the community and everyone participated in the priesthood of believers, Luther argued, all should have a sound education to prepare them for the tasks of ministry.[8]

On a theoretical level, the reformers made no distinction between men and women in the spiritual realm, even when relationships at the practical level were defined by traditional male and female roles. The emphasis on common justification quietly undermined any notion of an ontological difference between men and women. In this respect, Protestant theology was inescapably different from earlier Catholic theology, which viewed women as essentially different from men.

Luther's contemporary, John Calvin, argued that the rule of society or church by women was 'defective' to the natural order. Calvin apparently, however, downgraded Paul's teaching on women's silence in church from the sacred to the human level, which left it subject to the possibility of change.[9] In his own way, Calvin helped establish the basis for a future reappraisal of the roles of men and women in the ministry.

Radical sects within the Protestant Reformation likewise introduced, perhaps unintentionally, new opportunities for the leadership of women. For example, while most Anabaptists held a traditional view of the place of women in church, home, and society, many communities allowed women to be preachers. Radical Protestantism placed such great emphasis on prophecy and spiritual illuminations through direct revelation that it could not deny that such revelations might be given to women. Since divinely inspired leadership was central to the ecclesiastical polity of Anabaptist communities, men could not prevent women from preaching, even if they disapproved.[10]

Thus the evolution of Protestant theology towards a single anthropology apparently did not begin intentionally. None the less, the reformers' commitment to upholding marriage as normative for women, their theology of the priesthood of all believers, the doctrine of justification by faith, and their belief in immediate access to divine inspiration laid the groundwork for later changes. In turn, a new theology of gender developed as communities experienced the changing ministry of women. Protestant thought about women in ministry evolved in a dialectical relationship with the ongoing and changing reality of women as ministry partners in clerical marriages and as inspired preachers.

The Dialectics of Transformation

Some Protestant denominations have never explicitly denied that women can participate in the full ministry of the church. At different times, women have been active in various forms of ministry – even leading congregations – among Baptist, Methodist, Episcopal, and Pentecostal communities. For the most part, however, these women were atypical, and their ministries were the result of individual inspiration and personal achievement. Not until the turn of the twentieth century and the political enfranchisement of women in most Western countries did denominations begin to embrace the full participation of women in church life and ministry. The years between 1600 and 1900 were formative.

The Quakers

Less than a hundred years after Martin Luther, a group of radical Protestants known as the Religious Society of Friends, or Quakers, began to form in England around the teachings of George Fox. By the mid-seventeenth century, this often-persecuted group was advocating a sexual equality that was unparalleled in European history and preceded by many decades any call within secular society for equality. For this reason they are sometimes extolled as the forerunners of contemporary feminism.

Central in their theology were the biblical passages of Paul and Joel cited above. The Quakers despised all forms of ordained ministry; their leadership was by inspiration and prophecy. Fox himself argued that women should not be prohibited from leadership: 'The prophet Joel was not against the daughters prophesying, nor the apostles were not against it, but said, "despise not the prophesying," and saith the Lord ... "Touch not mine anointed, and do my prophets no harm." So you that persecute the daughters on whom the spirit of the Lord is poured, and believe them not, you are them that despise prophesying and so have broken the apostle's command.'[11]

The early teaching and practice of Quaker ministry are significant. First, they demonstrate that the religious conviction that women and men are not related to each other hierarchically was not copied from secular beliefs about gender relationships, despite popular opinion to that effect, but came from the Christian scriptures. Second, they show that, within non-sacramental traditions and in traditions lacking an ordained ministry, it was easier for women to take public roles in ministry than it was in sacramental and priestly churches. More hierarchical denominations took longer to embrace a unified anthropology, and those traditions grounded in prophecy and ecstatic utterance were indeed the first to embrace fully the leadership gifts of women.

Religious Enthusiasm

With the so-called Great Awakenings that swept through Protestantism in the eighteenth and nineteenth centuries, new stories of women's ministry and leadership came to the fore. The primary initiators in these cross-denominational and global revivals were men – for example, John Wesley and Jonathan Edwards. This is not surprising, as the revival movements grew out of discontent with spiritual life and worship in traditional Protestantism, usually instigated by dissatisfied male clerics. Their initiatives were enthusiastically received and expanded by a spiritually hungry lay population – composed largely of devout women.

In both periods of revival the circuit-riding preacher was prominent. Circuit riders travelled from place to place preaching an enthusiastic gospel of inspiration and sanctification. Their work affected the evolution of women's ministry in two ways: through the rise of local female leadership in post-revival prayer and action groups and through the gradual introduction of female preachers to the circuits.

When a circuit rider moved on after kindling a religious revival, enthusiastic lay people devoted themselves to maintaining the energy and work of the transient preacher in the local setting. Though few accurate statistics are available, the journals of many circuit riders note that many in their congregations at meetings were women.[12] It is therefore reasonable to conclude that throughout North America and also in England female involvement in the awakenings was crucial to their success.

Religious opinion of the day held that women were by nature more pious than men, and as such they were the designated 'keepers of religion' in both household and society. Until the mid-nineteenth century, however, this designation did not often translate into public leadership. Women outnumbered men in church attendance, but they were seldom leaders of congregations.[13]

In the mid-nineteenth century, religious enthusiasm among women led to a new phenomenon – the women's voluntary association. Many types emerged in the aftermath of revivals: Bible study groups, prayer groups, Sunday schools, missionary associations, temperance unions, movements for the abolition of slavery, altar guilds, and women's auxiliaries for fellowship and fund-raising. Their proliferation moved women into the public forum as never before. As leaders and participants, women began to acquire skills in organization, administration, fund-raising, public speaking, management, and leadership. They became comfortable expressing themselves theologically in public. Some began to interpret their activity as an exercise in the priesthood of all believers. This spontaneous development out of revivalism was a formative experience for many women, who began to envision a broader role in church ministry. Their male partners also participated in this learning experience.

Around the same time, other women moved in yet further directions out of their experience of religious enthusiasm, into full-time vocations as ministers: as preachers and revivalists in the holiness movements, as deaconesses and paid staff in major Protestant denominations, and as missionaries supported by funds raised by their sisters in the voluntary associations.

On the circuit, women occasionally conducted revival meetings, such as those held in the late eighteenth century by the Freewill Baptists of New England. The earliest circuit-riding women, however, were predominantly ministers' wives, who did not think of themselves as preachers at all. These women saw their husbands as the preachers, as did Hannah Whitehall Smith, who accompanied her husband, Robert, on the English evangelical circuit in the mid-nineteenth century. So also did Catherine Booth, wife of Methodist minister William Booth, who later joined him in founding the Salvation Army. These women usually saw themselves as offering a few words of consolation and praise at the conclusion of their husbands' addresses, but their often-lengthy exhortations received enthusiastic responses.[14]

Perhaps the best known of the women who rode the circuit with their husbands was Phoebe Palmer, acknowledged mother of the nineteenth-century Holiness Movement in North America. As a shaper of the evangelical movement, she participated in religious revivals because of what she identified as divine inspiration. In the spirit of prophecy, she began to proclaim, practise and write about the source and focus of her inspiration. She preached on progressive sanctification in the life of the Christian but, in the manner of the first pastors' wives of the Reformation, avoided calling attention to herself. She invited those in the movement to a life of humble submission to God, openness to divine inspiration, justification by faith, and salvation from the depravity of sin.[15]

Professionalization of Ministry

The middle of the nineteenth century witnessed a broad cultural movement towards the professionalization of educated labour. The church was not immune to this development in society, and the clerical ministry, which was still all male, began to be affected by the increased demand for professionalism. Women were beginning to gain access to higher education and professional occupations, and female Christians began to look for a place in professional ministry. Most mainline Protestant churches responded by resurrecting the order of deaconess and by instituting positions for professional lay women. By the end of the century, Christian women were working as full-time salaried workers in ministry to women and children, in Christian education, in service to the poor, and in foreign missionary work.[16]

Given women's growing involvement in ministry, it was only a matter of time before the question of ordination was raised. The discussions that ensued resurrected centuries-old questions about the nature and proper function of women, but now they gave rise to different answers. Mainline Protestantism was for the most part willing to define women as qualitatively and ontologically the same as men. Indeed, for many Protestants, the anthropology formally rejected in the twentieth century had been outmoded for a very long time. As Archbishop Edward Scott of the Anglican Church of Canada said, 'Ultimately we found that there was only one argument against the ordination of women which could not be debated away; it was the deeply rooted belief or prejudice that a woman simply could not BE a priest by virtue of her femaleness. We in the Anglican Church of Canada decided that that was a view which we could not and would not hold.'[17]

By the mid-twentieth century, a new day had dawned for many mainline Protestant denominations. The activity generated by the Great Awakenings and the changing position of women in society set the stage for the formalization in ecclesiastical policy of something that had been growing in the churches. Much of Protestantism was prepared to declare as normative the single anthropology anticipated early in the Reformation. Women and men were acknowledged to be ontologically equal and thereby able to participate fully in the church's ministry. New church policies first enfranchised women, allowing them access to all levels of ecclesiastical decision-making, and later admitted women to all ministerial offices.

Despite this movement, however, it would be a mistake to paint too rosy a picture of Protestant belief about gender in this century. Some churches still hold to a dual anthropology, and within those that do not there are individuals who still reject the notion that women and men are ontologically equal. Moreover, even where women are allowed full access to the ministry, discrimination on the basis of gender still exists. The picture that emerges on fuller examination is one of an imperfect, gradual transformation from a dualistic and divisive anthropology towards a more holistic, unified model of personhood.

Summary and Conclusion

The dialectical nature of theological transformation is evident from the discussion above. The reformers opened the door to a changed conception of Christian anthropology with their celebration of women as sexual beings in their capacity as wives and mothers, their insistence on common justification by faith, their acceptance of the priesthood of all believers without regard for gender, and the admission that God can bestow access to divine inspiration and revelation to anyone. Though the initial forms of Protestant church polity remained essentially androcentric, the theological framework that Protestants adopted forced them to modify their ecclesiastical practice to allow for divine inspiration and prophecy by women as well as men. As women were increasingly visible in the churches as vessels of ecstatic utterance, prophecy, and committed spirituality, Protestant structures gradually changed to accommodate them, and policy was later adapted to reflect reality.

If the story and analysis presented here are correct, Protestant denominations that maintain a dual anthropology need to ask whether they are being faithful to the theological principles underlying the reform tradition. Churches outside Protestantism may or may not be in the same situation, for they have different origins, different histories, and, perhaps, different theological foundations. Regardless of their position in the Christian spectrum, however, all church communities need constantly to examine whether they are faithful to God's word and to their calling as disciples. Though each dialectic is unique, it is only through such interaction that churches move forward to meet the challenges of succeeding generations.

NOTES

1 Elizabeth Clarke, ed., *Women in the Early Church* (Wilmington, Del.: Michael Glazier, 1987), 148.
2 Elisja Schulte van Kessel, 'Virgins and Mothers between Heaven and Earth,' in Natalie Zemon Davis and Arlette Farge, eds., *A History of Women*, vol. III (Cambridge: Belknap Press, 1994), 142–4.
3 Martin Luther, 'Lectures on Genesis Ch. 1–5,' in *Luther's Works*, vol. XIII (St Louis: Concordia Publishing House, 1958), 115–18.
4 Martin Luther, 'Table Talk,' in *Luther's Works*, vol. LVII (Philadelphia: Fortress Press, 1966), 8.
5 Ibid., vol. LIV, 317.
6 Otto Winckelman, *Das Fursorgewesen der Stadt Strassburg* (Leipzig: Heinsius, 1922), vol. II, 76.
7 On justification by faith, see *Luther's Works* (Philadelphia: Fortress Press, 1966), vol. XI, 10; vol. XXV, 30–5, 43–4, 67–8, 184, 188, 201, 206, 209–12. On the priesthood of all believers, see vol. II, 394; vol. IX, 124; vol. XII, 289, 403; vol. XIII, 65; vol. XVII, 98; vol. XXVII, 394; vol. XXX, 52. On women preaching, see vol. XXX, 135; vol. XXXIX, 234.
8 Ibid., vol. XLV, 175, 188–9; vol. XLVI, 232n.
9 Jane D. Douglass, 'Christian Freedom: What Calvin Learned at the School of Women,' *Church History*, 53 (June 1984), 167.
10 Joyce L. Irwin, *Womanhood in Radical Protestantism, 1525–1675* (New York: Mellen Press, 1979), 202–3.
11 George Fox, *The Works of George Fox*, 8 vols. (New York: Isaac T. Hooper, 1831; reprint ed., New York: AMS, 1975), vol. IV, 106, 109. Even within the Quaker tradition not all women assumed public or leadership roles in the community.
12 Terry D. Bilhartz, ed., *Francis Asbury's America: An Album of Early American Methodism* (Grand Rapids, Mich.: Zondervan, 1984), 85.
13 Rosemary Ruether and Rosemary Keller Skinner, eds., *Women and Religion in*

America: The Nineteenth Century, 3 vols. (New York: Harper and Row, 1981), vol. I, 2–3, 6.
14 Elliot Wright, *Holy Company: Christian Heroes and Heroines* (New York: MacMillan, 1980).
15 Phoebe Palmer, *Promise of the Father, or a Neglected Speciality of the Last Days* (Boston: Henry V. Degen, 1859), 2.
16 Wendy Fletcher-Marsh, *Beyond the Walled Garden* (Toronto: Artemis, 1995); Kathleen Bliss, *The Service and Status of Women in the Churches* (London: SCM Press, 1952).
17 Fletcher-Marsh, *Beyond*, 149.

8

Catholics and Protestants, Conservatives and Liberals: Christian Marriage Today

GAILE M. POHLHAUS

In twentieth-century North America the changing social climate has greatly affected marriage and the family. In recent decades especially, attitudes have altered and practices have diverged from what was earlier regarded as acceptable and normal. Many factors have contributed to these changes and differences – the two world wars, the communication explosion, the availability of contraceptive technology, and the cultural shift from family to individual values, to name but a few. No one factor by itself transformed North American society, but together they altered the social mores of millions of people. It goes without saying then that they also reshaped the attitudes and practices of Christians with regard to marriage and the family.

While one might think that religion influences social change, the closer one comes to the present the more one finds that the influence is usually in the other direction. For example, when knowledge increases (as it has through advances in public education), the changed perceptions of ordinary people reflect this increase in secular knowledge, and people spontaneously integrate these new perceptions into the totality of their beliefs, including their religious beliefs. This growth in secular knowledge tends to overwhelm the fixed body of ideas found in religious literature and institutions. Moreover, since the Reformation and the Enlightenment, marriage has come to be looked on as a more secular concern than a religious one, thus lessening the general influence of religion on marriage. In addition, churches as institutional organizations are usually slow to accept such changes, and some are slower than others, though some churches and denominations today are mounting something of a counterattack against social forces through marriage preparation programs and other means. None the less, change does occur, and it is often brought about by outside forces.

One example of the role of external forces on marriage is the way in which Christians respond to issues not according to denominational differences, as in the past, but in terms of what we might call sociological preferences. During the last four centuries, Catholics and Protestants have for the most part perceived each other as their primary antagonist. Catholics, for example, saw Protestants as denying the sacramentality and indissolubility of marriage. Protestants, in contrast, saw Catholics as stuck in a medieval and clerical understanding of marriage that denied the importance of the Bible and the relevance of contemporary experience. Today, however, Christian marriages are undergoing changes and challenges that are beyond the control of the churches, and they provoke conservative and liberal responses from Catholics and Protestants alike.

By 'conservative' we mean showing a preference for beliefs, values, and practices regarded as traditional, and by 'liberal,' a preference for the non-traditional. Conservative Protestants lean heavily on a literal reading of the Bible to support their desire to maintain marriage and family structures the way they have been in recent centuries, and conservative Catholics rely equally heavily on the traditional doctrines of their church for the same purpose. Liberal Protestants, in contrast, prefer a more relativistic reading of the scriptures to endorse marriage and family practices that have emerged since the 1960s, and liberal Catholics show a preference for recent church documents and theological opinions for the same reason. As a result, conservative Protestants and Catholics often find themselves on the same side of marriage and family questions (for example, premarital sex is always a sin), as do liberal Protestants and Catholics (for example, in some instances, premarital sex is morally permissible).

Though this chapter cannot do justice to all of the marriage-related issues that face Christians today, it attempts to raise enough of them to illustrate the changing dynamic that has just been described.

Sexuality and Gender Roles

While the academic study of gender is something peculiar to the twentieth century, throughout the ages men and women have been expected to learn and live according to sexually determined gender roles. What may be appropriate and expected male behaviour in one society may be seen as abnormal or prohibited in another. The same is true of female behaviour. Within Western culture, males have been assumed to be the norm for human behaviour and females the abnormal or less than normal. Traits described as typically feminine, such as sensitivity, emotionality, and nurturing, are often suspect when found in men. When these traits are valued in men, it is usually with a caveat that shows the superiority of the man who can embrace such traits and 'still be a man.'

Gender is understood today as the way in which individuals are perceived as male or female in their society. The society assigns various designations to traits of appearance, behaviour, personality, and tone and pitch of voice. If a person exhibits a preponderance of what are considered masculine characteristics, that person is assumed to be male, unless it is demonstrated otherwise. Conversely, if someone has been identified as a woman, then it is expected that she will have an overwhelming preponderance of 'feminine' characteristics. The bottom line for either designation is, however, a person's sexual organs. Since these are usually covered by clothes, we assign gender by an estimation of appearance and behaviour. Sometimes this is satisfactory and sometimes not. Professionals and lay people alike still debate whether these observable characteristics of maleness and femaleness are the result more of nature or nurture.

Though most Christian churches in the United States and Canada teach that women and men are equal in the eyes of God and should have equal civil rights, they often do not live up to their teachings. It is still assumed that child care is primarily the mother's responsibility and that economic support is primarily the father's. One can see evidence for this in church bulletins and newsletters and in religious newspapers and magazines. For example, the syndicated Christian radio program 'Focus on the Family' claims to be dedicated to 'traditional family values,' which often turn out to be the same as the values of male-dominated patriarchal society.

Conservative Protestant proponents of traditional family roles argue that the Bible endorses this form of marriage, but they are also quick to point out that in today's world an intelligent, God-fearing husband is always wise to consult his helpmate before making any major decision. Critics argue, on the contrary, that this model of the family is authoritarian, despite its scriptural foundation. Not only does the husband always have the final say, but even when the wife makes a decision it is the father's authority backing her up that gives her decision weight and value. Family decisions are considered good or bad not on the basis of objective criteria that are open to intelligent analysis by both men and women, but on the basis of whether or not they are made by a man.

More liberal Protestant churches tend to promote more egalitarian family models, but at the same time they often do little either to promote women's equality or to undo social structures that deny equal opportunities to women. Churches allow couples to make their own decisions about organizing family relationships and responsibilities, but they do little to help women make an intelligent decision by enlightening them about the hidden and often long-term disadvantages of inequality in marriage. At the societal level, churches are doing little to promote equal pay for equal work or to promote subsidized day care so that women can afford to work at lower-wage jobs. Within the churches themselves, women are often assigned roles that are traditionally regarded as feminine, such as teaching and organizing activities for children, and even in churches that accept women's ordination, female clergy find that they are not accepted as fully as males.

Official Roman Catholic teaching is equally ambiguous. Statements on the family from Leo XIII's *Arcanum divinum sapientiae* (1880), through Pius XI's *Casti conubii* (1931), to John Paul II's *Familiaris consortio* (1981) show changes in attitude towards the rights and responsibilities of married men and women, but they perpetuate patriarchal beliefs about traditional gender roles. All three documents portray women as the natural nurturers of children and men as economic providers and protectors. In Pius XI's classic phrase, the woman is the heart of the family, and the man is the head.[1] It is God's design that they complement one another.

Catholic social teaching for over a century has asserted that men (i.e., male heads of households) have a right to earn a wage that is high enough to support a family, so that women do not have to work outside the home.[2] It even saw the presence of women in the workforce as a factor sometimes driving men's wages down, because women increased the supply of available labour and were willing to work for less pay than men.[3] Thus women's rights to work and to equal pay were really not recognized, even though the church acknowledged that women sometimes needed to work outside the home. John Paul II seems to have rethought the church's position on women in the workplace, for he acknowledges that women should be allowed to develop their abilities outside the home and that they should be paid equal wages for equal work. He is, however, a vocal proponent of the view that the natural role of woman is as wife and mother.[4] The Catholic teaching on women therefore remains ambiguous.

Other recent documents of the Catholic church on the role of women have stressed women's equality to men, while emphasizing their difference.[5] These texts emphasize the complimentarity of women and men – that women by nature are nurturers and homemakers and men by nature deciders and accomplishers – a view with deep roots in the Catholic tradition. Some church documents have even moved towards admitting that fathers as well as mothers have responsibility for nurturing, yet other statements in the same documents have stressed the autonomy of the male as compared with the relatedness of the female – another version of the traditional theory of complementarity.[6]

Birth Control and Abortion

Basic to marriage is the question of having children. All Christian churches recognize the right of married people to have children, and the Catholic church even considers it an obligation. Prior to the Second Vatican Council in the 1960s, the church taught that the primary purpose of marriage was the procreation and education of children.[7] As might be expected, this responsibility fell more heavily on women, who were given the role of homemaker and caregiver, than it did on men. Other churches regard children as a blessing rather than an obligation.[8]

One way to put the human reverence for life and for children in perspective is to look at it in terms of its historical origins. For hundreds of generations, and indeed during the period when the great religions of the world, including the Judaeo-Christian tradition, originated, the individual human life was a precious commodity. Average human life expectancy was under forty years, and the childhood mortality rate was so high that it took five births to produce two individuals who survived long enough to reproduce and nurture their young. Every added person in a family or tribe was a net asset, because an adult could contribute to the total wealth of the community more than he or she consumed. The lives of children were important not in themselves but because they would enable the group to survive. Parents had no other medical insurance or old age pension than their own children. This is still the case in many Third and Fourth World nations.[9]

In social conditions of this sort, human life had to be zealously protected and promoted. Judaism prohibited murdering another Jew of any age or sex, and Christianity expanded this prohibition to include all innocent human life. In the agricultural societies of ancient and medieval Europe, the purpose of marriage was to produce offspring to ensure the survival of the family, to inherit and protect the family's property, and to carry on the family's (i.e., the father's) name. Both abortion and birth control endangered the continuance and well-being of the family not only by reducing the number of births but also by endangering the lives of women who were needed to bear children.[10] The prohibitions on these practices came therefore from a social and family perspective; the desires of individuals and the rights of women (if any) were hardly taken into account.

The sheer necessity of giving birth to enough children to ensure the continuance of the family and, in the long run, the survival of the human race, lasted well into the nineteenth century, when modern medicine began to curtail the death rate, first in Europe and then in all parts of the world reached by European colonialism. Even through the 1930s in North America, when the majority of people still lived on farms, each child that survived until old enough to work was a family asset: children's labour contributed more to the family than the cost of raising them. Today, by contrast, each child born into a middle-class family costs its parents between $100,000 and $300,000 by the time it leaves home, according to various estimates.[11] Instead of being financial assets, children in industrial societies have become financial liabilities to their parents.

Since the risk of human extinction through underpopulation has been eliminated through the invention of modern medicine, the planet is experiencing a population explosion of unprecedented proportions. Though the greatest expansion is occurring in poor countries, where basic medicine has lowered the death rate but families still depend on children for sustenance in old age, each child added to the consumer culture of wealthy countries depletes six to sixteen times as much of the world's resources as a child born into the survival culture of poor countries.[12]

For personal or social reasons or both, therefore, Europeans and North Americans have generally chosen to have smaller families by practising birth control. At the same time, abortion has been legalized in most countries, either as a method of birth control or as a means of protecting the right of women to make decisions about their own bodies. The social situation in which Christianity perceived the immorality of preventing conception and birth is thus vastly different from that in which many Christians find themselves today.

With regard to birth control, all Protestant churches have accepted that the regulation of birth is a decision to be made by individuals for personal or social reasons. The present position of the Catholic church is similar, except that it makes a distinction between morally acceptable and morally unacceptable methods. Those deemed morally acceptable are those that entail abstinence from sexual intercourse during a woman's fertile period; those considered unacceptable interfere with the process of conception. These latter are referred to in Catholic literature as artificial methods, and their moral prohibition is based largely on the church's traditional understanding of the purpose of marriage and sexual intercourse.[13]

Despite the church's prohibition, however, the majority of Roman Catholics in Europe and North America today practise family planning using the same methods as their Protestant neighbours. Most Catholics believe that women and married couples have the right to decide about which method of birth control to use, depending on medical and personal factors that they themselves choose, and they view attempts by the church's hierarchy to dictate acceptable methods of birth control as authoritarian rather than as instructive or helpful. Moreover, since most artificial methods entail specific actions performed by women (such as taking pills and inserting a diaphragm), women tend to come under greater pressure than men to use acceptable methods, and so this pressure is perceived as patriarchal and even sexist in effect, if not in intent.

With abortion the situation is rather different, since no church distinguishes in principle between acceptable and unacceptable methods. Rather, Christians tend to divide on the issue according to conservative or liberal outlooks. Conservatives condemn abortion as the murder of an unborn child, with Protestants basing their position primarily on the literal interpretation of scripture texts and Catholics, primarily on traditional church teaching.[14] The conservative position rests on the presumption that the fetus is human from the day of conception and is therefore entitled to the God-given right to life from the very beginning. The Roman Catholic church, Eastern Orthodox churches, and evangelical or fundamentalist Protestant churches support this position.

Liberal Christians, in contrast, divide over the morality of abortion. Some take the position that abortion is always morally wrong but sometimes permissible depending on the circumstances (such as saving the life of the mother); some, that it is morally acceptable during the early stages of pregnancy but not in the later stages; others, that it is permissible for certain reasons (as in the case of severe birth defects) but not for others (for example, because the child is not of the desired sex); and still others, that the decision to terminate a pregnancy or bring it to term is completely a woman's right and responsibility. The variability of positions depends to some extent on the determination as to when human life begins in the womb and to some extent on the balance between the value of life and other values. Moderate and liberal churches and denominations tend not to take institutional positions on abortion, preferring instead to give moral guidance while leaving the decision to those who are making it and will have to live with its consequences.

Not infrequently, liberal Christians have personal views that are different from those of the communions to which they belong, be those conservative, moderate, or liberal. Both liberal communions and liberal Christians tend to be less authoritarian and more individualistic in their mode of moral reasoning and decision-making. They therefore also tend to be less patriarchal and less sexist in their application of moral and religious norms to the issue of abortion.

Parenting

All Christian churches and denominations teach that parents have an ongoing responsibility to raise their children. This principle applies to all aspects of the children's lives, most especially with regard to values. There is no uniform position as to the amount or type of value education that should take place in public schools (for example, with regard to sexual behaviour), but in general the more conservative prefer traditional value education (i.e., teaching what is right and what is wrong), and the more liberal prefer values clarification (i.e., teaching children how to recognize and evaluate their own values and those of others) and decision making (i.e., instructing them in how to make intelligent decisions and to take responsibility for their actions). As may be surmised, more conservative Christians favour the teaching of traditional gender roles, and more liberal Christians favour modes that make it possible to question traditional gender roles.

Gender roles are taught more by example and are learned more by observation and imitation, however, than they are taught in the classroom and learned by studying. For this reason, gender roles in marriage and elsewhere are communicated more by the example of institutions and parents than they are by what is taught in school, even in Sunday school. Again here, the division does not seem to be between Protestants and Catholics but between conservatives and liberals. Conservative

Christian Marriage Today 151

institutions promote traditional gender roles through favouring male ministers, by referring to God using masculine pronouns, and through teaching Bible stories in a non-critical way. Liberal institutions soften traditional gender roles by choosing female ministers and leaders, by using gender-inclusive language in prayer and worship, and by helping children and adults to become aware of the sexual biases in the scriptures. Even the most liberal Christian institutions cannot avoid all gender stereotyping, however, for their very decision to be liberal entails their being non-authoritarian rather than imposing their views in what they perceive to be a stereotypically patriarchal fashion.

Churches as well as parents therefore engage in parenting: by precept and example they teach children what it means to be human, to be Christian, to be sexual, to be married, and to be parents. To the extent that institutions and individuals adopt and favour traditional teachings and practices, they promote traditional gender roles. In so far as they favour and practise non-traditional roles, they weaken gender stereotypes among their members. Churches can hardly hope to eliminate gender roles and stereotypes, however, because their members are exposed to many other influences than institutional religion, and religion today is hardly the cultural determinant that it was in the past.

Divorce and Remarriage

Since New Testament times, Christians have recognized the right of married persons to divorce in certain cases.[15] Divorce was possible but rare in the Christian Roman Empire, and in the Middle Ages it was virtually impossible, except among the nobility. Divorce remained impossible for Roman Catholics during the modern era, and it reverted to being possible but rare for Protestants up to the twentieth century. Even among the upper and middle classes, where divorce was most likely to be attempted as a solution to marital difficulties, it was socially frowned on, and divorced persons (especially women) were likely to be snubbed or treated as outcasts.

Attitudes began to change in the 1920s and 1930s. The devastation and carnage of the First World War shook the faith of many in the Christian governments and churches that had supported the killing of millions on both sides. The postwar years brought new technologies (especially radio, the movies, and the automobile) that opened people's minds to new possibilities and increased the attractiveness of breaking with the past. Both the poverty of the Great Depression and the anxiety of the Second World War put great stress on many marriages. Couples drifted apart, and families broke up, not always with the benefit of divorce, which, though legal, was still difficult to obtain. Nevertheless, beginning in the late 1940s, the divorce rate began to rise.

The 1960s accelerated the increase in divorces, partly a reflection of reaction to the social restrictions of the past (similar to the reaction of the 'roaring twenties' to the Great War), and partly a result of the women's movement, which brought many women a greater sense of their own dignity and worth apart from men and increased women's awareness of their human rights and economic value. More women started working outside the home, and in the 1970s new economic conditions made it increasingly difficult for a family to get by on one income. This renewed experience in the workplace also made women less economically dependent on their husbands, and it gave them the skills and confidence to support themselves if they had to. The 1970s also saw the introduction of 'no-fault divorce' – the possibility of a couple's filing for divorce in the same way in which they applied for a marriage licence, instead of having to prove in court that one of the spouses was guilty of destroying the marriage.

It would be difficult to discern a deliberate bias against women in the increased possibility of divorce. As legal restrictions relaxed, they affected women and men equally. Social constraints eased more slowly; women as homemakers were expected to be faithful to their husbands, regardless of how they were treated, and to keep the family together for the sake of the children. Nevertheless, through the 1980s, several times more women than men sought divorces in Europe and North America. To many women, apparently, the disadvantages of divorce were outweighed by those of an intolerable marriage, from which they could now legally and economically escape.

Today, all churches allow for the possibility that a Christian marriage may end in divorce. Theologically, divorce is never something that God wants; at most, God permits the sadness of divorce when it prevents more pain. Some conservative Protestant churches counsel strongly against divorce in almost all cases and urge against remarriage except in certain circumstances; the more liberal churches accept divorce when it happens and even see the possibility of a second marriage as a way to healing and fulfilment.

The Catholic church never officially forbade divorce, though it so strongly discouraged it that divorces among Catholics were rare until the 1960s. What the church does forbid is remarriage without an official annulment of the previous marriage. Described simply, an annulment is a declaration by a church court that a marriage between Christians, now separated by divorce, was not a sacramental marriage as it once appeared to be.[16] Since Catholics may not enter a second marriage if their first was validly sacramental and if their spouse from that marriage is still alive, they need a declaration of nullity in order to remarry in the church.

An annulment does not dissolve a civil marriage (hence the need for a civil divorce in addition to the annulment), nor does it render illegitimate the children born into it. The normal annulment process takes about a year, and the fee of a few hundred dollars, to cover clerical processing, is often waived in cases of financial hardship. Either party may apply for the annulment, but if it is granted, both parties are free to remarry in the church.

Grounds for annulment used to be rather stringent and factual (for example, having been coerced into the marriage or not being able to perform sexual intercourse), but in recent decades they have become more broad and psychological (such as not being able to enter into a relationship of intimacy and commitment). None the less, not everyone who seeks an annulment obtains one, for sometimes the church court cannot find sufficient evidence that a marriage was sacramentally null. Liberal theologians argue that disappointed individuals, if they are convinced that their first marriage was never a sacrament, may follow their own conscience and, even though they may not remarry in a Catholic wedding ceremony, may remain active in the church. Conservative theologians, including Pope John Paul II, disagree, arguing that Catholics may not exempt themselves from church laws and that those who remarry outside the church may not receive the church's sacraments. The ecclesiastical argument is somewhat moot, however, because about ninety per cent of divorced Catholics never even apply for an annulment.[17] They either leave the church or, if they want to remain active, find a parish where no one knows that they are divorced and remarried.

If there is a bias against women in divorce, it is financial and legal. Numerous studies have shown that, after a divorce, average income increases sharply for men and decreases drastically for women.[18] Whereas in the past, women who sued for divorce were awarded alimony because they were not expected to have to support themselves, today, when couples file jointly for divorce, the woman is expected to find a job if she does not have one already. The difficulty is that many women do not have skills for high-paying jobs and, even if they do, do not get paid as much as men do for the same jobs. Also, since women have the gender role of nurturer in our society, they usually receive custody of children after a divorce. Even though they are often awarded child-support payments as well, the payments still do not raise women's household income to the level of men's, and courts have been lax about enforcing child-support payments on delinquent fathers. Partly as a result of the combination of high divorce rate and low child support, the two groups in the United States most likely to be living in poverty are women and children.[19]

In the past, women contemplating divorce who sought advice from their pastors were often counselled to remain even in abusive relationships, on the basis of biblical texts such as Matt. 5:32, which says that people should not divorce except in the case of immorality (usually interpreted as adultery); Eph. 5:22–4, which counsels women to be subject to their husbands; and I Cor. 7:16, which suggests that spouses should remain with their partners in order to save them. Today, the literal application of ancient texts to marriage problems is generally regarded as inappropriate, but women are still more likely to be advised to remain in the marriage in order to save it, if for no other reason than that they generally seek advice more often than men do. Nevertheless, pastors who are aware of research on physical and emotional abuse know that when women remain in abusive relationships they are usually codependent or psychologically locked into the relationship, and they are unwittingly enabling the abuse to continue rather than helping their partner break the vicious habit.

Homosexual Marriages

'The past four years have witnessed unprecedented productivity on the part of Protestant denominations in the generation of papers on human sexuality. Four such documents, that of the Protestant Episcopal Church in the U.S.A. (ECUSA), the United Methodist Church (UMC), the Evangelical Lutheran Church in America (ELCA), and the Presbyterian Church in the U.S.A. (PCUSA) are striking in their similarities. These documents all pose challenges to what are understood to be traditional views on marriage, acceptable sexual practice, and homosexuality.'[20]

Though the issue of the churches and homosexuality deserves an entire book in itself,[21] something needs to be said about it in a book that discusses gender issues and Christianity. Certainly homosexuality is a sexual issue having to do with the morality of certain types of genital behaviour and sexual bonding, but it is also a gender issue, because it raises questions about the very nature of maleness and femaleness, non-genital behaviour between persons of the same sex, and even marriage. Many of those who oppose legalizing homosexual marriage believe that the traditional roles of mother and father, as well as the traditional structure of the heterosexual family, would be threatened if homosexual couples were allowed to call their committed relationships marriages.[22]

There are very few sociological data on the permanence of committed homosexual relationships. Some of the existing research indicates that homosexual unions on average do not last as long as marriages in the general population.[23] One reason may be that couples who choose to live together in a sexual relationship without the benefit of a wedding do not receive the same social approval and support that married couples do. Rather than comparing homosexual couples to married couples, perhaps it would be more appropriate to compare the longevity of homosexual relationships to that of unmarried heterosexual people who live together.

There is also little statistical evidence to suggest that children who are raised by same-sex couples (if one partner has children from a previous marriage, for example) are either sexually confused or even inclined towards homosexuality. If sexual attraction to persons of the same sex is largely determined before birth, as much current research seems to indicate,[24] then environmental factors may actually have little influence on sexual preference. As homosexuals themselves often point out, virtually all of them were raised in heterosexual households, but the example of their parents and the pressure of society around them was not strong enough to turn them into heterosexuals.

Though some gay men publicly adopt mannerisms that are socially identified as feminine, and though some lesbian women do the same regarding masculine mannerisms, most homosexuals choose gender-related behaviour that is socially appropriate in all areas of life except sexual preference. These persons do not have public lives that are noticeably different from those of heterosexuals, and indeed they often adopt many of the gender roles dictated by Western culture, making their homosexuality socially invisible.

The question of homosexual marriage seems to be whether two persons of the same sex can legitimately be called spouses or parents. That is, can homosexuals adopt social roles traditionally linked with gender roles? Posing the question in this way emphasizes the fact that gender roles (except for those determined by physiology) are culturally determined – dictated by society. Thus the issue is whether individuals have a right to choose their own social roles regardless of tradition, or whether society may rightly pose limits on individuals' choices of social roles. The patriarchal tradition of Western culture places the right of society over the rights of individuals and claims that society has a right to decide who may and may not be married. The patriarchal tradition of Christianity goes further and claims that all rights come from God and that it is impossible to prove from the Judaeo-Christian revelation that God has given homosexuals a right to be marriage partners.

At present, none of the U.S. states or Canadian provinces recognizes the legality of homosexual marriages, though a number of laws and local ordinances give unmarried couples (whether of the same or different sexes) the same insurance benefits and housing rights as married couples. The United Church of Christ in the United States and the Society of Friends (Quakers) provide for commitment ceremonies in homosexual unions, but most denominations prohibit such ceremonies. Individual local churches have on occasion held such rites and were censured by or expelled from their denomination.[25]

The Roman Catholic church completely opposes such marriages. Its official position is that homosexuals deserve love and support, since they are human beings, but as single human beings they must be held to the standard of celibacy required of all unmarried persons.[26] While the church teaches that it is impossible for women to be ordained (since they lack certain required characteristics), it has never claimed that it is impossible for homosexuals to be married. Rather, its argument has been that their marriage would undermine the institution of marriage as God has intended it.

Communication and Christian Marriage

Though conservatives and liberals may differ over a number of marriage issues, they do agree on the importance of communication. Nevertheless, they differ in the ways they see communication in the husband–wife relationship.

Contemporary communication theory distinguishes five levels of interpersonal communication. The shallowest level, *small talk*, can be reached even when strangers ask about the weather, make noncommittal observations about things that are happening, and stick to topics that are neither personal nor controversial. In *factual conversation*, one begins inquiring and talking about family, work, and interests (hobbies, sports, people, places, and so on) on the level of external information rather than personal beliefs and values. Sharing *ideas and opinions* moves communication to a level that involves some risk, for one is revealing judgments that one has made, beliefs that one holds, and values that one thinks are right. Yet another level is reached when people share *feelings and emotions*, for these are private matters, normally not revealed except to those with whom one feels close and secure. The most intimate level is that of *deep insight* into oneself, one's relationship with God and others, the meaning of life, and one's fundamental values, principles, and commitments.[27]

In marriage relationships of the past, it was not necessary for husband or wife to communicate any deeper than level two: they needed only to be able to talk about the house, the farm, the business, the neighbours, the in-laws, the children, and the rest of ordinary life, in a truthful and matter-of-fact way. While such conversation can supply the information to keep a household going, it cannot offer either partner the satisfaction of being close to another person or knowing another person deeply. Nor can it provide emotional support in times of stress or grief. People with underdeveloped communication skills cannot be close companions, sharing ideas and discussing personal beliefs, nor can they develop a deep interpersonal relationship through the sharing of feelings, sorrows, and insights. Today, however, many people enter marriage seeking companionship and intimacy, which can be found only through communicating at the deepest levels.

In the past, typically the husband was the dominant partner. In this hierarchical (essentially patriarchal) model of marriage, communication was relatively unimportant. Both spouses knew what was expected of them, and few words were necessary. When a decision had to be made, the husband made it, and the wife obeyed it.

A second style of marriage, sometimes called a companionate model, allows the person in charge to be the one with particular expertise or talent. In a rather traditional version, the wife might make decisions about homemaking and child-rearing, and the husband, about balancing the chequebook and mowing the lawn. In a non-traditional version, the wife might earn the larger salary and balance the chequebook, and the husband might take care of the home and children. In an ideal companionate marriage, the person in charge is open to consulting with the spouse, but the ultimate decision always rests with one person.

Egalitarian marriage is a third type that is emerging in Western culture, according to some analysts.[28] There is no subordinate or dominant role. The spouses make decisions collaboratively, with each viewpoint being given equal consideration. No one is considered superior to the other, nor are tasks portioned out by one person. Yet it is reasonable to expect that, given the time constraints of family life today, not all decisions are reached by consensus. Even an egalitarian marriage will find occasions and patterns when one spouse decides and the other trusts the decision. Nevertheless, both companionate and egalitarian marriages require well-developed communication skills.

Though the traditional hierarchical model of marriage was promoted by both Catholics and Protestants in the past, few churches today consider it divinely sanctioned. Rather, the division among Christians over marriage styles is, as suggested above, between conservatives and liberals. Conservative Christians tend to find in the Bible divine directives about which spouse should be in charge of certain aspects of marriage and family life, and so they tend to prefer the companionate model.[29] Liberals generally regard most statements in the scriptures about marriage as culturally conditioned, and they suggest that the family is a community of disciples who are radically equal before God (as is true in any Christian community), and so they tend to prefer some version of the egalitarian model.[30] Again, however, both companionate and egalitarian marriages require good communication skills.

Conclusion: A Brief Theology of Communication for Conservative and Liberal Christians Alike

Communication is often thought of in terms of a message that is sent from one or more persons to another. If there are two or more listeners (and often the sender is a listener also), there can be two or more meanings given to the same sequence of words, raising the possibility of misunderstanding as well as understanding through communication. It is quite possible (and all too common in the experience of marriage counsellors) that what is said is understood quite differently from the way it was intended. Different family and cultural backgrounds – and even gender differences – can lead people to interpret messages differently than they were meant to be taken, and the only way to straighten out the misunderstanding is through communication.

Effective communication relies not only on words but also on nonverbal, or body language as well. (According to one estimate, 93 per cent of interpersonal communication is non-verbal.) This includes physical posture, tone of voice, spacing of words, emphasis on words, and expression of face. Most of the time the average listener just takes body language in the total context of the communication that is going on. It is one of many things that contributes to his or her understanding of what is being said. Learning about communication and developing good communication skills therefore require sensitivity about sending and receiving non-verbal as well as verbal messages.

If a Christian marriage means following Christ in the context of a family community, then everything that can be said about discipleship can also be said about Christian marriage and family life. For example, Jesus taught, 'Thou shalt love thy neighbour as thyself.' The closest neighbour in a marriage is one's spouse. Moreover, the love of which Jesus speaks here is *agape*, which in Greek is not a feeling but a decision – to care about and take care of others, to put their needs ahead of one's own wants and desires. Communication in a Christian marriage should therefore be an exercise in caring for and caring about one's spouse and one's family – as well as about oneself. It is legitimate, in other words, to communicate one's own needs and desires while caring for others.

If Christ asks his followers to be truthful, then communication in a Christian marriage should be truthful and open. In open communication, messages go in both directions, with opportunities existing for clarification when misunderstandings occur. Christian caring keeps the door open between spouses and among family members. 'Love is patient, kind, not envious or boastful or arrogant or rude. It does not insist on its own way; it is not irritable or resentful; it does not rejoice in wrongdoing, but rejoices in the truth. It bears all things, believes all things, hopes all things, endures all things' (I Cor. 13:4–7). If people love one another and care for one another, they will be honest with one another.

The gospels portray Jesus as honest with his followers, even when it came to saying hard things. If something needs to be said, then it should be said. Yet here, too, tone and pitch and timing can make all the difference in the world. One way of communicating a hard truth may provoke stubborn rejection; another may invite responsible cooperation. Being a Christian does not relieve one from having to learn about communication. In fact, being a married Christian today requires skills that few people possessed in earlier eras.

Fortunately, these skills are neither mysterious nor difficult to acquire.[31] Attentiveness, respect, openness, and honesty are traditional virtues to which even liberal Christians can relate. Assertiveness, active listening, and self-disclosure are recently developed techniques in which even conservative Christians can see value. Spouses should acknowledge that communication is foundational to happiness in marriage, be it companionate or egalitarian, and be willing to develop the personal skills needed to achieve a fulfilling interpersonal relationship.

NOTES

1 Pope Pius XI, *Casti connubii*, sec. I, par. 53 (1931).
2 For example, Leo XIII, *Arcanum divinae sapientiae*, par. 6 (1880) and *Rerum novarum*, par. 10–14, 28–32, 47 (1891); Pius XI, *Quadragesimo anno*, par. 71 (1931); Pope John XXIII, *Pacem in terris*, par. 20 (1963).
3 See 'The Family Income' in Edwin F. Healy, *Marriage Guidance* (Chicago: Loyola University Press, 1948), 90–105.
4 This is a familiar theme in John Paul II's writing on both women and the family – for example, his apostolic letter *Mulieris dignitatem*, 15 August 1988.
5 Again many documents could be cited here, among them John Paul II's *Familiaris consortio* (22 November 1981) and the more recent 'Letter to Families,' which can be found in *Origins*, 23, no. 37 (3 March 1994).
6 *Familiaris consortio* is a good example.
7 Leo XIII, *Rerum novarum*, par. 10 (1890). With regard to the ends of marriage, Vatican II's *Constitution on the Church in the Modern World* (nos. 47–50) put the fostering of the relationship between the spouses on a par with having children, without giving one of these primacy over the other.
8 The church will not marry two people who declare their intention to remain childless. It is also grounds for annulment if one of the spouses discovers after the wedding that the other refuses to have children.
9 I first became aware of this through African students in my classes. These students were appalled at the American reliance on social security and assured my classes that in their culture it is the offsprings' obligation to take care of their elders.
10 All methods of abortion and many methods of birth control (such as inserting materials into the vagina and taking potions) entailed doing things to women's bodies, which, in an era without much knowledge of the causes of disease, put the woman's life at risk. See Joseph T. Noonan, *Contraception* (Cambridge: Harvard University Press, 1965).
11 Mark Lino, 'Expenditures on a Child by Families, 1993,' *Family Economics Review*, 7, no. 3 (1994), 2–19. This follows up his earlier study: U.S. Department of Agriculture, Agricultural Research Service, Family Economics Research Group, *Expenditures on a Child by Families, 1991* (1992). Many reports on the cost of raising children do not take in enough factors, how-

ever, as shown by James Banks, Richard Blundell and Ian Preston, 'Life-cycle Expenditure Allocations and the Consumption Cost of Children,' *European Economic Review*, 38 (1994), 1391–1410.
12 See Paul Erlich, *The Population Bomb* (New York: Ballantine Books, 1968).
13 See Noonan, *Contraception*; also Paul VI, *Humanae vitae* (1967), and Mary Ann Glendon, *Abortion and Divorce in Western Law* (Cambridge, Mass.: Harvard University Press, 1987).
14 Jer. 1:5, Job 10:8–12, and Psalms 22:10–11 are commonly cited as biblical warrants against abortion. The *Catechism of the Catholic Church* treats abortion in part III, sec. 2270–75.
15 Matt. 5:32 allows for divorce in the case of immorality. (The Greek word, *porneia*, has often been translated as adultery, but language experts say that its meaning is actually rather vague.) I Cor. 7:12–15 allows for divorce in the case of a Christian convert married to a non-believer who actively opposes the Christian's religion.
16 In Catholic theology, a sacramental marriage, being a sign and reflection of the indissoluble union between Christ and the church, is indissoluble.
17 Steven Priester, 'Marriage, Divorce and Remarriage in the United States,' *New Catholic World*, 229 (1986), 9–19.
18 Much of this information is summarized in Frank D. Cox, *Human Intimacy: Marriage, the Family and Its Meaning*, 5th ed. (St Paul, Minn.: West Publishing Co., 1990), 560–2.
19 For statistics and analysis see Terry Arendell, *Mothers and Divorce: Legal, Economic and Social Dilemmas* (Berkeley: University of California Press, 1986), 36–53; Arlie Hochschile, *The Second Shift* (New York: Avon Books, 1989), 249–53.
20 Mary McClintock Fulkerson, 'Church Documents on Human Sexuality and the Authority of Scripture,' *Interpretation*, 49, no. 1 (January 1995), 46.
21 See, for example, John Boswell, *Same-Sex Unions in Premodern Europe* (New York: Villard Books, 1994); also Patricia Beattie Jung and Ralph Smith, *Heterosexism: An Ethical Challenge* (Albany, NY: SUNY Press, 1993).
22 In the spring of 1996, Mayor Ed Rendell of Philadelphia proposed extending work benefits that married couples enjoyed to any domestic partners. Anthony Cardinal Bevalaqua of of Philadelphia called on the Catholics in his diocese to oppose such a move as destructive to the foundations of marriage. See *Catholic Standard and Times*, 101, nos. 45–48, 13, 20, 27 June and 1 July 1996.
23 See P. Blumstein and P. Schwartz, *American Couples: Money, Work, Sex* (New York: Morrow, 1983). Some studies, such as this one, also suggest that lesbian couples break up less frequently than either heterosexual or gay couples.

24 The debate continues as to the prenatal disposition to homosexuality. Whereas some think that the cause must be genetic, others believe it to be hormonal, triggered by prenatal stress on the mother. See Chandler Burr, 'Homosexuality and Biology,' *Atlantic*, 271, no. 3 (March 1993), 47ff.
25 In 1994 several Lutheran churches in California agreed to celebrate such marriages on a case-by-case basis, even though their governing body outlawed homosexual marriages.
26 Sacred Congregation for the Doctrine of the Faith, *Letter to the Bishops of the Catholic Church on the Pastoral Care of Homosexual Persons* (1 October 1986), par. 12.
27 John Powell, *Why Am I Afraid to Tell You Who I Am?* (Valencia, Calif.: Tabor Publishing, 1969), 50–62.
28 See William Johnson Everett, *Blessed Be the Bond* (Philadelphia: Fortress Press, 1985).
29 The story of Eve's creation to be a helpmate to Adam quite easily supports this approach, as do a number of other biblical texts. The notion of headship based on Eph. 5 can also be interpreted in a companionate rather than a patriarchal manner. See, for example, Wes Roberts and H. Norman Wright, *Before You Say I Do: A Marriage Preparation Manual for Couples* (Eugene, Ore.: Harvest House Publishers, 1978), 47.
30 See Michael Lawler, *Marriage and Sacrament: A Theology of Christian Marriage* (Collegeville, Minn.: The Liturgical Press, 1993), and Everett, *Blessed Be the Bond*.
31 There is a wealth of contemporary literature on communication in marriage, with more titles appearing every year, not to mention communication workshops and marriage-enrichment programs that are available through many churches. A few of the better books are John Gottman, *A Couple's Guide to Communication* (Champaign, Ill.: Research Press, 1976); Patti McDermott, *How to Talk to Your Husband, How to Talk to Your Wife* (Chicago: Contemporary Books, 1994); Nancy L. Van Pelt, *How to Talk So Your Mate Will Listen and Listen So Your Mate Will Talk* (Grand Rapids, Mich.: Fleming H. Revell, 1989); H. Norman Wright, *Communication: Key to Your Marriage* (Ventura, Calif.: Regal Books, 1979).

9

Weaving New Cloth: Overcoming Sexism in Ordination Policies

MOLLY T. MARSHALL

Most major Christian denominations in North America have recently witnessed a phenomenal transposition of women into the status of clergy, adding new texture to the fabric of Protestantism, which earlier had seen women in the leadership of smaller churches and pentecostal denominations. At the same time, insistent voices in the Catholic church are calling for the ordination of women to the priesthood and the diaconate. Though this movement has thus far been denied official approbation, Catholics are already reaping the benefits of the enriching ministries of women, as pastoral associates and parish life coordinators perform many of the functions of priests and deacons, even though they are not allowed to preside at the Eucharist.

My concern in this chapter is with ministry and leadership in the church today, with particular emphasis on ordination. The first two sections offer a historical perspective. The first takes a brief look at the deliberate choosing of patriarchal order over egalitarian discipleship during the earliest Christian centuries, and the second considers some implications of the Protestant Reformation for the ministry of women in the life of the church. The third section focuses on the contrast between contemporary Baptist and Catholic perspectives on the ordination of women. The final section offers a constructive proposal for the full integration of women in the ministry and leadership of the church, whether Protestant or Catholic.

It is a working assumption of this chapter that women should not replicate the cultural patterns of ministerial authority that have prevailed among men. Rather, women and men as colleagues in church and ministry must weave new cloth together. Otherwise, women simply patch an old garment, which is, in the memorable words of Sandra Schneiders, 'beyond patching.'[1]

Patriarchal Order

Elisabeth Schüssler Fiorenza has contributed the concepts of the '*basileia* vision of Jesus' and the 'discipleship of equals' to scholarly studies of early Christianity and their implications for the lives of women then and now. Her critical feminist hermeneutics has profoundly influenced how we read the scriptural and other texts written in this formative epoch.

Her argument is basically this: Jesus' ministry was a movement of inner renewal within the religious structures and practices of Judaism, of which he was a faithful adherent. He did not envision starting a new religion or overthrowing the old.[2] Jesus' preaching of the *basileia tou theou* – the kingdom, reign, or realm of God – proclaimed a radical 'eschatological reversal,' in which the hopeful words of Mary's canticle would find historical realization: the mighty would be cast down, the rich sent away empty, and those of low estate exalted (Luke 2:52–3). This vision was a prophetic critique of the corrupt hierarchical structures that existed in the society that Jesus knew and at the same time an imaginative construct that opened up the possibility of God's own transforming rule.

The women and men who gathered around Jesus were his disciples, or – to use an English word closer in meaning to the original Greek – his students. With him as their teacher, they were a 'discipleship of equals,' a community of learners, who attempted to live his *basileia* vision. One of their instructions for living was written into Matt. 23:8–10: 'You are not to be addressed by the title "rabbi," for you have one teacher, and you all are learners. And call no one among you by the name "father," for you have one father who is in heaven. Neither are any of you to be called "leader," for you have one leader, the Christ.'

Notice here that Jesus is not likened to a priest.[3] Though he certainly is an intermediary between people and God, reveals the love of God to them, and bears the human face of God for them, the gospels do not present him in priestly terms. Nor is it likely that the historical Jesus accorded a special status to the priestly order within Judaism; rather, he probably viewed it as part of the world that would pass away with the advent of the *basileia*. Thus the famous 'cleansing of the temple' not only has to do with the impropriety of buying and selling in a holy place; it also has to do with a religious structure gone awry. The early Christian community probably remembered this event not simply because it was a judgment on priestly Judaism but because it served as a warning lest the followers of Jesus fall into the same institutional trap as those of Moses.

Contemporary scripture scholars often cite Jesus' inclusion of women as disciples, his defence of them in his public ministry, and ultimately his commissioning of them as primary proclaimers of the resurrection[4] as evidence of the radical equality afforded women in the early Christian community. The male followers of Jesus received the women's announcement of the resurrection as no more than an 'idle tale' (Luke 24:11). Men's record did not appreciably improve in subsequent centuries, when male clergy, claiming to be the successors of the apostles, consistently showed a similar lack of receptivity to the gospel when it was proclaimed by women.

Paul inherited a tradition that had attempted to preserve the egalitarian impulses of the Jesus movement, but he and his more rigid successors allowed subordinating accommodations to creep in and distort the *basileia* vision. Rules that restricted the behaviour of women were promoted in order to 'preserve the fragile Christian community by not destabilizing the fabric of society, thus risking persecution for the embryonic Christian movement.'[5] It is no secret that the church has tended to read these proscriptions as prescriptive for all time rather than as descriptive of an accommodation to political prudence in early Christianity.

Wayne Meeks points to four counterforces in Pauline churches that served to modify the hierarchical structures of Graeco-Roman culture as they began to be erected in Christian communities: the external authority of itinerant apostles and their co-workers (some of whom were women); the charismatic gifts of individuals within local churches (such as the women prophets of I Cor. 11:2–16); anti-hierarchical sentiments inherited from the Jesus tradition and frequently expressed; and the sense of unity among all the Christian 'households' of a single city.[6] To this list we can add the significance of baptism as the new covenantal sign of belonging to the people of God. Perhaps it is not surprising that male theologians have not considered the significance of the displacement of circumcision (with its attendant gender exclusivity in Jewish tradition) in their reflections on baptism.[7]

The consensus of feminist scholarship is that Christianity as presented in the Pauline traditions of the Bible reflects unresolved tensions. A permanent break with the past and divergence from conventional patterns of behaviour did not occur. Some scholars suggest that the more visible any new religious group became in an ancient society, the more its members were pressed to conform to the general norms of 'good behaviour.' Avoiding tensions with the larger community by insisting on conformity to 'good order' by slaves and women (as in the prescriptions of Ephesians, Colossians, and I Peter), early Christians chose patriarchal order over egalitarian discipleship.[8] This cultural adaptation to the structures and institutions of Judaism and Hellenism progressively limited women's role and influence.

As the church became an established social institution, it became increasingly hierarchical. This change reduced charismatic leadership (i.e., people holding positions because of their personal gifts or natural talents), in which women had figured prominently. It also led to a gradual patriarchalization of ministry. Women ministers were limited to serving other women, and the leaders among them could not have normal sexual roles in society – they were required to be widows or virgins.[9]

The strong sense of calling to ministry felt by women was to be suppressed by the bargain that male leaders of the church struck with the surrounding culture. Women continued to form communities, first as recluses devoted to prayer and later as monastic orders parallel to the great orders of men that spread throughout Europe during the Middle Ages. In these communities, women were organizers as well as organized, ministers as well as ministered to, and they offered their gifts in manifold ways to those who came within the monastery walls and to people living in the surrounding area. For many centuries, women religious and their leaders were powerful forces for the living and spreading of Christian faith.

A Partial Reformation

One would suppose that Luther's bold declaration of the 'priesthood of all believers' and the 'freedom of the Christian,' as well as the reformers' insistence on the primacy of Christ, faith, and scripture, would have led the church to rethink the position of women and include them in ministerial leadership. Actually, however, the Protestant Reformation harmed the position of women in Christian society. By closing monasteries and 'liberating' nuns from convents, the reformers denied the good to be found in religious communities, negated the value of contemplative living, and destroyed whatever opportunities medieval women had had for independence, leadership, and control over their own affairs.[10] Perceiving some measure of these consequences, Protestants tried to compensate women by reviving the diaconate for the distribution of alms and for nursing.

In Protestant Europe, men tended to occupy the 'public' sphere of civil and church leadership; women were consigned to the more 'private' domain of *Kinder* (children), *Kuchen* (cooking), and *Kleiden* (clothing). Roland Bainton has argued that the reform had 'greater influence on the family than on the political and economic spheres.' The home thus became 'the area *par excellence* for the exemplification of the gentler Christian virtues.'[11] Though the doctrine of Christian vocation elevated the religious status of the housewife as well as the cobbler, it did nothing for the social status of women or labourers.

Most reformers saw the husband as head of the household, with the wife obedient to him. Putting aside his wonderful insight about the priesthood of all believers, Luther grounded his view of men's dominance in the story of the fall: 'Never any good came out of female domination. God created Adam Master and lord of living creatures, but Eve spoilt it all, when she persuaded him to set himself above God's will. 'Tis you women, with your tricks and artifices, that lead men into error.'[12] Luther also argued for male superiority in the social sphere, based on an analysis of human anatomy: 'Men have broad and large chests, and small narrow hips, and more understanding than the women, who have but small and narrow breasts, and broad hips, to the end they should remain at home, sit still, keep house, and bear and bring up children.'[13] Obviously, Luther's theology was more revolutionary in some areas than in others!

But what about the position of women in the ecclesial sphere? Did the reformers simply extend their vision of domestic relationships to women's role in the church? According to Jane Dempsey Douglass, Calvin followed Luther's teaching on the freedom of the Christian, but he saw many more implications of this doctrine for the life of the church than Luther did. Based on a close reading of his works, Douglass comes to four conclusions about the place of women in Calvin's theology. First, the subordination of women is limited to the realm of human governance; it is not God's eternal decree. Specific injunctions about veils and silence in the church could therefore be adapted to changing circumstances. Second, Calvin acknowledges the ministries of women in teaching, ruling, and prophesying. He is aware that many have not read the scriptures in this manner, but his understanding of Christian freedom maintains that God did use women in this manner (though he prefers a social order in which women are subordinate). Third, wrestling at length with I Cor. 11:7, Calvin affirms that women are also made in the image of God – an idea that this text does not seem to allow. In this signal affirmation, he moves well beyond the Augustinian theological framework that guided so much of his thinking. He does not, however, work out the further implications of this insight. Fourth, Calvin believes that the Bible does not preclude women from holding positions of authority in the church, including preaching, but he is very hesitant to advocate this, for fear of causing social upheaval.[14] Douglass writes: 'Given his concern for the consciences of his brothers, who would indeed be greatly offended by women in authority, and given his own prejudices, he seems generally content to tolerate and perpetuate the social subordination of women both in church and society as a style of decorum approved by the Bible.'[15]

It is fair to say that the new freedom of the Reformation was experienced far less by women than by men, yet the theological resources for the full inclusion of women as ministers are present in the thinking of the reformers.[16] Perhaps the most significant effect of the Reformation for women was the opportunity allowed them to engage in serious study of the Bible. Translations into modern languages and the availability of texts through the printing press spurred educational endeavours. Women relished this new avenue and profited greatly, further equipping themselves to seek full access to the clerical realm. The reformers could not envision the prospect of the ordination of women to ministry. Indeed, the reform they made possible and implicitly set in motion has not yet been fully realized.

Baptists and Catholics

In recent years, (U.S.) Southern Baptists and conservative American Catholics have made common cause on protecting the unborn and on vouchers for parents electing to send their children to Christian or parochial schools. This unexpected alliance has caused consternation on both sides of the historic divide between these traditional enemies. Either side has yet to admit, moreover, that on the ordination of women, they are closer than they realize.

A Southern Baptist Perspective

Representative of Southern Baptist churches is the argument against the ordination of women put forward by Dorothy Kelley Patterson.[17] In her brief article, based on an address that she gave at the Historical Commission of the Southern Baptist Convention, she blisters those women who have left Southern Baptist churches in order to attain pastoral positions in other denominations. This illustrates, in her words, 'a determination to be ruled by emotional and intuitive impulses, i.e., a "call," instead of by the authority of the immutable written Word.' Casting aside the Baptist traditions of freedom of conscience and the autonomy of local congregations, she adds, 'In any case, though the practices of God's people through the years deserve careful attention, tradition, without scriptural authority, is not binding.'[18]

Patterson bases her case on a theological principle and several exegetical examples. Her primary theological evidence is the subordinationist pattern found in the Bible, which she believes is ordained by God: the superiority of God over the covenant people, Israel: of Christ over his bride, the church; and of the husband over the wife in marriage. 'By placing a woman in the teaching/ruling office, the church negates this truth taught by subjection of wives to husbands, i.e., that the church is subject to Christ, thereby destroying the image.'[19]

Those who are familiar with the scriptures can almost anticipate the texts that Patterson claims prevent women from aspiring to pastoral responsibility. She turns first to the 'warning' of I Tim. 2:8–15, stressing verses 11–12: 'Let a woman learn in silence, with all submissiveness. I permit not woman to teach or to have authority over men; she is to keep silent.' Teaching and authority over men are naturally tied to the pastoral office, Patterson argues, and the author of the epistle explicitly forbids it. Any attempt to regard this as other than a 'timeless principle' she rejects as 'hermeneutical gymnastics,' and she avers that order in worship is grounded in the order of creation. She does not apply this principle, however, to any situation other than church or home – for example, school or government or business.

The priority of woman in humanity's fall from grace in the Garden of Eden is inscribed in a resolution of the Southern Baptist Convention.[20] Passed at the 1984 annual meeting, it states that this is the reason for the exclusion of women from ordination as pastors. Patterson echoes this reasoning: 'Paul does not absolve Adam of guilt, but he points to Eve's prior sin, which was not only a violation of the divine command concerning the forbidden fruit but also a reversal of divine order (Gen. 2:15–17).'[21]

She treats I Cor. 14:33–5 in a similar manner. In this passage, Paul lays down a somewhat ambiguous rule for the church at Corinth regarding the role of women at prayer meetings, though he seems to be saying that women should be silent. Patterson takes this as a divine rule for all women in any type of worship service. Divine order is to be preserved; hence women must not presume to be able to teach or rule. Were women to take charge of a worship service, this would be a disruption of orderly worship, which the apostle condemns.

Patterson's conclusion is that the church has never sought to suppress gifts that God has given; rather, God has given gifts to women that can be used with the requisite submission, modesty, and order. She aims her coup de grâce at Baptists who believe that scripture offers clear warrant for the inclusion of women in ministry. Ignoring the dozens, if not hundreds, of stories in Baptist tradition where congregations have split and individuals have dissented over the interpretation of scripture, she writes: 'Nowhere in Baptist history, except perhaps in this generation, has religious freedom come to mean that one can be a Baptist and believe and teach anything he personally desires.'[22] She equates espousing the ordination of women with disavowing the authority of the Bible.

The ordination of women to ministry has come to function as a test case in Southern Baptist life for one's view of the authority of scripture. Persons on both sides of the acrimonious debate claim biblical support.[23] Conservative interpreters find in these texts an apostolic and also a divine prohibition against women serving with equal status in the Body of Christ. They reject any interpretation that limits these statements (often addressing problems in the nascent Christian communities) to the particular social and cultural contexts in which the epistles were written.

The influence of tradition is not significant to Baptists who argue against the ordination of women. They assume that contemporary interpreters go straight back to the text and ignore the long history of scriptural interpretation. Since women traditionally have not occupied positions as official ministers, however, this negative precedent is given authority as 'the faith once delivered,' and it is perceived as divinely directed. That this biased history might reveal the sin of the subjugation of women is unthinkable, and so the majority of congregations remain bound to this patriarchal perspective.

A Catholic Perspective

On 15 October 1976, the Sacred Congregation for the Doctrine of the Faith published, with the approval of Paul VI, a 'Declaration on the

Question of the Admission of Women to the Ministerial Priesthood.' Since this document remains the definitive statement on the subject, it can serve as the basis for a brief overview of the Catholic church's official position.

The declaration opens with an introduction on the role of women in modern society and in the church. Six sections follow, attempting a cumulative argument against women being admitted to the priesthood.

The first section refers to the 'constant tradition,' which always and everywhere in the whole course of Christian history (apart from some heretical sects) indisputably and uniformly excluded women. The fact that the church's magisterium, or authoritative teachers, had never pronounced on the subject did not make women's ordination an open question, however, because the magisterium had simply never intervened to reinforce a principle that had never been questioned.

The second part of the document treats of Christ's attitude towards women. Modern biblical scholarship acknowledges that Jesus was more inclusive of women than was his cultural milieu, and the text notes that he did not call any women to be part of the Twelve. The document describes this exclusion of women as reflecting a deliberate decision by Christ to exclude women from the priestly ministry. Commenting on this section, however, the respected Catholic theologian Karl Rahner writes: 'A purely historical exegesis of the texts of Scripture does not "make the matter immediately obvious."'[24]

The third section contends that even though the apostles had high regard for women and, like Jesus, rose above the social biases of their culture, it did not occur to them to advocate the ordination of women. Faithfulness to the example of Jesus rendered that out of the question. The fourth section extends this interpretation of the historical data and infers that Christ's attitude toward apostolic leadership is normative, excluding women from the priesthood. It ends with a reminder of the teaching that the church has power over the sacraments with regard to their liturgical shape and other outward details, but not over the inner reality or substance of the sacraments.

The fifth and sixth sections consider the priesthood in light of the mystery of Christ and the church. Women cannot be ordained, not because of any inferior status in nature, but because of the sacramental 'mystery.' The historical fact that Jesus was male demands that only another male may represent him in actions wherein the one acting represents Christ. This follows Thomas Aquinas: 'Sacramental signs represent what they signify by natural resemblance.'

Having thus denied the priesthood to women, the Catholic church attempted to affirm the dignity of women in its fold. In August 1988, Pope John Paul II published *Mulieris dignitatem*, an encyclical 'on the dignity and vocation of women on the occasion of the Marian year.' Ostensibly written to eulogize Mary, the Virgin Mother, as the great role model for women, this argument, Jacqueline Field-Bibb suspects, 'is subsidiary to the encyclical's primary function, namely a reiteration of the central argument of the Declaration.'[25]

Somewhat in response to the declaration and American women's dissatisfaction with the social roles that it assigned to them, the U.S. Catholic bishops in 1988 approved a pastoral letter on women. The first draft appeared rather balanced, recognizing the church's traditional affirmation of the rights and dignity of women and acknowledging the historical presence of sexism in the church. Each of the next two drafts toned down any implicit criticism of the church and eliminated language that could possibly be construed as giving women a claim to ordination, probably in response to pressure from the Vatican to bring the letter more in line with the pope's own position. Finally, the fourth draft failed to get the two-thirds' vote necessary for passage. For conservatives it was still too liberal, and for liberals, too conservative.

On 30 May 1994, the anniversary of the burning of St Joan of Arc for witchcraft, John Paul II instructed the world's bishops that there must be 'no more discussion' about female priests. If anything, however, this declaration prompted even more discussion. An 'Open Letter to Pope John Paul II and the U.S. Conference of Catholic Bishops' was drafted and published in November 1994, signed by hundreds of prominent American Catholics.

A Shared Vision

Southern Baptists and Roman Catholics are the two largest U.S. religious groups – the largest U.S. Protestant denomination and the largest U.S. Christian denomination respectively. Throughout their history, they have diametrically opposed one another. Both appeal to authoritative teachers – Baptists, to the Bible, and Catholics, to the Vatican – in prohibiting women from being ordained. Both choose to ignore historical evidence of women functioning as deacons, priests, and bishops.[26] Likewise, both deal selectively with scripture, preferring to focus on the ancillary role of women in service to the church. Further, by exalting motherhood as the chief calling of women, placing a high priority on homemaking and child-rearing, they give scant notice to other areas of women's calling and presume them either unattainable or undesirable.

The Baptist and the Catholic traditions perpetrate a theological anthropology that subordinates women to men. One does it through woman's priority in the fall (a fundamentalist contention); the other, through a notion of essential female inferiority (the teaching of Aristotle and Thomas Aquinas). They also invoke theories of complementarity, asserting that women are 'different but equal,' which allows them to treat the two sexes differently, but in theory honouring both sexes equally. Official statements assume that the relationship of superior to inferior is parallel to that of male to female and that in both relationships the latter is to be in submission to the former. Thus the covenant people, the church, and the wife (all feminine) are to be in submission to God, to Christ, and to the husband.

Leaders of both communions contend that ordaining women to ministry upsets this natural order. Southern Baptists argue that women must not usurp the headship of the male in church or home, for the God-ordained pattern is that of submission for the woman. Catholics claim that in 'the sacrament of holy orders, Christ's headship of the church, his body, is made visible,' and therefore the priest must be male in order to 'resemble' Christ – to function as 'a sacramental symbol of Christ.' This sacramental symbolism relies on 'the natural symbolism of gender to signify the relationship between the priest and Christ, the head and bridegroom of the church.'[27]

Southern Baptists and Roman Catholics, despite their differential treatment of men and women, assert that there is fundamental equality between men and women – either in the sight of God (Baptists) or in their common human nature (Catholics). Very often, however, this assertion conflicts with church practice. The disparity is politely termed an inconsistency between theory and practice; less politely it is called hypocrisy. As one editorial in the *National Catholic Reporter* put it: '"Equality" without ordination defies language and logic.'[28]

Both communions regard open disagreement on this issue as a serious breach of church order. Besides attempting to foreclose any questioning of official pronouncements, they have also taken punitive action against public dissenters – most notably, the dismissal of teachers (primarily women) in both Catholic and Southern Baptist seminaries who have protested their church's position.

They also resist inclusive language for God, lest God not be regarded as patriarchal sovereign. Somewhat more difficult to explain is their resistance to inclusive language for humanity.[29]

A New Garment

As our comparison of Southern Baptists and Roman Catholics reveals, both traditions have been more willing to patch the old garment of patriarchy with meagre attempts at inclusivity than to reweave the fabric of the church's identity. Including women as ordained clergy would call into question their implicit denial that women as well as men bear the image of God.[30] It would thus also question the patriarchal image of God[31] and the hierarchical structures that have buttressed male prerogatives in the Christian community since the first century.

Baptists (including Southern Baptists) who disagree with the Southern Baptist Convention argue that welcoming women into church leadership would affirm be faithful to important dimensions of the Baptist tradition. Baptists have historically celebrated freedom of conscience (sometimes called 'soul freedom') as essential to voluntary faith. According to Baptist tradition, any Christian's religious experience is not to be denied by another Christian. Each person has the freedom, ability, and responsibility to respond to God for herself or himself. Therefore, if one of the church's daughters declares that God has called her to the ministry, the validity of her calling should be taken as seriously as that of any male candidate. Rather than being denied, her call from God should be tested within the Body of Christ by seeing whether she is invited to serve a congregation and then by determining how well she does in that position.

Those who invoke the Baptist tradition against the policy of male-only clergy also point to the Reformation tradition of the priesthood of all believers, to which Baptists have always subscribed. If in past eras this doctrine served to moderate exalted notions of ministerial authority, in this day it can temper inflated ideas of male authority. No less than people in other communions, Baptists have copied secular paradigms of authority rather than creating new models based on the life and ministry of Jesus. Baptist critics point out that the particular cultural captivity of their denomination has been to think of churches as modern corporate structures rather than as the communities of equals described in the New Testament. Congregations have sought leaders with the qualities of corporate managers rather than those of disciples and shepherds. Furthermore, just as women have been kept out of power in government and business for not having male leadership styles, women have been kept out of church leadership for not having 'ruling authority.' Reclaiming the teaching that all Christians are priests to each other could raise up a paradigm of leadership that corresponds better to scriptural teaching and thereby invites women as well as men to be shepherds of flocks.

Baptists historically have encouraged what Walter Shurden calls 'Bible freedom'[32] – the principle that people have a right to interpret the scriptures in different, even opposing, ways. Though the principle applies primarily to the local church, allowing congregations to decide for themselves how they will organize themselves, how they will worship, and what they will believe, it applies also to the individual, guaranteeing liberty of conscience and freedom from doctrinal coercion. Historically minded Baptists find it somewhat ironic that the majority of Baptists today are leaning so far in the direction of fundamentalism that their tradition of Bible freedom is becoming lost. Those who oppose the ordination of women refuse to acknowledge the right of local congregations to think differently and remain within the Southern Baptist Convention.

Baptists who are aware of contemporary biblical scholarship know too that the texts that pertain to women's roles in ministry have historically been used to support men's biases. Moreover, they acknowledge the culturally androcentric character of scripture: it is 'patriarchal in its assumptions and often in its explicit teachings, and at times, deeply sexist, i.e., anti-woman.'[33] They also know, however, that the same scriptural corpus to which conservatives appeal contains the liberative resources to address the exclusion of women from ordained ministry. These Baptists argue with the current practice of denominational conformity in the hope that a more careful and critical reading of the scriptures can help reverse centuries of prejudice against women.

In the same way that progressive Baptists have been using their tradition against resistance to change, liberal Catholics have harnessed resources in their own tradition against reactionary tendencies in their church. They insist that they are good Catholics even if they do not agree with the church's insistence on ordination for men only, pointing to times in the past when new ideas were first condemned and later embraced by the hierarchy. They want to continue the church renewal begun by the Second Vatican Council in the 1960s. They suggest that this updating – which has already revitalized the liturgy, improved ecumenical relations, re-emphasized the Bible, and increased lay participation in ministry – ought to move forward and allow women to be priests. As Schüssler Fiorenza noted, 'The ecclesiology of Vatican II has reaffirmed the New Testament teaching on the election, sanctity, and priesthood of all the faithful.'[34] These are the same biblical themes to which progressive Baptists appeal. Even as cautious a theologian as Karl Rahner advised further study of women's ordination after the promulgation of the declaration discussed above.[35]

Most vocal are the feminist theologians who continue to work within the Roman Catholic tradition while articulating the propriety of ordaining women. They point out that Jesus' selection of twelve male apostles can be explained by the cultural milieu in which he lived and in which the canonical gospels were written, and they argue that this selection therefore has no normative significance for all time. They remind the church of its history of prejudice against women, and they prophetically call its hierarchy to a radical conversion and repentance for the sin of sexism. They insist that women, as baptized and confirmed members of the church, are called to ministry and to exercise the charisms that God has given them, even the charism of leadership in the ecclesial community.[36]

Conclusion

In their own ways, both the Baptist and the Catholic communities are struggling with gender issues that transcend their own doctrinal beliefs and ordination policies. Clearly a divine prohibition against women's ministry is not self-evident in the scriptures, because the two communions appeal to different biblical texts to buttress their essentially similar practices. Even the fact that ordination means quite different things for Baptists and Catholics – confirmation of a divine call on the one hand and elevation to a priestly order on the other – suggests that the root issue is not ordination but men's reluctance to surrender power or position to women. None the less, ordination remains symbolic of much that is going on beneath the surface.

For this reason, the ordination of women is perhaps the most politicized issue in North American Christianity today. Getting beyond the politics of gender will require a journey of conversion not only for Southern Baptists and Roman Catholics but also for all the churches that maintain the practice of sex discrimination in ministry. They will have to confess that they have wronged women in believing them to be inferior and in failing to treat them with equality. They will have to repent of their reluctance to embrace the *basileia* vision of Jesus, and they will have to acknowledge their error in adopting instead the cultural vision of patriarchy. They will have to reject theological and institutional frameworks that perpetuate discrimination and prejudice against women. They will have to rethink their language and symbolism for God, so that women can readily be seen as appropriate embodiments of the representative functions of ministry. Above all, the male ministers in these churches will have to relinquish their exclusive hold on structural power and begin to share it freely with female colleagues in ministry.

This revolution has been a long time coming, but the history of Christianity suggests that the energy behind it is not merely the aspiration of women but the Spirit of God moving humanity towards the *basileia* announced by Jesus.

NOTES

1 See the insightful work by Sandra M. Schneiders, *Beyond Patching: Faith and Feminism in the Catholic Church* (New York: Paulist Press, 1991). Her thesis is that wholehearted renewal is necessary for the church to retain any credible claim on women, given the history of morally unacceptable treatment they have received.
2 See Elisabeth Schüssler Fiorenza, *In Memory of Her* (New York: Crossroad, 1983). A similar argument is put forward by Marcus Borg, though without the focus on the impact of his movement on the lives of women. See his *Jesus: A New Vision: Spirit, Culture, and the Life of Discipleship* (San Francisco: Harper and Row, 1987). Cf. his *Conflict, Holiness and Politics in the Teaching of Jesus* (New York: Edwin Mellen Press, 1984).
3 Elisabeth Schüssler Fiorenza, 'The First Women's Ordination Conference,' *Discipleship of Equals* (New York: Crossroad, 1993) 85: 'Whereas the various New Testament authors do not understand Christian leadership in a cultic sense and therefore apply the title "priest" only to Christ and to all Christians, the second and third century documents begin at first to liken Christian ministry to that of the Old Testament or Hellenistic priesthood and than to gradually identify Christian leadership with the hierarchical priesthood and cultic sacrifices of Jewish and Greco-Roman religion.'
4 Calvin intimated that Jesus revealed his resurrection first only to the women because the men had fled, and this disclosure was meant as a punishment to the latter. God deigns to choose the weak things of the world in order to humiliate the loftiness of the flesh, Calvin suggests. See the treatment by Jane Dempsey Douglass, *Women, Freedom, and Calvin* (Philadelphia: Westminster Press, 1985), 58.

5 Pheme Perkins, 'Women in the Bible and Its World,' *Interpretation*, vol. 42, no. 1 (1988), 37.
6 Wayne Meeks, *First Urban Christians* (New Haven, Conn.: Yale University Press, 1983), 23–5, 75–7.
7 Women and men share equally in baptismal identity as 'one in Christ Jesus' (Gal. 3:28). 'Putting on Christ' (Rom. 13:14) and being 'clothed ... with Christ' (Col. 3:10) echo this liberative pronouncement. This understanding of baptism conferred new status on women and transformed the behaviour of both women and men in the church, greatly enriching early Christianity.
8 See Schüssler Fiorenza, *In Memory of Her*, 251–70.
9 Schüssler Fiorenza, *Discipleship of Equals*, 86.
10 See Molly T. Marshall-Green and E. Glenn Hinson, 'The Contribution of Women to Spirituality,' in Bill J. Leonard, ed., *Becoming Christian: Dimensions of Spiritual Formation* (Louisville, Ky.: Westminster/John Knox, 1990), 116–30.
11 Roland H. Bainton, *Women of the Reformation* (Minneapolis, Minn.: Augsburg Publishing House, 1971), 9.
12 *Table Talk of Luther*, trans. and ed. William Hazlitt (London: William Clowes and Sons, 1890), 300.
13 Ibid.
14 Jane Dempsey Douglass, *Women, Freedom, and Calvin* (Philadelphia: Westminster Press, 1985), 62–3.
15 Ibid., 63.
16 Douglass notes that Calvin was the sole reformer who put women's role in the church under the category of 'things indifferent' – about which there can be judicious difference of opinion and also something that can change. Usually people have appealed to Calvin for support of their view of the exclusion of women to ministry; Douglass suggests that actually he is more of an ally for women's cause (9).

   The left wing of the Reformation did not at first offer its women any more concrete freedom in the expression of their ministries. It did provide more opportunity for its members in principle, however, because of its dissenting tradition and because it refused to emulate the hierarchical leadership patterns of other churches. It also resisted aligning itself with civil government; Baptists, for example, insisted on separation of church and state.
17 Patterson, 'Why I Believe Southern Baptist Churches Should Not Ordain Women,' *Baptist History and Heritage*, 23, no. 3 (July 1988), 56–62.
18 Ibid., 57.
19 Ibid., 58.

20 *Proceedings,* Southern Baptist Convention, Kansas City, Mo., 12–14 June 1984, 65.
21 Patterson, 'Why I Believe,' 60.
22 Ibid., 61.
23 Not all Southern Baptists share Patterson's view. In the same issue of the journal, an article by Jann Aldredge-Clanton argued that Southern Baptist churches should ordain women. She is a member of the disaffected moderate wing of this body, aligned with the Baptist Alliance and the Cooperative Baptist Fellowship, both on record as supporting the ordination of women.
24 Karl Rahner, *Concern for the Church,* Theological Investigations XX, trans. Edward Quinn (New York: Crossroad, 1981), 36.
25 Jacqueline Field-Bibb, *Women towards Priesthood: Ministerial Politics and Feminist Praxis* (Cambridge: Cambridge University Press, 1991), 193.
26 See 'An Open Letter to Pope John Paul II and the U.S. Conference of Catholic Bishops,' *National Catholic Reporter,* 31, no. 3 (4 Nov. 1994), 12. See also Karen Jo Torjensen, *When Women Were Priests: Women's Leadership in the Early Church and the Scandal of Their Subordination in the Rise of Christianity* (New York: Harper, 1993).
27 Quotations from 'One in Christ Jesus,' fourth draft of the pastoral letter on women's concerns, Nov. 1992.
28 Ibid.
29 *National Catholic Reporter,* 31, no. 3 (4 Nov. 1994), 24: 'Instead of moving forward in efforts to deal with women, the church appears to be moving backward. Just last week the Vatican rejected the [New Revised Standard Version] for use in liturgical and catechetical texts – already approved by the U.S. bishops in 1991. Why? For its use of inclusive language!'
30 Kari Elisabeth Borresen, 'The Ordination of Women: To Nurture Tradition by Continuing Inculturation,' *Studia Theologica,* 46 (1992), 3–13, contends that women's ordination to the priesthood is a test case for the recognition of women's full human likeness to God.
31 The most significant attempt to correct Christianity's penchant for masculine imagery for God is Elizabeth A. Johnson's award-winning *She Who Is: The Mystery of God in Feminist Theological Discourse* (New York: Crossroad, 1992).
32 See his helpful work, *The Baptist Identity: Four Fragile Freedoms* (Macon, Ga.: Smyth and Helwys, 1993).
33 Schneiders, *Beyond Patching,* 38.
34 Elisabeth Schüssler Fiorenza, 'Should Women Aim for Ordination to the Lowest Rung?' In *Discipleship of Equals* (New York: Crossroad, 1993), 33.
35 Rahner, *Concern,* 45.
36 Sandra Schneiders describes the active protest of feminist Catholics as 'pour-

ing immense energy into the reform of life in the grassroots communities of the church. They are refusing to tolerate gender exclusive language in daily discourse or liturgical celebration; they are taking effective action, sometimes even legal action, to protect their rights against clerical privilege and the arbitrary use of hierarchical power; they are changing the dominative procedures of the ecclesiastical workplace in the direction of feminist models of cooperation and participation; they are building alternative models of religious community' (*Beyond Patching*, 102).

10

Understanding the Dynamics of Gender Roles: Towards the Abolition of Sexism in Christianity

PIERRE HÉGY AND JOSEPH MARTOS

As was noted in the first chapter of this book, gender roles are appropriate and nondiscriminatory if they are based on sex-related physical attributes (such as the ability to father or mother offspring) and if they result in a balance of status and power between males and females (that is, the gender roles of one group do not automatically give it higher status or more power than the other group). In a just society, any other distribution of gender roles is inappropriate and discriminatory, that is, unfair and unjust. Today, the unjust assignment of higher-status and higher-power roles to one gender (and, conversely, the assignment of lower-status and lower-power roles to the other gender) is understood sociologically as sexual discrimination, or sexism. In the context of the Christian religion, it is becoming increasingly common to regard sexism as sinful and contrary to the will of God.

At the same time, there do not appear to be any roles in a Christian community that are justly assignable purely on the basis of sex, that is, on the basis of a person's having either male or female genitalia, musculature, or other sex-related characteristics. For this reason, any assignment of gender roles in Christianity is on the face of it an instance of sexism. The fact that gender-based roles have existed throughout the history of Christianity is therefore taken as evidence that sexism has been a perennial part of social and ecclesiastical practice rather than as evidence that God wants some roles to be reserved to men and other roles to be reserved to women. Though individuals and organizations (including churches and denominations) may argue on biblical or historical grounds for the appropriateness of gender roles (such as family headship and ordained ministry),[1] the working assumption of this volume has been that all such arguments are erroneous and that all justifications of gender roles in Christianity are inherently rationalizations of various forms of sexism. It is therefore not in the purview of this chapter to offer a critique of particular arguments in favour of gender roles in the Christian community.[2]

This concluding chapter instead looks at the organizational structures of churches and denominations in so far as they exhibit signs of sexism or patriarchy (culturally institutionalized sexism) and asks what Christian community might look like if it were free of sexism. This type of analysis could be undertaken from a number of different perspectives, but here we limit ourselves to that of family systems theory.

Family Systems and Social Fusion

For Murray Bowen, the creator of family systems theory, the fundamental human social unit is not the dyad, or the one-to-one relationship, but the triad, or triangular relationship. One reason is that dyads invariably perceive themselves as dyads in relationship to some third element, which is thus essential for defining the dyadic relationship itself. For example, siblings can understand themselves as siblings only in relationship to parents. A seemingly horizontal relationship between two individuals is actually two corners of a triangular relationship, in which the third corner is something outside the individuals themselves. Another reason for the primacy of the triad is that 'the triangle between self and parents ... is the most important primary triangle in life, and the one in which a person develops the triangle relationship patterns that remain relatively fixed in all relationships.'[3] Thus families are multigenerational social systems that remain stable because they consist of interlocking triangles: mother and father with their child, adult child and spouse with their child, and so on.

For Bowen, emotional triangles are created by psychological dependence rather than by objective relational status. From this perspective, triangles are emotional prisons from which one must 'detriangle' in order to achieve autonomy. As long as one's sense of self is defined in terms of one's relationship to one's parents, for example, one is not yet a psychologically autonomous individual. A person who fails to differentiate himself or herself from his or her parents remains bound or tied to them; the feeling of closeness is based on psychological or emotional fusion.

Bowen saw psychological fusion or excessive closeness among humans as analogous to physical fusion among micro-organisms.

Research published in 1970 indicated that when organisms without an immune system come into contact with one another, they fuse and lose their separate identities. Moreover, when they are brought close to one another (but not into contact), the smaller one often disintegrates without any observable action on the part of the larger one. This suggested to Bowen that without something like an immune system to protect itself, any organism, regardless of its size, will tend to lose its independent existence. In more general terms, 'whenever you increase togetherness without also increasing self-differentiation, you run the risk of losing that togetherness through the autodestruction of one of the partners.'[4]

Bowen observed that in most traditional marriage systems (ones that we would today classify as patriarchal) a woman lost her independent identity and was socially fused into her husband. She renounced her family (maiden) name, became identified as Mrs So-and-so, surrendered all ownership rights, and became a legal minor, incapable of entering into contracts without her husband's permission. Traditional marriage was thus a form of autodestruction for the woman.

In a state of fusion, individuals such as parents tend to 'triangle in' their children. Fused parents create a 'parental we-ness,' presenting a unified front to their children, who in response are not able to differentiate between the beliefs and values of their mother and those of their father. They see their parents as thinking and feeling the same thing.[5] Moreover, fused parents foster fused children. Children are emotionally coerced into identifying with their parents, and they experience disagreement as betrayal or rebellion, in no small part because their parents tell them that disagreement with them is wrong.

Expanding on this model, we can use the concept of fusion to explain the relationship between individuals of different status or power who are in close proximity to one another. It is possible to distinguish three types of fusion: *psychological*, which was studied by Bowen; *emotional*, which is closely related to it, and *intellectual*, which is more distantly related to it.

Psychological fusion occurs when weaker individuals derive their sense of identity from their relationship to others or, conversely, when stronger individuals see others as extensions of themselves. Patriarchal and matriarchal heads of families practise psychological fusion when they perceive family members not as autonomous individuals but as representatives of the family. All must behave in ways that make the family look good, and no one is allowed to do anything that would bring disgrace to the family. In turn, family members practise such fusion when they derive their identity and self-worth from their parent or parents, from the family tradition, or from the extended family. Though a certain amount of such fusion is normal and necessary in young children, it becomes pathological when older and adult children remain heavily dependent on others for their sense of identity and personal value. Psychological fusion is found in authoritarian-submissive relationships even outside the family – for instance, in relationships between employers and employees and between military superiors and subordinates, in apprenticeships, and in friendships between unequals.

Emotional fusion results from psychological fusion. It occurs when a weaker individual identifies with the emotions of the stronger one as if these emotions were his or her own, as when a submissive wife denies her own feelings and follows her husband's lead in reacting to situations; when children adopt their parents' likes and dislikes, biases and prejudices; and when teenagers adopt as their own the preferences of their peers. Emotional fusion also takes place when a stronger individual projects his or her emotions into others and does not see the others as having their own feelings, as when a husband assumes that his wife feels about things the way he does, or when a mother expects her children to like and dislike what she likes and dislikes. Emotional fusion at the organizational or societal level occurs when leaders assume that their feelings are shared by all their followers and when followers feel what they believe they are supposed to feel rather than what they would feel if they were free to experience their own autonomous emotions.

In *intellectual fusion* a person embraces the ideas of another without any attempt at critical examination, as when children uncritically accept the prejudices of their parents, or when cult members blindly accept the pronouncements of their leaders. Intellectual fusion can also be an extension of psychological fusion on the part of higher-status individuals who expect those with lower status to think as they do, whether in the family, in political or business organizations, or in churches or religious organizations. When blind obedience is a virtue, intellectual fusion usually lies behind it. Political and economic 'hard line' attitudes often betray an unhealthy dose of intellectual fusion, as does religious fundamentalism.

Fusion, Triangles, and Gender Roles

The traditional gender roles of the so-called traditional family, prevalent since the Industrial Revolution, can be understood in terms of fusion and triangling. Men and women both practised intellectual fusion with the prevailing social order, uncritically accepting the existence of and the norms of socially dictated expectations for men and women, but the result was different for the two sexes. On the male side, the dominant fusion was between the father and his work, which defined who he was. Male identity also derived from psychological and intellectual fusion with family ancestry, ethnic tradition, or national heritage. As a consequence, the husband triangled in his wife and children, in practice denying them an existence or meaning separate from his. On the female side, the dominant fusion was between the wife and the children, who, when they arrived, defined her as mother. Female identity also derived from fusion with the husband, as she socially surrendered her separate identity and denied (in public if not always in private) her own thoughts and feelings. The mother subsequently triangled in members of the extended family (in-laws, grandchildren, and so on), encouraging them to identify with the family through the practice of its traditions. Children, both male and female, were expected to fuse first with their parents, then with the role model offered by the same-sex parent, and so the pattern continued from generation to generation.

In traditional families there was little closeness between husband and wife, who often felt like strangers to one another, even though there may have been intense fusion between mother and children and between father and work or profession. The intellectual fusion of women with their husband was fostered by exclusion from formal education and from the political process. Psychological fusion was facilitated by the loss of the last name at marriage and subservience to either father or husband. Emotional fusion was encouraged among mother, children, and the extended family. Because the daughters left home only to marry (and if they did not marry, they did not leave home), they remained close to their mother and relatives. When they did marry, they extended the fused family through the addition of children, numerous in traditional families. Family loyalty and closeness, which both nurtured and resulted from fusion, were highly valued.

The parents' fusion with the prevailing social order made the transmission of traditional gender roles not only possible but necessary, though it was primarily through the husband that the wife and children identified with the larger society. The husband had to identify with the prevailing order if he hoped to succeed. By internalizing the values of the existing order, he fused with it, and in patriarchal cultures male dominance had a high value. The more authoritarian the values that the husband internalized, the more authoritarian he became at home. Thus the social inequality of patriarchal culture was replicated in the home and so passed on from generation to generation.

Gender roles still play an important role in the experience of emotional closeness or distance between spouses. The more they identify with traditional gender roles, the more they tend to feel like strangers to one another, even though they also experience a certain intimacy with one another.[6] Since the wife values emotional closeness and sometimes expects from the husband more than he is able to provide, the asymmetry between the spouses can create a constant dynamic of distance and closeness. When the wife seeks closeness, the husband may shy away; when she then seeks closeness with friends and children, the distanced husband may want greater closeness, but he may also be unskilled in achieving it, mistaking sexual for emotional intimacy.[7]

The dynamic of distance and closeness, when it is present, can affect all third corners, be they work, political and social involvement, religion, friends, relatives, or children. Moreover, it is through the mother's relation with the children that gender roles and the ambivalence of closeness and distance pass from one generation to the next. By treating them differently, the mother imparts different roles and expectations to her son and her daughter. The closer the mother is to either child, the more distant in the child's mind the father appears to be. In today's society, adolescents often repeat this type of triangle, only now they often fuse with their peers and distance themselves from their parents. Because the inherent inequalities of traditional gender roles are found in the marriage relationship itself, gender differences and inequalities are transmitted through the emotional core of the family, along with gender identity.

Romantic Fusion and Peer Relationships

One reaction to the traditional social order and distance between the spouses is romantic love. Though not unknown in earlier ages (for example, Héloise and Abélard in the Middle Ages, Romeo and Juliet in the Renaissance), romantic love did not become an ideal until the nineteenth century (the so-called Romantic period in literature), and it did not become a widespread social phenomenon until the twentieth century. Initiated among the upper classes, in which young people could pursue literary ideals in their choice of love life, it eventually found its

Towards the Abolition of Sexism in Christianity 187

way to all strata of society that were and still are affected by the mass media of print, film, radio, and television, which portray 'falling in love' as the apex of male–female interrelatedness.[8]

Romantic fusion is often the first stage of romantic love – the 'I can't live without you' stage, experientially identical to what is popularly called a crush or infatuation. Mutual lovers can be emotionally and even intellectually enmeshed in one another. Romantic fusion or infatuation is most common among adolescents; among adults, the falling-in-love stage is often brief. The psychological process involved has been explained in Jungian terms as discovering an image of oneself in the other, and in Freudian terms, as lowering the ego boundaries between the self and the other.[9] People in this stage of romantic love spend days and nights in mutual admiration, narcissistically contemplating their other half, and feeling emotionally whole. They live in a world of dreams and hopes, with fairy tales and romantic myths, with movie images and song lyrics. Through romantic fusion they seem to have achieved equality, at least temporarily.

This feeling of equality, however, is an illusion that lasts only as long as the experience of infatuation itself, which is never very lengthy. As described by Bowen and documented by Marks, 'one partner typically gravitates to the full-time position of leader and definer.'[10] Traditionally this dominant partner is the male, but because two people are in love, this seems fine to both of them. She feels that she has the right to disagree with his decisions, but typically she does not exercise it, and in the end he provides her definition of herself. Romantic involvement thus leads women to psychological fusion (lack of individual boundaries), intellectual fusion (absence of critical mindedness), subservience (diminishment of self-worth), and even codependence (enabling the destructive behaviour of the partner).[11] Under the spell of apparent emotional equality, social inequality may seem natural, even mutually beneficial. None the less, when romantic fusion has run its course, lovers are likely to find that they have taken on quite traditional gender roles that contradict their early sense of equality.

A more healthy way out of traditional gender roles is self-differentiation or disentangling oneself (in Bowan's terms, detriangling) from the persons or social realities with which one has become fused. If fusion, simply understood, has psychological, emotional, and intellectual dimensions, differentiation necessarily entails these same three dimensions. Through psychological differentiation, one distances oneself from one's family of origin, from those social and political organizations (nationality, country, church, and so on) that earlier provided an identity through psychological fusion, and from any person with whom one is currently fused. Through emotional differentiation, one learns to get in touch with one's own feelings and to experience consciously these feelings rather than the emotions that one has been taught are appropriate to one's sex, one's background, one's position, and so on. Through intellectual differentiation, one examines the premises of ideas and values that one has been taught, retains those that stand the test of critical scrutiny, and rejects those that are shown to be groundless prejudices and biases. One learns to think one's own thoughts rather than the thoughts of others.

There is no simple and easy method of overcoming fusion and achieving self-differentiation. Moving out of one's parents' home is part of it, and for many people today higher education contributes to this process. Self-education is also important because schooling is often specialized and work-related rather than consciousness raising. Reading helps overcome fusion to the values and images presented by television and radio, and deliberately broadening the range of one's personal experience helps overcome the biases of reading. Assertiveness training and other ways of developing communication skills enable one to take personal stands rooted in self-awareness and critical thinking rather than in reaction to what others think. By taking conscious possession of one's feelings, ideas, and values, one becomes less fused with one's environment and more one's own person. The process can be painful, however, because the fused family, group, or partner often sees emotional distanciation and respectful dissent as disloyalty, disobedience, even betrayal.

If self-differentiation is needed to overcome social fusion, a redefinition of marriage is needed to support individuals who do not subscribe to the gender roles of patriarchal culture and the traditional social order. Experimentation with different styles of marriage began during the 1960s and 1970s, and since the 1980s many of these styles have been gathered under the headings of non-traditional, companionate, and egalitarian marriage. More recently, Pepper Schwartz has proposed the term 'peer marriage' to designate a unique and purposeful style of equality in marriage.[12]

According to Schwartz, the two major causes of inequality in marriage are income and child care. As noted in chapter 1 above, in prehistoric times tribal cultures accorded different roles and often greater privileges to males who provided meat from the hunt than they did to females who bore and raised the young. This division of labour and its concomitant sexual discrimination endured in traditional marriage and family structures, in which the male's gender role was that of provider, and the female's that of nurturer. Schwartz argues that it is not the husband's income as such (today still statistically higher than that of the wife) which creates inequality in marriage, but the traditional provider role, which requires that the breadwinner subordinate everything (including wife and family) to work, and today to career and advancement. In traditional marriage, 'If the man is financially successful, the wife gives up all previous demands on his time and cooperation and releases him to as much success as he can provide.'[13] Likewise, it is not child care itself that creates gender inequality, but the necessary confinement of mothers to the home when they are cast in the gender role of nurturers while at the same time the non-confinement of fathers leaves men free to increase their status through the accumulation of wealth and the exercise of power. This endurance of the social roles of breadwinner and nurturer helps account for the statistic that in the United States today, married women spend on average nineteen hours more per week on housework than do their husbands, even though the majority of women also work outside the home.[14]

The concept of peer marriage entails the notion that women and men enter into the relationship essentially as peers, free from gender roles and social stereotyping. Both the husband and the wife contribute to the family income because work outside the home is personally as well as financially rewarding. Similarly, both raise the children, because of the benefits of shared nurturing to spouses and children alike. Traditional gender roles in marriage give way to spouses contributing more or less equally to the quality of the marriage and family relationship.

Note the emphasis on the quality of the relationship, not on the material quality of life. Peer marriage represents a radical change from traditional marriage, because the ultimate purpose of income is not material benefit but personal and relational enhancement. Similarly, the ultimate purpose of child-rearing is not social indoctrination but relationship building and, to use Virginia Satir's memorable word, 'peoplemaking.' 'Peer couples are evaluating marriage according to the quality and type of time spent together; they are reinterpreting marriage.'[15] When both partners value marriage above economic success, and when family nurturing is also a shared value, this situation alters the reality of marriage and creates a potential for the transformation of society, because gender roles are not transmitted from one generation to the next.

The need for something like peer marriage may be a byproduct of the growing necessity for two incomes to support a household, plus the recognition that full-time employment is incompatible with full-time homemaking. Its desirability also probably springs from the increased desire of women and men alike to actualize their full human potential, not just their gender-related possibilities. Peer relationships are compatible with the political ideals of democracy and equality, though often not with other beliefs and values connected with society, family, and religion. For example, Western society perpetuates male and female stereotypes through biased media images and job opportunities, virtually all families are organized around traditional gender roles to a greater or lesser extent, and most branches of the world's religions either teach that sex roles are divinely ordained or act as though they were. At the same time, however, the New Testament seems to lay the groundwork for a community based on peer relationships rather than on relationships defined by sex or gender.

The Bible and Relationships

It is clear from what has been said above in this volume that the Judaeo-Christian scriptures arose out of and have been used to support patriarchal social traditions. At the same time, there is ample evidence that Jesus himself envisioned life under the reign of God as a community of equals.[16] As the early Paul wrote, 'In Christ there is neither Jew nor Greek, slave nor free, male nor female' (Gal. 3:28). In this closing chapter, however, it is appropriate to compare the dynamics of patriarchal society and of peer community in terms of fusion and differentiation in order to argue for the abolition of sexism in Christianity.

Primeval Fusion and the Differentiated Serpent

Both accounts of creation in Genesis open with a scene in which nothing in the world is differentiated from anything else: all is either chaos or desert (1:2; 2:5). God (Elohim in the first account, Yahweh in the second) appears differentiated from the world, but since the world's elements obey God without question, it can be asked whether the world is differentiated from God. Certainly the world does not have a will of its own; it and all its elements immediately obey the divine will. From the opening scene through the unfolding process of creation in either the first or second account, immediate and automatic response to God's will is presented as an unmitigated good (1:31; 2:16–17). Should humans also respond to God's will as if they had no conscience of their own? The Yahwist account of Genesis 2 and 3 implies an answer.

Initially, male and female are not differentiated, for the Hebrew name *Adam* (from *adamah*, ground) means human, not male. Even when God makes a partner for the originally undifferentiated human, the woman is formed from part of the original (at this point in the story, presumably male) human's body, leading Adam to exclaim, 'This at last is bone of my bone and flesh of my flesh' (2:23). They feel no shame, even though they are naked (2:24), just as young children, who are not reflexively aware of sexuality, feel nothing odd about playing together undressed. At this stage, Adam and Eve are in volitional fusion with God, and they are in psychological fusion with one another. This, according to the Bible, is paradise.

Enter the serpent. Though one of God's creatures (3.1), the serpent is obviously differentiated from God, for he does not take God's word as law and tempts Eve to eat the forbidden fruit. Eve is naïve, intellectually fused with God's will ('We may not eat of it, lest we die'). She has no critical awareness of the reason behind the command, and so she is easily duped. She temporarily fuses with the serpent and sees things his way, and she quickly triangles in Adam. Adam, equally naïve, is also easily duped. When they eat the fruit and do not die (as God had said they would), their 'eyes are opened.' They realize that there is a difference between what they heard God say and the way things happened and that there is a difference between what God told them to do and what they actually did. When differentiation enters, the paradise of fusion is in trouble. Adam and Eve notice that they are naked, so they make clothing out of fig leaves for themselves. Aware of their disobedience, they are now ashamed of what they have done, and so they hide from God, acting out their sudden differentiation from him (3:6–7).

Enter Yahweh, who is not at all pleased (anthropomorphically speaking) that his human creatures are no longer in unison with his will. Adam at this point is differentiated enough from Eve to blame her for his eating the forbidden fruit, and Eve bears the same relationship to the serpent, but neither is intellectually capable of critically examining either God's command or their behaviour: they accept that their behaviour was wrong simply because it was against God's will (3:11–13). For their disobedience, they are banished from the garden of Eden, which symbolically confirms the loss of original naïveté they have already begun to feel, for they have been heading out of paradise ever since they relinquished naïve fusion with God. Nevertheless, they remain fused to some extent, for they believe without question the curses that Yahweh heaps on them and live their lives according to his dictates (3:16–19).

The Cycle of Unequal Relationships

The next major story in Genesis is that of Noah and the Great Flood, which, from the perspective of family systems theory, is a reprise on the story of the first parents. The assumption of the story (and a fortiori, of the storyteller) is that human beings are supposed to be so attuned to God that they need not have a mind of their own. Those who disobey God's will are characterized as behaving 'wickedly' (6:5–7). Noah, however, finds favour with God because he 'walks with God' – that is, he does what God wants without question. For his intellectual fusion with God, Noah is rewarded, as is his entire family, which is not socially differentiated from him. Yahweh, for his part, does not differentiate between wicked human beings and other living beings, for all are drowned except the animals in the ark. No subtlety of thought appears here: all the people outside the ark are wicked. Similarly, the animals inside the ark fully share the blessing of Noah's goodness. The moral of the tale, in psychological terms, is fuse with God and be saved, or act differently and be damned.

Though the cycle of stories about the patriarchs (Abraham, Isaac, and Jacob) are usually thought of in terms of faith, they can also be read as stories of fusion. They are national epics, told and preserved in order to inspire faith of heroic proportions, and they are therefore exaggerated. The very exaggerations, however, tend to turn what might otherwise be considered as thoughtful obedience into thoughtless fusion.[17]

In each of the stories, the patriarch is to a greater or lesser extent fused with God – that is, he accepts God's will as his own. Abraham surrenders his mind so totally that he is willing to kill his own son, and this behaviour in the Bible is accounted as great virtue. Jacob wrestles with God, not knowing against whom he is striving, but on the whole he is law abiding, and, most important, he maintains Abraham's promise to obey only one God. In return for their intellectual and volitional fusion with Yahweh, the patriarchs receive power over others: they are masters over their households of wives, cattle, sheep, and other possessions.

The third corner of the patriarch–God relationship is thus the household, which is entirely subservient. With God on his side (that is, with God and the patriarch as two sides of the triangle), the patriarch has a direct line to God, which no one else has. This direct connection to God therefore means that whatever else might become the third corner (a foreign ruler, a drought, and so on), it is no match for the patriarch. The patriarch may not realize it at the time (for example, when Jacob loses his son, Joseph, or later, when Joseph himself is thrown in prison), but the patriarch always has more power than any other character in the story.

The sagas of the patriarchs are matched in their relationship dynamics by the stories of the proto-history of Israel from the Exodus to the conquest of the promised land. Always the relationships are unequal: the person with God on his side is always the person with power. Moreover, since that person is always male, men in the Bible always have more power than women.[18] Thus Moses triumphs over the armies of the Pharaoh, Joshua defeats the Canaanites, David slays Goliath, and so on. The key to this power is always partial or total fusion with God – uncritical obedience to God's will. God is all knowing, and so the person who intellectually fuses with God shares God's knowledge. Moses ascends Mount Sinai and is wrapped with God in smoke and fire as he receives the law (Ex. 19:16–19), and he descends with the commandments that tell people how they too can be fused with God by surrendering their will to his (20:1–23). In this way the Israelites become a chosen people, different from all others.

The Hebrew Bible is a continuous cycle of uneven relationships not only between men and women but also between prominent men and other men, armies, cities, and forces of nature. Even the covenants entered into between Yahweh and Noah, between Yahweh and Abraham, and between Yahweh and Moses are technically covenants between unequals.[19] When kings such as David and Solomon are fused with God in understanding and will, they are undefeatable, but later, when other kings of Israel stray from the law, they are captured by their enemies and killed. Even though prophets such as Jeremiah and Amos are reviled by the powerful in their day, the longevity of their words and their honour as prophets come from their intellectual fusion with God's truth.[20]

The Old Testament, for all its length and diversity and complexity and profundity, is not a helpful source for learning about relationships between equals or among peers. What comes closest to promoting such relationships is the Jewish Torah, or law, not in so far as it organizes the worship of God, recognized as supreme and unequalled, but in so far as it regulates relations among Israelites themselves. Even the Decalogue and other individual laws, however, cannot be said to promote peer relationships. For one thing, many of the commandments address the concerns of men, not those of women, who more often than not are referred to as objects of men's behaviour rather than as subjects of the law.[21] For another, Jewish laws prescribing moral behaviour vis-à-vis other men primarily regard behavior towards other Jews; except for the rules of hospitality toward strangers and wayfarers (which in their own way are very demanding), Jewish laws do not necessarily govern how Israelites need to interact with non-Israelites. Finally, the fundamental purpose of the Decalogue and other lists of rules prescribing proper behaviour among men is to regulate behaviour among unequals. The underlying assumption of many laws is that society is divided among the more powerful and the less powerful, and that the former take advantage of their position, which is why Yahweh provides rules of conduct in order to maintain a certain level of fairness among them.

The book of Proverbs advises its readers how to behave towards their betters and their lessers, and it advocates wisdom and justice not for the sake of equality but for the sake of peace, order, and prosperity. Similarly, the prophets' message of social justice assumes the existence of a situation of injustice and exhorts rulers to treat their subjects fairly and the wealthy to be considerate of the poor. Even when the prophets envision a future situation in which God's justice will reign, the vision is not so much of a society of peers as of a society in which the downtrodden are lifted up, raised from their lowliness because God, the powerful and just ruler of the universe, is with them.

Status Reversal in the New Testament

The Christian Testament, while not the exact opposite of its Jewish predecessor, does advance in the direction of equality among unequals and peer relationships between men and women.

John the Baptist continues the prophetic tradition of denouncing the abuses of secular and religious rulers, but he does not perceive inequality as a social evil and does not recommend peer relationships as an alternative. Thus John couches his solution to the social problems of his day primarily in terms of individual repentance (Luke 3:1–20). Jesus likewise condemns the hypocrisy of the scribes and Pharisees as well as their abuse of power (Luke 11:39–52), maintaining the prophetic insistence on social justice and furthering the notion that those in power do not necessarily have God on their side. Jesus advances beyond John and the earlier prophets, however, by inviting his listeners not only to repent of their sins but also to treat one another as they would like to be treated – that is, to treat others as equal to themselves (Matt. 7:12).

The sins that Jesus principally attacks are not violations of divine law but abuses of power and distortions of relationships: anger, hatred, greed, hypocrisy, and especially unforgiveness and hardness of heart. The cure for such sins is not simply individual repentance, for it also entails entering into community, that is, caring for one another.[22] The gospels call this extended community of caring and sharing the kingdom (or realm or reign) of God, and Acts and the epistles call its concrete realization the church.

The authors of the New Testament present Jesus as someone who is in union with God and who is therefore powerful and authoritative. In the synoptic gospels, Jesus teaches with authority, cures the sick, casts out demons, and walks on water; in John's gospel, Jesus does all these, and he can also tell what other people are thinking and knows the future. Whether this union with God is a unity of purpose, a fusion of wills, or a union in godhead (as the Christian doctrine of the Trinity proposes) is less important here than what Jesus asks of his followers. Does he demand unthinking fusion with him (or with God)? Or does he invite his listeners to learn from him but to make up their own minds?

Certainly Jesus' teachings have been understood as words to be taken literally and obeyed without question. The synoptic gospels contain compilations of sayings that appear to be apodictic statements to be taken on faith, and the fourth gospel contains lengthy discourses that are clearly didactic if also poetic. It is not difficult for the Christian believer to perceive these as doctrines coming from a mind that is one with the mind of God, nor is it difficult for the Christian preacher to urge total and unquestioning acceptance of these doctrines. History is replete with biblical literalism and doctrinal fundamentalism, not to mention coercion in the name of orthodoxy.[23]

Jesus' method of teaching in parables, however, is the opposite of indoctrination. Though scholars debate which parables can be traced to Jesus himself and whether the gospel versions of the parables contain his actual words, there is no debate that the historical Jesus taught in parables, and parables of their nature stimulate rather than stifle thought.[24] The parable of the good Samaritan (Luke 10:29–37), for example, would have been quite disconcerting to listeners who believed that all Samaritans were wicked, even as that of the wise and foolish virgins (Matt. 25:1–13) is troubling to people today who believe that God is always merciful and forgiving. There is ample evidence in the New Testament that Jesus did not encourage mindless fusion with himself or with the God whom he addressed as 'Abba.'

Moreover, even though a number of New Testament texts have been used to promote dominance and submission between church leaders and followers and between men and women, many passages in the gospels and epistles promote mutual service and peer relationships. More than once in the gospels, Jesus admonishes his disciples not to be like other rulers, and the gospels may have included his denunciations of the scribes and Pharisees as a warning against growing legalism and hypocrisy in the church of the first century.[25] Though Jesus selects twelve as a sort of inner circle among his followers, the gospels do not give much attention to most of the twelve, and indeed offer two slightly different lists.[26] The disciple mentioned most often – Peter – is also the one who is portrayed as having the most failings, but all twelve fail to understand Jesus' message,[27] and all of them desert him when he is arrested and crucified.

Jesus apparently treated women on a par with men, which ran counter to the cultural norms of his day, and women enjoyed greater equality in Christian communities than in society at large. The gospels show Jesus addressing women in public (John 4:4–26), letting himself be touched by women (Luke 7:36–50; 8:40–8), and allowing women to be his disciples (Luke 8:1–3; 10:38–42).[28] Women are the only disciples who stay with Jesus when he is on the cross, and women are the first to discover the empty tomb. The gospels also portray women as the first bearers of the good news about Jesus (John 4:28–30; Matt. 28:8–10). The epistles in a number of places suggest that women were deacons, apostles, and heads of local Christian communities (Rom. 16:1–16; Col. 4:15).

The behaviour of Jesus and his earliest followers fits in with Jesus' general teaching of status reversal in the kingdom of God. In its most general form, this aspect of the good news is that 'the last will be first and the first will be last' (Matt. 20:16). Applied to status and roles in the Christian community, it means, 'Whoever wants to be great among you must be your servant, and whoever wants to be first among you must be your slave' (Matt. 20:26–7). This principle apparently applies even to gender roles, since in the ancient world it is women who serve and men who are served. But reversal of status in the New Testament is also broader than this, for Jesus teaches that tax collectors and prostitutes will enter the kingdom of God before civil and religious leaders (Matt. 21:31).

Jesus in his dialogues often encourages perspective taking – looking at a situation from the point of view opposite to that which one normally takes. In the story of the repentant woman who washes Jesus' feet with her tears (Luke 7:36–50), Jesus invites the self-righteous host to look at the woman's behaviour from a different perspective by asking him whether a person who had been forgiven a greater debt might feel more gratitude than a person who had been forgiven a much smaller debt. When he is criticized for curing a woman on the sabbath, Jesus asks his critics to look at her cure as freeing her from bondage (Luke 13:10–17). In the story of the woman caught in adultery (John 8:1–11), Jesus interrogates the judges and in the process of getting them to put themselves in her place transforms the accusers into the accused. Standing before God, all are sinners, and so all are equal: 'Judge not, lest you be judged.' (Matt. 7:1). Inequality is based on the judgment of an inferior by superiors, and perspective taking allows one to realize that judgments of inequality are always biased.

The equalizing power of the kingdom breaks through the social customs that keep ordinary people subservient to religious leaders, the powerless subservient to the powerful, the disreputable subservient to the respectable, and women subservient to men. On numerous occasions Jesus disobeys religious rules concerning the sabbath in order to help people, risking the anger of the Pharisees, who authoritatively interpret the rules. On other occasions Jesus reaches out to the poor and counts them among the blessed, and he touches the lives of the socially marginalized, elevating their status to that of the socially acceptable. Jesus, through his authority as son of God, is able to humble the proud and exalt the lowly (cf. Luke 1:51–2), so that all before him are children of God and peers to one another. It is as though Jesus treats all equally, with the result that they become equals.

Towards Peer Relationships in Marriage and Ministry

We have been considering the scriptures in terms not of their contents but of the relationships that they describe as normative and desirable. What is usually described as faith in God or following God's will we have called intellectual fusion with God, and we have left aside the behavioural content of the Mosaic law and prophetic exhortation. Whereas the common assumption is that human beings are saved by attending to what is divinely revealed because the content of the revelation is true, for people of faith the truth of revelation is secondary to the authority of the one revealing – namely, God. At the time when they first decide to trust God's word, believers do not fully understand the truth of what they are accepting. It is through believing and living out their beliefs that people of faith come to understand what has been revealed to them.

This dynamic of faith is crucial. Church leaders often uncritically imitate the example of religious leaders in the Bible, thinking that they are thereby being obedient to divine revelation. They psychologically fuse with God (i.e., with their image or notion of God), and in their own minds they come to possess the uprightness of Noah, the courage of Moses, the resourcefulness of David, the wisdom of Solomon, the insight of the prophets, the power of Jesus, and the authority of the apostles.[29] Especially in matters not explicitly treated in the Bible (such as abortion, contraception, annulment of marriages, ordination), they set themselves up as interpreters of God's will and judges of human behaviour.[30] Moreover, inasmuch as unequal relationships between persons are illustrated in most of the scriptures, religious authorities who base their self-understanding on the scriptures often uncritically assume that unequal relationships are normative and even desired by God.

Let us ask then what Christianity would look like if dysfunctional triangling and sexism were eliminated from social dynamics among Christians.

It is easiest to begin with marriage, because this volume has reviewed the concepts of egalitarian, companionate, and peer marriages. These three styles of marriage presume spouses to be equals or peers and regard them as individuals with unique qualities and characteristics, rather than as women and men with certain roles. They argue also that relationships between spouses, including duties and rewards, should be negotiated within a marriage rather than dictated by social expectations or religious leaders. Spouses in such marriages are related primarily to, but not fused with, one another, nor are they fused with a third corner such as work or children. Since they negotiate their shared responsibilities in the family, they do not attempt to perpetuate traditional gender roles in their children; rather, they model negotiation, flexibility, and mutual concern for the happiness of one another. Just as important, such spouses are not intellectually fused with church leaders, and therefore while they respect religious authority they do not follow it blindly.

When gender roles and sexual preference disappear from Christian ministry, the type of dynamics that prevails among equals in marriage also prevails among peers in ministry. Unless one argues for an undifferentiated ministry of the laity, however, one needs to allow for some differentiation of responsibilities among ministers, including the possibility that some find themselves placed in responsibility over others. This does not necessarily look like the type of hierarchy found in traditional churches, but it does allow for the existence and evolution of organizational structures that are necessary for the work of the church to be accomplished.

In this type of organization, the most important ministers are those directly engaged in interacting with people, and administrators or managers assist the direct ministers in their work. This concept of leadership fulfills the gospel precept cited above: 'Whoever wants to be great among you must be your servant, and whoever wants to be first among you must be your slave' (Matt. 20:26–7). Except for the type of ministerial work in which they engage, therefore, ministers are essentially peers; thus while direct ministers are accountable to administrators, administrators are accountable to direct ministers and even to church members.

Whether or not a particular church or denomination engages certain principles of democracy (such as majority rule) or of discussion (such as parliamentary rules) is less important than its adoption of a polity that promotes peer relationships, accountability, and the accomplishment of the church's ministerial tasks. In such a church, tasks and roles may be assigned, but gender as such is not a determining factor, except in certain rare instances directly related to the type of ministry performed.[31]

Most important, ministers in such a church do not perceive themselves as fused with God or, as has been more often the case, invested with the authority of the scriptures, the apostles, or tradition. Rather, they are receptive of and respectful towards their religious heritage while at the same time being critical of it. In this way they model for the laity an attitude towards their common heritage that discourages fusion while it encourages responsiveness to scripture and appropriation of tradition.

They recognize that a certain amount of fusion (i.e., uncritical acceptance, identification, and enthusiasm) is unavoidable at certain early stages of religious development, but they do not promote fusion with themselves or with their church and its teachings as an ideal of mature religious belonging. Nor do they encourage the type of moral non-differentiation that views all acts of a certain type as wrong, or worse, that views all persons who perform certain types of acts as evil. Rather, they seek the highest levels of religious and moral development, and they invite people to commit themselves to finding and living a Christianity that is faithful to the gospel of Jesus, concerned about the well-being of others, and true to themselves.

NOTES

1 For a Catholic argument, see Sacred Congregation for the Doctrine of the Faith, *Declaration on the Question of the Admission of Women to the Ministerial Priesthood* (15 Oct. 1976), and David M. Maloney, *The Church Cannot Ordain Women to the Priesthood* (Franciscan Herald Press, 1978). For an Orthodox position, see Thomas Hopko, ed., *Women and the Priesthood* (Crestwood, NY: St Vladimir Seminary Press, 1983). For a fundamentalist argument, see John W. Robbins, *Scripture Twisting in the Seminaries*, Part I, *Feminism* (Jefferson, Md.: Trinity Foundation, 1982). For a humanist position, see Daniel Amnéus, *Back to Patriarchy* (New Rochelle, NY: Arlington House Publications, 1979).

2 For some critiques, see Mary Daly, *The Church and the Second Sex* (New York: Harper & Row, 1968); Alice L. Hageman, ed., *Sexist Religion and Women in the Church: No More Silence!* (New York: Association Press, 1974); Rosemary Radford Reuther, *Sexism and God-Talk: Toward a Feminist Theology* (Boston: Beacon Press, 1979); and Terrence A. Sweeney, *A Church Divided: The Vatican against American Catholics* (Buffalo, NY: Prometheus Books, 1992).

3 Murray Bowen, *Family Therapy in Clinical Perspective* (New York: Jason Aronson, 1978), 531.

4 Edwin H. Friedman, 'Bowen Theory and Therapy,' in Alan Gurman and David P. Knesken, eds., *Handbook of Family Therapy*, vol. II (New York: Brunner/Mazel, 1991), 157.

5 Bowen, *Family Therapy*, 497.

6 See Lillian Rubin, *Intimate Strangers* (New York: Harper & Row, 1984).

7 See Dorothy Dinnerstein, *The Mermaid and the Minotaur*, (New York: Harper & Row, 1976).

8 See Cindy Hazan and Philip Shaver, 'Romantic Love Conceptualized as an Attachment Process,' *Journal of Personality and Social Psychology*, 52 (March 1987), 511–24. The fact that people of the same sex can also fall in love need not detain us here.

9 See, for example, M. Scott Peck, *The Road Less Traveled* (New York: Simon and Schuster, 1978), 84–90.

10 Stephen R. Marks, *Three Corners: Exploring Marriage and the Self* (Lexington, Mass.: Lexington Books, 1986), 103.

11 See Anthony Giddens, *The Transformation of Intimacy* (Stanford, Calif.: Stanford University Press, 1992).
12 Pepper Schwartz, *Peer Marriage* (New York: Free Press, 1994).
13 Ibid., 126.
14 See Scott J. South and Glenna Spitze, 'Housework in Marital and Nonmarital Households,' *American Sociological Review*, 59, (June 1994), 327–47.
15 Schwartz, *Peer Marriage*, 126.
16 See Elisabeth Schüssler Fiorenza, *Discipleship of Equals* (New York: Crossroad, 1993).
17 It is difficult to interpret biblical texts in a way that regards the behaviour of protagonists in a negative way when the reader, conditioned by years of religious training, has intellectually fused with such a positive image of the religious heroes that any other interpretation of their behaviour seems sacrilegious. Another example of intellectual fusion with biblical texts is taking them literally.
18 When women do exercise power – for example, the Hebrew midwives in the Exodus story or, much later, heroines such as Ruth and Judith – they have power because God is with them, but they must still exercise that power in stereotypically feminine ways – for example, using wiles and deceit.
19 See 'Covenant' in John L. McKenzie, *Dictionary of the Bible* (Milwaukee: Bruce Publishing Co., 1965), 153.
20 The prophet's mission is not to convey his own thoughts and judgments but to proclaim, 'Thus says the Lord,' as is clear from the many places in the writings of the prophets where such proclamations are found. This notion is also found in descriptions of the prophet's call by God; see, for example, Jer. 1:4–11, Is. 6: 1–13, and Ezek. 2:1–3:11.
21 'The commandments in Ex. 20:1–17, considered to be at the very heart of both Jewish and Christian belief, state explicitly that it is a male community to whom they are addressed.' Drorah O'Donnell Satel, 'Exodus,' in Carol A. Newsom and Sharon H. Ringe, eds., *The Women's Bible Commentary* (Louisville, Ky.: Westminster/John Knox, 1992), 33.
22 While it is often noted that *agape* is the Greek word behind the word 'love' in the New Testament, 'love' is a poor translation of *agape*, which is better translated as 'care' or 'caring.' See Morton T. Kelsey, *Caring: How Can We Love One Another?* (Ramsey, NJ: Paulist Press, 1981).
23 At the extreme stands Tertullian's bold defence of doctrine, *Credo quia absurdum est* (I believe because it is absurd). Even Anselm's more reserved *Credo ut intelligam* (I believe in order to understand) implies that one ought to accept things on faith before one understands them. During the Middle Ages

conquered barbarians were sometimes forcibly baptized, and heretics were tortured into submission.
24 See John Dominic Crossan, *In Parables: The Challenge of the Historical Jesus* (New York: Harper & Row, 1973); also Neal F. Fisher, *The Parables of Jesus* (New York: Crossroad, 1990), 20–31.
25 'It is important to remember that all of [Matthew's] fierce invectives against Pharisaic Judaism reflect a pastoral concern for his own church. The church is in danger of imitating the mistakes of the Pharisees and so falling under the same judgment.' John P. Meier, *Matthew* (Wilmington, Del.: Michael Glazier, 1980), 265.
26 Mark 3:16–19 and Matt. 10:2–5 give one list mentioning Thaddeus but not Judas the son of James; Luke 6:13–16 and Acts 1:13 include Judas the son of James but not Thaddeus.
27 See, for example, Mark 6:51–2, Matt. 16:21–3, Luke 9:43–9.
28 As noted by Ben Witherington III, 'For a Jewish woman to leave home and travel with a rabbi was not only unheard of, it was scandalous. Even more scandalous was the fact that women, both respectable and not, were among Jesus' travelling companions.' *Women in the Ministry of Jesus* (New York: Cambridge University Press, 1984), 117.
29 They also often have the humility to acknowledge that this is God's gift rather than their own achievement, and they sometimes claim that they are not free to teach or do otherwise than has been revealed to them, but these attitudes of subservience to God's will do not obliterate the fact that they insist that others should respect and obey them (i.e., fuse with them) as God's representatives.
30 Note that this dynamic occurs not only in Christianity but also in Judaism, in Islam, and in other religions in which divine authority can be invoked. Nor is the dynamic restricted to religious settings, for it is also used by politicians, generals, economists, business managers, and indeed any persons in authority who claim that their insights and decisions are privileged and unquestionable. Remember that what we are talking about here is a dynamic that takes place primarily in the intimacy of families, even though it can also happen in the public forum of religion and other areas of social interaction.
31 For instance, women or men could lead same-sex support groups of women or men tackling gender-related problems in society.

Afterword

As promised in the Preface, this book is not so much a thorough history of sexism in Christianity as a series of historical essays, each one offering a certain window through which to view a succession of periods. We wrote the Preface after the authors were contacted but before the chapters were written – that is, when the plan of the book was clear but the final products were not yet in hand. Perhaps something more needs to be said at this point, now that the writers have finished writing, the editors have finished editing, and the reader has finished reading.

Any window offers a view that both reveals and conceals: it shows what can be seen, but it does so in a limited way and only from a certain viewpoint. A window that opens out to a garden and a road with mountains in the background, for example, could be hiding the fact that on the other side of the house are a beach and an ocean. Lest the reader think that the chapters of this book always display the most prominent features of the historical landscape in each era, we must say something about what they leave out.

The chapter on gender in the origins of Christianity (chapter 2) comes largely from materials in the four canonical gospels and from historical documents that shed light on them. It only briefly alludes to what can be seen happening in early Christianity when it is viewed from the window of the New Testament epistles. Much has been written about how the egalitarianism of the early Jesus movement – or, as Mary D'Angelo prefers to call it, the reign-of-God movement – steadily diminished as Christianity slowly adopted the social norms of the dominant culture in which it found itself. A reader who wants a fuller picture of the first Christian century should look at some of the works mentioned in that chapter's notes.

Likewise with chapter 3, on the images of women in Christian antiquity. The period from the second through the sixth or seventh century is traditionally referred to as the patristic era, a name that we avoid because of its sexist overtones, but a name of which readers must be aware if they are to learn more about this period. The church in this era was highly patriarchal, and church leaders (by this time exclusively male) were sometimes deeply misogynistic. These facts are so obvious to scholars that Kenneth Steinhauser chose to write about something less obvious, but readers would do well to look at Christian antiquity through other windows in addition to the one presented here.

Most women in the Middle Ages did not fare well under the dominance of men, but Marie Anne Mayeski shows us in chapter 4 that some women (usually those of noble birth, about whom we have records) were able to do relatively well for themselves during the early Middle Ages in the church and in society at large. After the twelfth century, however, when ecclesiastical scholars (all men) began to discover and draw from the misogynistic texts of antiquity, restrictions on women once again increased. Even then, however, a number of women in addition to the few mentioned here soared to new heights.

Few women during the Renaissance were able to succeed in their own right; those who did, such as Queen Elizabeth of England, were privileged by birth, gifted in ability, and fortunate by circumstances. Moreover, as William Swatos points out in chapter 5, they had to accept the rules of patriarchy even if they could find ways to use them to their own advantage. Every year, more is published about the modest but real achievements of Renaissance women in the arts and in society, and much more can be learned about the positives and negatives of this brief period than is said here.

With the arrival of the modern era the history of Christianity becomes more complex, which is why we asked two scholars to write about this period. In chapter 6 Ellen Leonard shows how Catholicism after the Protestant Reformation reasserted the antique notion that woman's nature is different from man's, but this same notion made it possible for women to band together in religious orders and to experience their own feminine lives and achievements. In chapter 7 Wendy Fletcher-Marsh concurs with this analysis, noting that though Protestantism theoretically advanced the equality of women by asserting that males and females have the same human nature, in practice it reduced the roles of women to those of wife and mother. Again, much more can be said, and indeed much has been written, about the oppression and accomplishments of women during this lengthy period.

The two areas in which women in contemporary Christianity have experienced the greatest discrimination are marriage and ministry, and so again we commissioned two chapters. Gaile Pohlhaus, coming from a Catholic background, looked in chapter 8 at marriage from a Catholic perspective and highlighted positive developments in the twentieth century. Much more could be written from a Protestant viewpoint or from a negative angle, as has been done by others. In chapter 9, Molly Marshall, raised in a Protestant family, looked at ministry primarily from a Baptist and Catholic perspective. In doing so, she had to leave out the many advances by ordained and unordained women that would round out a fuller picture of women's ministry today. At the same time, by singling out marriage and ministry, both chapters ignored the churches' failure to address sexism in the wider society.

Even the introductory and concluding chapters, which attempted to set the stage and close the curtain on the eight historical dramas they encompass, did not say all that could be said. Chapter 1 could have said much more about gender roles from a biological or sociological perspective, but it necessarily had to mention only the most salient features in order to play its role as a preview of chapters to come. Chapter 10 looked at sexism and gender roles through the lens of family systems theory, fusion, and peer relationships. Some may find this viewpoint somewhat narrow, but it does serve the purpose of bringing closure to the discussion. In doing this, it invites further discussion among readers and, as sometimes happens, between readers and the authors to whom they write.

Much is written throughout this book and in other works named in each chapter's notes about the long history of gender roles and sexism in Christianity, but not much is said here about the future of male–female relationships in the churches – except that they ought to be egalitarian. One reason of course for the lack of information about the future is that it has not happened yet. Another, less obvious reason is that while Christianity in the past has been confined largely to Eurocentric cultures, it now faces a multicultural future. It is difficult to write simply about a situation that is becoming increasingly complex.

It would be easy to trace a straight line from patriarchy to egalitarianism and to label this as development. It is not difficult to see, as this book attempts to show, that Christians in Europe and North America have slowly if not always steadily progressed from unenlightened sexism to a conscious attempt to treat women and men as equals. Yet Christians in the future around the world may not perceive gender equality as a pressing need, and so at a global level the churches may remain as male-dominated as ever.

Other world religions tend to be sexist as Christianity has been, even if some (like Buddhism) had founders who were radically egalitarian in outlook. Other human cultures tend to be even more sexist than Eurocentric culture is today, even if some (such as tribal cultures) tend to divide gender roles somewhat equally between the sexes. In their encounters with world religions and human cultures at a global level, Christians may prefer to emphasize similarities rather than differences, and one of the most prevalent similarities is the male dominance of society and religion. Women may object, but their voices may be pushed to the background of interreligious and intercultural dialogue.

Another complicating factor is economics. In today's global economy, a relative few who are wealthy (including the writers and readers of this book) consume the resources of the planet, while most of the world's six billion people are denied access to those same resources. Despite the disintegration of the Soviet Union, most people in the world live under oppression that is both economic and political. Faced with poverty and malnutrition, insecurity and repression, Christians who live in such conditions may look at gender equality as less important than basic human rights and social justice. Indeed, they may regard it as a luxury when their primary concern is daily survival. Today such Christians are in the majority.

It is not easy to predict, therefore, when and how sexism will be perceived as dysfunctional in society and named as sinful in the global Christian community, which continues to be dominated by men. Certainly women, who daily contend with discrimination against their sex, will perceive it as unjust and name it as wrong, but they may not have the power to change it, except in places where men themselves become sensitized to the harm that sexism causes to relationships and society.

Scripture scholars note that the reign of God announced by Jesus has the peculiar attribute of being both 'already' and 'not yet.' It is clear that Jesus himself was egalitarian in his attitude towards women, perhaps even radically so, and there is every reason to believe that, in the kingdom he envisaged, women and men are equals. Seen in this light, the achievement of even partial gender equality, already real but not yet fully realized, is for all its ambiguity a sign of God's reign in history.

Contributors

Mary Rose D'Angelo
Department of Religious Studies
University of Notre Dame
Notre Dame, Indiana

Wendy Fletcher-Marsh
Faculty of Theology
Huron College of the University
  of Western Ontario
London, Ontario

Pierre Hégy
Department of Sociology
Adelphi University
Garden City, New York

Ellen Leonard
Faculty of Theology
University of St Michael's
  College
Toronto, Ontario

Molly T. Marshall
Program of Theology and
  Spirituality
Central Baptist Theological
  Seminary
Kansas City, Kansas

Joseph Martos
Russell Institute of
  Religion and Ministry
Spalding University
Louisville, Kentucky

Marie Anne Mayeski
Department of Theological
  Studies
Loyola Marymount University
Los Angeles, California

Gaile M. Pohlhaus
Department of Religious
  Studies
Villanova University
Villanova, Pennsylvania

Kenneth B. Steinhauser
Department of Theological
  Studies
Saint Louis University
St Louis, Missouri

William H. Swatos, Jr
Religious Research
  Association
Association for the
  Sociology of Religion
Holiday, Florida

www.ingramcontent.com/pod-product-compliance
Lightning Source LLC
Chambersburg PA
CBHW022055290426
44109CB00014B/1111